IN THE HOUSE TTLE

D0118085

By James Solomon

MTV Books / Pocket Books
Based on MTV's *The Real World*
Produced by Bunim/Murray Productions Inc.
In association with MTV

* This area is being used for the taping of a television program. If you do not wish to be taped as part of the program, please exit the area until taping has been completed.

* Excerpt from the sign posted at the door of the Seattle house

An original publication of MTV BOOKS / POCKET BOOKS

POCKET BOOKS, A DIVISION OF SIMON & SCHUSTER INC.
1230 Avenue of the Americas, New York, NY 10020

ISBN: 0-671-02597-X

First MTV Books/Pocket Books/trade paperback printing, December 1998

10 9 8 7 6 5 4 3 2 1

Pocket and colophon are registered trademarks of Simon & Schuster Inc.

Printed in the U.S.A.

Special thanks to:

Andy's Deli, Amanda Ayers, Brian Blatz, Andrew Blauner, Craig Borders, Eduardo A. Braniff, Mary-Ellis Bunim, Karen Clark, Craig Cegielski, Gina Centrello, Tracy Chaplin, Tom Colamaria, Andre Colton, Valentine Costello, Oskar Dektyar, Twisne Fan, Libby Fernau, Lisa Feuer, Tom Finlayson, Scott Freeman, Gaga, Janine Gallant, Erin Galligan, Robert Garcia, Mayo Gray, John and Carly Gumina, Greer Kessel Hendricks, Laura Hirschfield, Julie Johns, Jim Johnston, Steve Karadimos, Jeff Keirns, Patrick Kendall, Kate Keough, Mark Kirschner, Matt Kunitz, Andrea LaBate, Steve Lichtenstein, Anthony Manupelli, Kevin McGillycuddy, Kramer McGillycuddy-Walker, Jimmy Malecki, Michelle Millard, Laura Murphy, Jonathan Murray, Daniele Nero, Kim Noone, Donna O'Neill, Ed Paparo, David Park, Luigi Porco, Janice Potter, Billy Rainey, Katherine Raymond, Matthew Saal, Adam Salvatore, Tammy Scannavino, Robin Silverman, Donald Silvey, Jerome A. Singletary, Abby and John Solomon, Ann and Richard Solomon, Dave Stanke, Liate Stehlik, Van Toffler, Two Downtown, Inc., Christina Walker, Kelly Weinhart, Kara Welsh, Leola Westbrook, Kyla White, Natalie Wigotsky-Reed and Nancy Willen.

Photo Credits:

Seattle:
Cover photos, and other Seattle cast publicity photos for MTV Press by Jimmy Malecki/MTV Press.

All Aqua Games, In the House except toilet and "after"photos, airport, press day, wrap party, RACE in the house, Slacking in Seattle except archival photos, portrait of Jon, and Jon and Mary-Ellis at door, by Jimmy Malecki Photography Studio.

Back cover, Contents page, Title page, RW Fashion Accesories cut-out portraits, Tale of Two Cities photos except "batphone", U.S. map, Seattle hates *RW* T-shirt by Stacy Thomas.

Personal photos were provided for their respective pages by Janet, Lindsay and Rebecca.

Many photos of the Seattle cast were generously provided by members of the cast and crew of *The Real World-Seattle*.

RW house drawings courtesy of Two Downtown, Inc.

Sri Maha Kali illustration by J.B. Khanna & Co.

Photo of Sunset Boulevard, Jimi Hendrix, Bruce Lee, Tom Hanks, and Neil Diamond by Photofest.

All Application Form images except Sunset Boulevard, Copyright 1997 PhotoDisc Inc.

Seattle City Timeline:
Chief Sealth courtesy of the Burke Museum of Natural History & Culture, Catalog #L-4772. Seattle earthquake by *The Seattle Times* file photo. Kurt Cobain by Tom Reese/*The Seattle Times.* Kingdome /Hamilton neg. # 2421, Seattle Fire neg. #6991, Boeing plane neg. #15276, World's Fair neg. #15544 and Mt. St. Helens, Special Collections, University of Washington Libraries.
Sub Pop logo reprinted by permission of Sub Pop Records. All rights reserved.
Basketball, life preserver, golf clubs and beer images, Copyright 1997 PhotoDisc Inc.

Mary-Ellis Bunim photo by Gary Null, courtesy of National Broadcasting Company, Inc.

Water background and radio images Copyright 1997 PhotoDisc Inc.

Boston:
Many photos of the Boston cast were generously provided by Elka.
Personal photos were provided for their respective pages by Jason, Sean, Kameelah, Syrus, Elka, and Montana.

Boston cast publicity photos for MTV Press by Michael Walls/MTV Press.

Sean black and white portrait by Dietrich Gesk Photography.

Photo of Syrus in basketball uniform by Reed & Jay Photography. Black and white portraits of Syrus by Sherrod Calland Photography. Goddog logo courtesy of Goddog, Inc.

1955 Denoyer Geppert Beginner's USA Wallmap Copyright Rand McNally R.L. #98-S-118.

Book Design: Rick Jost, Tom Ryse, Mariko Marrs, and Glenn Castonguay

Canon   **Kodak**   **RITZ CAMERA**

Cast and crew cameras   Cast and crew photo film   Cast and crew film processing
courtesy of Canon.   courtesy of Kodak.   courtesy of Ritz Camera.

Contents

With the Creators of *The Real World*

MARY-ELLIS BUNIM & JON MURRAY

Could you have survived *The Real World*?

MARY-ELLIS: Knowing what I know about it—and remembering what I was like at 18—I didn't have the self-confidence to go through this experience. I was a very naïve 18-year-old. I think it would have been very difficult for me to go through this before I was 25 or 26.

JON: I think I would've gotten very frustrated with the people in the house, and I probably would've exploded at them at some point. I did that when I was a kid. Every seven years or so, I'd have some major explosion. I'd start throwing desks, or things like that. I'm sure I would've had one of those every-seven-years eruptions on *The Real World*. Now I don't explode like that anymore. I've learned how to let the steam out more gradually.

What were you like during your *Real World* years (age 18- 24)?

MARY-ELLIS: My biggest issues revolved around the divorce of my parents when I was 17. I realized I had no financial security, and my future was totally up to me. If I was going to get an education, I had to pay for it myself. That was the biggest shock I faced at 18 or 19: coming to terms with the fact that nobody else was going to bail me out.

I grew up on Long Island, New York, and lived in a very small community surrounded by potato fields. My brother and sister were both much older, and I grew up very sheltered. When I went to college, I hadn't had sex and had never even heard of marijuana. My life experience didn't begin until I left home.

JON: I was born in Mississippi in the late 1950s, and raised outside of Syracuse, New York, during the 1960s. My Mom is British, so I spent a little time in England during my childhood, too. So, in other words, I had many different cultural influences.

The biggest issue affecting me then, however, revolved around my brother, who died of a drug overdose when I was 17. My family had been through some real emotional rides with him, including his leaving the Navy and fleeing to Canada. His travails made me a little less naïve at 18 than Mary-Ellis was at that age.

My brother's difficulties also caused me to postpone dealing with some important issues of my own—like my sexuality. I was my parents' only remaining child after my brother's death. So, I felt it was very important for me not to cause them any undue harm or sadness. I saw how destroyed they were by what happened to my brother. So, among other things, I chose not to deal with the fact that I was gay until after college.

In effect, I concealed it from everyone until then, even though I knew I was gay when I was a teenager. But concealing that kind of knowledge was the norm at that time. Things weren't nearly as open as they are now. There weren't gay and lesbian clubs all over campus, like there are at colleges today. I was also having such a good time with my schoolwork and the social aspects of college, that I didn't really focus on my sexuality.

But make no mistake, I was much happier when I was ultimately able to embrace and reveal my sexuality.

What cast member—past or present—were you most like?

MARY-ELLIS: I think I started more like Julie from *The Real World-New York*—just sort of a wide-eyed innocent. But I evolved to be more like Rachel of *The Real World-San Francisco*, in terms of her sense of focus and ambition. I was very driven by the time I was 23.

JON: So was I. I had real focus on what I wanted to do. So, in that way, I don't relate to many of the people we've cast on *The Real World*. A lot of them haven't figured out what they want to do, but I knew very early on that I wanted to be in broadcast journalism.

I guess in some ways, I most identified with Judd from *The Real World-San Francisco*. Certainly in the sense that he, like I, knew what he wanted, and was very focused about getting it. I also think Judd got impatient with other people. He'd push them in a direction if they weren't doing something with their lives. That's something I tend to do. And I think Judd also can have a caustic sense of humor, which I definitely have. When I was in college, people used to tell me I needed to tone 'it' down. My barbs could really sting.

Would you have cast yourselves for *The Real World*?

JON: I wouldn't have cast me for the show. I don't think I'm charismatic enough. I would've been boring.

MARY-ELLIS: I would've cast Jon. I think he was dealing with some very interesting issues at that stage of his life—from sexuality to mourning a loved one. But, I don't think I would've cast me. Partly 'cause I probably wouldn't have made a very interesting cast member, but also, because I've always preferred being behind the camera, rather than in front.

Do you wish you'd been on the show?

MARY-ELLIS: I think I would have retreated. I would have hidden from the cameras. But I certainly would have been fascinated to look back on the show now, and examine my struggles and the choices I made.

JON: I'm glad I got to deal with my own issues on my own timetable, rather than on *The Real World*. But as a producer of the show, I wish I'd done it. I think we empathize with what the cast members go through, but we can never really know what they experience, unless we've gone through it ourselves. At some point, it might be instructive for us to turn the cameras on ourselves (crew included) for a couple of days, just to see what it's really like.

What kind of roommates would the two of you have made?

JON: Good roommates. After all, we've shared an office and a desk for ten years...and we still get along really well.

MARY-ELLIS: I agree. I think we listen to each other really well.

JON: We don't fight. I'm not a fighter. I grew up with parents who fought a lot, and I just have no interest in conflict. I don't like it. Mary-Ellis handles conflict a lot better than I do.

MARY-ELLIS: I just handle it more often [laughing]. I tend to get provoked more easily than he does.

JON: I think our strength is that we come at this show from very different points of view. But we both listen to each other. So, we come to conclusions that work for each of us.

MARY-ELLIS: We really trust each other, but we trust each other enough to not agree on everything.

Do you consider yourself *Real World* den parents?

MARY-ELLIS: Yeah, I'm definitely a den mother for some of the cast. And there are certain people I've stayed particularly close to, but usually, I spend the most time talking to the people who've just come off the show. It's often very difficult for those cast members to deal with their newfound celebrity status, especially as the show is just beginning to air. It's kind of like they've been

house, and no one quite understands that before they move in.

They think—based on what they've seen on the air—that it's just a lot of fun. It looks like a privilege. They get a phat pad. They live rent-free. They get to be rock stars. But it isn't all of that. Fact is, they give more than they get.

They not only put their faces out there for examination—but their souls as well. They invite scrutiny, which is very difficult for an adult—let alone someone who is only 19 or 20.

Just read the remarks of both the Seattle and Boston casts in this book. Many of them describe just how little they were prepared for the pressures of this experience. *The Real World* is a pressure cooker, no question about it. I think you live five years of your life in five months. Everything happens really fast.

So I think that it takes incredible courage to withstand this experience, particularly once you start to understand what it's all about. Jason from the Boston cast said he woke up his first morning in the house feeling terrified. With his face buried beneath his down comforter, he thought to himself, 'Maybe I can just stay here under the covers all five months.'

Jason soon realized, like everyone else does on the show, that it's hard to hide on *The Real World*. The combination of strong-minded roommates and ever-present cameras exposes you—warts and all. So, it takes a lot of courage each morning to be willing to pull the covers off of your face.

> ## They think that it's just a lot of fun. It looks like a privilege. They get a phat pad. They live rent-free. They get to be rock stars. Fact is, they give more than they get. — *MARY-ELLIS BUNIM*

orbiting in space for 20 weeks, and they've just landed. Everyone seems to know who they are and what they did on their space mission.

I'm eager to help any former cast member I can. After all, they've given so much of themselves to us by doing this show.

JON: Personally, I don't think of myself as their den parent. Mary-Ellis fills that role much more ably and easily than I do. Certainly, I'm very thankful to all of them for what they've given us, and I feel a responsibility to help them, particularly when it's about an issue caused by the show, but otherwise, it's really up to each of them as to how much they want to stay connected with the show.

Would you let your own children appear on *The Real World*?

MARY-ELLIS: Well, my 18-year-old daughter, Juliana, has recently become eligible—age-wise—to be on *The Real World*. But hell no, I wouldn't let her be on the show. I wouldn't want her sharing all of my personal secrets with the whole world [laughing].

JON: My partner and I are adopting our first child next year, so I'm still developing my philosophy on child rearing. Now I figure my kids should get to do whatever they want—as long as they consider the good and bad of the experience—but ask me in twenty years when they've grown, and I might be singing a different tune.

What advice would you give to people applying for the show?

MARY-ELLIS: There is no way to adequately prepare yourself for the experience of doing *The Real World*. There's very little that compares to the feeling of invasion you must endure in that

JON: Anyone considering doing this show, I recommend you examine your motives first. The most dangerous reason to do *The Real World* is because you think it's going to position you for stardom. Because from what we've seen so far, that hasn't happened to many members of our cast.

Frankly, it's only helped launch the careers of a few people from the show—like Eric from *The Real World-New York*, as a TV host/actor, and Judd from *The Real World-San Francisco*, as a cartoonist, and both of them had shown talent in those areas prior to appearing on *The Real World*.

The people that seem to do the best on the show are the ones who do it for the experience alone; who just want to see what it's like to be put together with people from different places and walks of life; who want to examine their motives and feelings; and who, in a way, are pretty comfortable with themselves. If you're really uncomfortable with yourself then *The Real World* will probably bring those insecurities out.

To make the most of this experience, you've got to be willing to give up control. It's a big deal not being able to control your situation, and that's what happens the moment you enter the house.

And then there's the pride factor. Someone calls you a name, you have to decide whether or not you're going to respond...or walk away. With a camera on you, it becomes a statement in either case. Do you want to leave something on the record that isn't refuted? That's a constant dilemma for each cast member. As a result, conflicts escalate into arguments; opinions turn into pronouncements; and insecurities evolve into major drama.

Real life happens about 10 times faster on *The Real World* than it does in real life, and it's a ride that isn't for everyone.

Rock & Suck

 What rocks about being on *The Real World?*

Mary-Ellis: It rocks that it's a home-movie for your grandchildren. Can you think of a lot of TV shows that you could put in a time capsule, and it would have some meaning to future generations? I can't. *The Real World* really chronicles someone's life—their tastes, their vernacular, and the tastes of a generation.

You also become part of a very small club of people that have gotten to do this, and that creates a very special family, not only with your own cast, but with previous casts as well. Each season just adds to the network of *Real World* alums. We have people from different casts now rooming together, and even dating—like Sean from *The Real World-Boston* and Rachel from *The Real World-San Francisco*.

Jon: It gives you a chance to grow, and a chance to experience people different from yourself and I think it's a helluva lot of fun.

 What sucks about being on *The Real World?*

Mary-Ellis: It depends on the individual but it can be a pretty painful experience for some people, especially when you have to watch your mistakes on national TV...and then hear about them later from hundreds of strangers.

Jon: Sometimes the show raises unreasonable expectations among cast members. Some of them believe it's going to open up all sorts of doors, and it doesn't always turn out that way.

Spin-offs

How many *Real Worlds* exist in the real world?

 Mary-Ellis: Ours is the only alternative universe at the moment. There were three *Real World* spin-offs running overseas for a while—in Italy, Germany, and Sweden—but none are on anymore. Italy and Sweden lasted two seasons. And Germany, one. However, our own *Real World* does air in more than forty countries now.

 Jon: Each of the other *Real World* spin-offs reflected its own culture. The Italian version featured beautiful people, but was really talky. They just sat around all day and discussed politics. The German version had beautiful lighting and a stark loft, but not a lot of storytelling. And in Sweden, they had a lot of nudity.

Fact or Fiction

How real is *The Real World?*

Mary-Ellis: In terms of what you see on the air, the cast's actions and reactions are real; but yes, we enhance the drama by the choices we make with music and editing. The stories, however, are completely true.

Jon: And I think that's true of *60 Minutes*, too. When they put together one of their 12-minute pieces, they make the same decisions we do about how to tell their story in a dramatic fashion.

Is *The Real World* any less real than it used to be?

Mary-Ellis: No, I don't think so. I think the people and the stories are just as real and relatable as they've ever been.

Jon: I think it's harder to make it work. We have to cast more carefully. We have to shoot more carefully. But I don't think the result is any less real or compelling. In fact, I think we've gotten better at it. I think our storytelling has gotten better and in some ways, our casting has gotten better, too.

Soap vs. Documentary

Is *The Real World* a soap opera or a documentary?

 MARY-ELLIS: It's a docu-soap. What it is...is a direct product of mine and Jon's pre-*Real World* work experiences. Jon came out of news and documentaries, and I came out of soap operas, like *Search for Tomorrow, As The World Turns, Loving,* and *Santa Barbara.* In all, I executive-produced 2,500 hours of soaps over thirteen years before Jon and I created this show.

 JON: And I came out of broadcast journalism. I'd been everything from a news producer to station manager... working everywhere from Green Bay, Wisconsin, to New York City. As for *The Real World,* I think it's a documentary, but it's constructed like a soap. What happens is real but we apply the dramatic standards of good storytelling to the material. If there's a flirtation between two people, well, we're going to play that up. We're going to use the right interviews to tell that story.

Celebrityhood

JON: The kind of recognition we receive is very different from what our cast goes through. I'm never recognized walking down the street, which frequently happens to former cast members!

MARY-ELLIS: Well, I was spotted in a restaurant once. A college-age waiter recognized me from a casting special. I must say I was shocked. I just laughed out loud.

Jon and Mary-Ellis discuss casting with Matt Kunitz, RW producer, Clay Newbill, RR supervising producer, and John Miller, senior V.P. of programming for MTV.

The Future

What other places would you like to do *The Real World*?

JON: We'd like to do a season in Hawaii 'cause it would certainly be a nice place for us to visit. And I'd love to do a show one summer in Chicago for the same reason. I like to pick locations based on where I'd actually like to visit.

MARY-ELLIS: I'd like to do a season in Cape Town, South Africa, since it's an English-speaking country. I think a lot of American kids would be interested and surprised by South African culture. A lot of South Africa's racial issues mirror our own...but in a more focused way.

How many more *Real World* seasons will there be?

MARY-ELLIS: Until my daughter's college education is fully paid for [laughing]. Correct that: Until Jon's newly adopted child gets out of college. Seriously, I don't know, but it's conceivable that even if the show took a rest for a while, it could still come back years later.

JON: Honestly, it'll go on as long as it should go on, and that's up to the audience. The number of viewers is greater than it ever was, and once it goes into syndication, we'll find an even bigger audience.

Any *Real World* spin-offs under consideration?

MARY-ELLIS: We want to do a *Real World-Golden Girls*. We'd like to choose a whole bunch of sassy, senior citizens in a new independent time of their lives. People who are really vital and outspoken.

And we're also developing a show, *Vegas Life*, which takes a look at show-girls in Las Vegas. In it, we go behind the scenes of the big showrooms at the Riviera Hotel. It's a world that hasn't been seen on TV before. It would be sort of a *Real World* meets *Showgirls*. We've already done a presentation tape based on hours and hours of footage we shot over a week and a half.

JON: We're also developing a prime-time live-action game show, called *Catch Me if You Can*. The show pits sets of trackers against sets of runners.

Each day, two runners are set free in a city and have to accomplish a mission. Meanwhile, two trackers use high-tech means to try to catch them. One tracker is on foot. The other is back at command central in constant communication with his tracker in the field. Each day the runners elude the trackers, they win thousands of dollars.

The premise is based, in part, on a show that aired in England for two seasons, which we optioned and retooled.

LEGACY

What's the legacy of *The Real World*?

Jon: Well, personally speaking, you'd think we'd be much richer [laughing].

Mary-Ellis: I think everything from *Reality Bites* to *Friends* has been influenced by our show. Certainly, *The Truman Show* with Jim Carrey and the upcoming *ed TV*, directed by Ron Howard, are similar in concept to *The Real World*. Frankly, I can't keep count of all the incarnations of *The Real World* that there have been.

Jon: ...Or, how many times *Saturday Night Live* or David Letterman has spoofed the show. It's become part of our culture. People say, 'Hey, I just had a *Real World* experience,' and you know what they mean. Not to mention the way commercials have been influenced by our use of music and editing on the show.

What aspect of the show are you most proud of?

Jon: The San Francisco season and our involvement with Pedro.

Mary-Ellis: That season was profound. It dealt with life and death. Pedro was an extraordinary individual with extraordinary courage to allow us to be a part of his life. He knew his time was finite, but he also knew the impact he could have on millions of people if he did the show. We still get letters years after from viewers telling us that Pedro was their first personal introduction to HIV and AIDS. Or that Pedro and Sean were their first insight into a gay relationship. Pedro and Sean's relationship was...and continues to be...the best love story we've ever done—gay or straight.

Janet

BEING ON *THE REAL WORLD* was like having someone read your diary every day. Or like having your best friend tell everyone in the world your darkest secrets.

I had no idea it would be that way. I think everyone assumes you have to be a big fan of the show to want to be on. I wasn't a fan at all. I think everyone assumes you know a lot about how it works before you enter the house. I had no idea. In fact, I seriously feel like an idiot because I didn't know what to expect.

I applied on a whim. I did practically no research to figure out what the show entailed, and I was completely unaware of the demands it would make on my life. That's all so unlike me. I'm usually so prepared and premeditated about things. But because I was so clueless, I was totally caught off guard. The first half of the show was absolutely grueling for me. Going in, I didn't realize how insecure I was, how afraid I was of showing my weaknesses. But when you have a microphone strapped to your back and a camera in your face, you have two choices—either let them see who you really are...or hide. For the first half of the show, I chose the latter.

I did consider leaving and I wasn't the only one. I know David and Nathan considered leaving 'cause of their girlfriends. I think Stephen and Rebecca thought about it, too, for different reasons. And, of course, Irene did leave ultimately. So, basically everyone except Lindsay seriously thought about bagging *The Real World.*

The directors said to me, 'Janet, if this isn't right for you, you should go home.' They took me out for coffee and walks off camera and tried to give me pep talks. It made me feel like they were really looking after my best interests. They made me feel like they really cared about my welfare...not my entertainment value. I began to see the crew as human beings, too.

What the crew goes through is just as bizarre as the cast, possibly more. After all, they have to suppress their lives for five months, and in effect live through us. Not only is that a huge personal sacrifice, it means they get really wrapped up in our lives and our well-being.

That was a major turning point for me. As I started to trust them, I began to trust myself more. Basically, I made a conscious decision not to give a s**t. I've always

"I was constantly editing myself. I was constantly trying to hide all the things that were negative about me.

I'd try to run away from the cameras, or cover my microphone. Lindsay and I would always whisper—not knowing until the show was over that the microphones picked up every whispered word."

We'd run into a women's bathroom whenever there was a male cameraperson filming us. Of course, that didn't stop any of them. They'd just follow us in and yell at us. We'd even secretly pass notes back and forth to each other. But the directors caught on and 'encouraged' us to stop.

In interviews, I gave them short answers. Or, I'd say, 'I don't know,' and smile a lot. I laughed off all their hard questions, and shrugged my shoulders. I was smoking like mad, up to two packs a day. I'd break into tears in the oddest situations. Like, I'd lose a pair of shoes or socks and suddenly explode. I felt tired all the time. I didn't want to talk to anyone, and when all else failed, I slept a lot and hoped the cameras would go away. Physically, I was hurting, and mentally, I was quite depressed. It was all so unlike me.

One weekend, Irene started pushing me to leave. She said, 'Janet, you just don't seem happy here. I love you too much to see you suffer like this.' I appreciated her concern, but I thought it was kind of weird just how hard she was pushing—almost like she was doing it for herself. If she really wanted what was best for me, you'd think she would want me to get through it. So I questioned her motive, but I got her message—that maybe I should quit.

been worried so much what other people thought. That was my biggest hurdle going into this thing. Well, I just decided, 'I can't please everyone. I might as well be proud of who I am, and be secure enough to show it—imperfections and all.'

Of course, you can say those things, but it's hard putting them into action. I think I opened up a lot the second half of the show. I worried a lot less about failure and rejection, which is a constant fear of mine. By the end, I'd completely fallen in love with my roommates and the crew. I gave them more of myself than I'd ever given anyone else. I know it sounds cheesy, but I was real proud of what I accomplished.

I think I represented my family pretty well. I couldn't represent the Korean community, even if I tried. Honestly, I should be more in touch with my Korean culture than I am. But I did feel obligated to represent the ethics and morality of my grandparents, who are so dear to me. For the most part, I think I did fairly well.

All in all, this was quite a positive experience. Incredibly difficult at times, but completely satisfying in the end. You know, I think it's ridiculous that people say to me *The Real World* isn't real. What's not so real about *The Real World*? That it's a fantasyland? Well, sure, there are fantasy aspects to this experience, but I can assure you, it didn't always feel like a fantasy to me—more like a bad dream sometimes. The feelings I had inside that house felt very real to me.

On Janet

DAVID: Janet is such a sweetheart. She's such a kind and giving woman. I think she grew a lot living in the house. She got over a lot of her insecurities. She learned that the best way to get over them is to put your mind on someone else. I think she really helped out everyone in the house, and I know she grew more confident as a result of this experience.

✳ IRENE: Janet came back from one of her interviews saying, 'Irene, I feel like I don't know you.' Listen, Janet. You feel like you don't know me 'cuz you ain't turned your ears on this entire time. That girl does not listen. Janet, if you want to be in journalism—this is my journalistic tip—learn to listen. Forget about your opinion. Forget about what you have to say. Learn to sit there and learn to listen. You're gonna make a terrible journalist if you keep opening your mouth. Janet has so many gifts and so many talents. She has so much potential in life. But she's so defensive. She's so caught up in exterior things that she's not living. She needs to say to herself every night, 'I am not perfect. I will never be perfect. And I'm okay not being perfect.

REBECCA: Janet is multifaceted, you know. She can be this kind of happy, giddy, 'Whoo-Whoo,' party girl. She can also be very reflective, and very ambitious. She's just got a lot of different sides. I think she's very interesting.

LINDSAY: If I can't date Janet, I guess someone else can. But I hope some day she'll be one of my bridesmaids.

STEPHEN: Janet is disco! I love her! She's a friendship that I earned. We earned it together. That's why I love her so much. We worked hard on understanding each other. She's a girl with so many facets and can relate them all so well. I think she's beautiful—inside and out.

We had some bad times in the beginning. But we're buddies now, and that's an awesome thing. Before this experience, if I didn't like someone at first, like with Janet, I'd have walked away. But being forced to hang around with Janet forced both of us to find different ways to form a friendship. So, I've learned from this experience that I've got to give a better effort from now on. If I don't like someone right away, I can't be, 'Get away from me.' I'm going to be like, 'What's up?' If it's a hard friendship, it might be a stronger one in the end. That's definitely what happened with Janet and me.

NATHAN: Janet is a great girl, and great friend. She just loves to have a good time. That's Janet in a f**king nutshell.

MARY-ELLIS: Janet had very relatable issues with her parents, especially regarding communicating with them. She'd felt that her parents hadn't emotionally extended themselves to her. So, when her father sent her those flowers on Valentine's Day, you could just tell how much it meant to Janet.

Janet also has very high expectations for herself...and for her potential boyfriends. Like other women in the house, she felt that if a guy was too easily attainable, then he probably wasn't good enough. That came true in her relationship with Justin. He fell head over heels for her, and that scared her away.

JON: I think Janet really grew from her *Real World* experience. At the start, she was editing herself too much, but she knew she was being overly self-protective, and fought to overcome it. By the end, she'd managed to break through and become much less self-conscious. As a result, she got so much more from her roommates and her experiences—and we got to know her much better, too.

And...

JANET: Given the limited TV time, I know it's impossible to portray me in my entirety, but I don't want people seeing me as the token Asian girl, or simply the girl struggling with a cross-cultural clash with her parents. That's not a big part of me. It's only about ten percent. I'm basically someone who really loves to get to know people. To learn what they're all about. And to keep expanding this knowledge every minute of my life.

✳ Irene opted not to participate in this book project. The quotes included throughout the book are taken from her on camera interviews with the show's producers and directors.

Inquiring Minds

What question would you most like to ask Janet?

LINDSAY: Where did you buy your leopard underwear?

JANET: The same place I got my zebra, tiger, and rhino underwear.

DAVID: What were you saying to your mother and grandmother in Korean?

JANET: Which time?...And wouldn't you like to know?

REBECCA: What made you want to do *The Real World*?

JANET: My life was boring, and I was ready for a party.

NATHAN: Are you ever going to quit smoking?

JANET: Absolutely...someday.

STEPHEN: What's the nickname we gave you at the station when we saw your vagina?

JANET: 'Lean Pocket.' And I still can't believe you embarrassed me like that.

And...

JANET: How many cigarettes do you really smoke a day?

JANET: About a pack a day.

Pet Peeves

What annoys you the most about Janet?

REBECCA: That she's so insecure, when she has nothing to be insecure about.

DAVID: That she can take an hour to get ready to go out. She was so high-maintenance it used to aggravate me, but she got better about that toward the end.

LINDSAY: She thought she was so much taller than me, but she's only got three inches on me.

NATHAN: When she reacts to every situation with, 'Oh, my God! Oh, my God,' like fifteen times in a row.

STEPHEN: That she always said, 'Oh, you're kidding me. Oh, you're kidding me,' over and over again.

And...

JANET: That I second-guess myself all the time. I'll scream out an opinion, then sit around for hours chastising myself for saying it.

Rock & Suck

When did it ROCK?

JANET: It rocked when we went to Nepal. There was barely any conflict on that trip. Everybody was just so happy to get out of Seattle, and be in such an awesome place. All of us had just the best time of our lives.

When did it SUCK?

JANET: It sucked right after the honeymoon period ended for the cast. The directors say the honeymoon period always lasts the first two weeks of *The Real World*. Everything is really exciting and brand-new. And you're still able to hide just about anything you want, but after that excitement dies down, harsh reality sets in. That's when you begin to freak out about what you've just gotten yourself into.

Janet's real world

On Grandmother

My grandmother is my soul mate. My parents worked twelve hours a day, and still do. From the time I was a child, my grandmother took care of me. She's just the most vivacious women I've ever met. She's like a 5-year-old trapped inside an 80-year-old's body. She's so kindhearted and generous, too. I don't think she's ever had a selfish thought.

She came to America from Korea in 1973. When she first got here, she worked in a sewing factory. Before the Communists took over North Korea, she was a wealthy landowner, but the Communists took away all her land. She and my grandfather—my father's parents—have had just an incredible life.

On Dad

He's just an incredibly hardworking, admirable individual. He's completely tolerant of the way life has been dished out to him, but he wants everything and more for his children—nothing less. Toward that goal, he's sacrificed so much of himself. When I was younger, my father was definitely my disciplinarian. Now he's my cheerleader.

On Mom

I don't know how to explain my mom. She's a beautiful, energetic woman, who's really tired by her circumstances. She'd just like to take off with my dad and go live in some beach house. She definitely needs a vacation.

It's been very hard on my mom living with so many generations in the house. Between my father's parents and her kids, she's struggled to maintain her equilibrium between all three generations. She was a distant mother—pretty much caught up in our family's finances—but I think she's tried to become closer to me in the last few years...and we definitely have.

On Parental Expectations

Growing up, their expectations were a burden. Now, they inspire me. They just want me to be happy and financially stable. Basically, they don't want me to have to go through what they went through. They sacrificed a million things for me, and I want to repay them by making sure they don't have to worry about me.

On Culture Clash

The biggest culture clash I've experienced was that my parents wanted me to be their son. They've always expected me to take care of them in their old age, like a son would. They've always expected me to carry on the family name. My grandfather says I'm the family 'son without a penis.' That's all right with me. They still let me wear skirts [laughing]. So, I definitely feel an obligation to maintain the family name and keep it when I get married.

On Family Reaction to Being Cast on *The Real World*

In Korea, they don't have anything close to *The Real World*. So, my family couldn't even fathom it. The directors had to explain it to them, step by step. I was so happy they didn't show my parent's reaction on the casting special because their reaction was awful. My dad gave me a half-a** pat on the back. My mom could barely look at me.

May 8, 1977–Born	1983	1984	1985		1988
Janet's 'Line'					
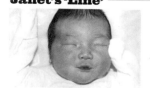	**First tricycle:** A strawberry-shortcake tricycle.	**First Barbie:** Just one of those good ol' plain Barbies.	**First trauma:** When I was eight, there was a fire in my parents' restaurant. My parents weren't making any money at the time. So it was a huge problem for them.		**First period:** In sixth grade, and it happened on a bus coming home from summer camp. It wasn't until my mom was washing my clothes that she told me I'd just had my period.

My mother and father are very private people. It scared them that their oldest daughter might reveal everything about them on national TV. On the other hand, my grandparents were ecstatic. It was something they could brag about. But as far as understanding what I was doing...they just figured I was going to be acting on some sitcom.

On Younger Sister's Reaction

My younger sister was happy for me. Of course, there's a tad bit of jealousy there. There's still some sibling rivalry between us. She's always been told to be more like me. And as the older sister, I've always been held accountable for her actions.

On The Red Dragon

My family runs a Chinese restaurant called The Red Dragon which they've owned for eighteen years. Even though we're Korean, a lot more people eat Chinese than Korean food. So, it made more sense for my dad to open up a Chinese restaurant. Food-wise, I got the best of both worlds growing up—I got my grandparents' Korean food and my dad's Chinese.

My father is real proud of the fact that the restaurant is family owned and operated. So, he likes for me and my sister to work there a lot. Over the years, I've been a hostess, a carryout girl and a cashier, which I really sucked at. But, to be honest,

I've tried to spend as little time at the restaurant as possible. I just want to do other things. My sister is a more family-oriented person than I am. So, I hope she takes over the restaurant from my dad.

On High School

I had the best four years of my life in high school. I wouldn't change a thing about it. I had classes with the academic kids, but I hung out with this 'crew,' which was a pretty popular crowd. We partied a lot, but I still maintained enough of a GPA to get into Northwestern. I was involved with every organization possible. I was all about pom-pom, yearbook, junior class president and senior class president.

On "The First Time"

It was awkward. It was very quick. And I cried for hours afterward because it was such a huge emotional thing for me. All in all it's a good memory, except that he dumped me two weeks after, the a**hole!

On "Bad Boys"

I like fly-by-the-seat-of-their-pants-type guys. I don't like calculated people, because I'm pretty calculated myself. I like guys that have no idea where they'll be the next day. I like rock stars. I love their passion. I'm attracted to passionate people.

On Smoking

I started smoking at the end of my sopho-

more year in high school. I've had problems with oral fixations since the day I was born. I was weaned very late, and sucked my thumb until I was 9 or 10. Then, I bit my thumbnails and pen caps until I chipped my teeth. On top of that, I've got a very addictive nature. I know I'll quit eventually. I've got to quit. My voice has gotten a lot scratchier since I started smoking.

On College

College is the first time I've appreciated an education. I truly love what I'm learning. I'm currently a double major in broadcast journalism and international studies, with a minor in sociology. Most of the people at Northwestern are very motivated, but you get that at every 'top ten' school.

S T A T S	
Birthday:	May 8, 1977
Hometown:	Elmhurst, Illinois
Siblings:	Alice (age 15)
Pets:	Black Scottish terrier, "Herman"
High School:	York High School
College:	Northwestern University

F A V E S	
Band:	Dave Matthews Band
Book:	*Catcher in the Rye* by J.D. Salinger
TV Show:	*I Love Lucy*
Movie:	*Breakfast at Tiffany's*
Actor:	Robert Redford
Actress:	Audrey Hepburn
Personal Motto:	Everything happens for a reason.
Meal:	Cheese and spinach dip at the Cheesecake Factory
Way to Chill Out:	Coffee and cigarettes over a conversation
Pick-up Line:	I would normally never say this, but...
First Date:	Dinner and a glass of wine
Sleeping Outfit:	Green satin nightshirt
Stuffed Animal:	Yellow silk Binkie (My favorite blanket, which I brought to Seattle.)

1992	1993	1994	1995	1996	1996	1997
First kiss: I was 15...and all I kept thinking was, 'Am I doing this right?'	**First crash:** Just six days after I got my license. I was driving my mom's Honda Accord. She was not happy.	**First love:** He was on the football team. I was a pom-pom girl. Ain't that cheesy!	**Graduates high school:** From York Community High School in Elmhurst Illinois.	**First sex:** In my boyfriend's bedroom.	**First break:** I broke my pinkie toe 'cause my sister pushed me off the bed.	**First time watching** *The Real World*: The Boston season was the first time I'd ever really watched the show.

Janet & Justin

JANET:

I liked Justin a lot. He's an amazing guy. But he wasn't right for me. He was overly into me. And after four days there was no way I was about to get into a serious relationship with him. I think the cameras also caused problems for us. Our relationship started towards the beginning of the show, and I wasn't comfortable with the cameras yet. I wasn't totally at ease being myself in front of them, let alone doing any romantic stuff. So, we had to sneak kisses while the cameras weren't around. In fact, I don't think they caught a single kiss on camera.

One time, Justin grabbed me and gave me this huge smooch. We could see the cameraman running toward us to get it on film. We stopped kissing right before he reached us. And the director was soooo pissed. Basically, it was just impossible for me to get intimate with someone on camera. So, Justin and I never went beyond kissing, or anything like that..

Skydiving

JANET: Skydiving sucked! It's not my piece of cake. And the bastard forgot to turn on my radio to tell me which way to turn.

Right before I went up in the plane, the guide told me, 'Don't worry, this radio never fails.' Right then and there, I should've known something was going to happen. You should never say 'never.' And on top of that, the guide was such a complete a**hole. He'd gotten all wrapped up in the glamour of the cameras and was trying look like a hard-a**. He was saying things like, 'Janet, be serious. Unless you're serious, I'm not taking you up in this plane. We're all about safety here.' Well, he's the jacka** that turned off my radio.

It was definitely a huge rush jumping out of the plane. But as soon as I realized my radio wasn't working, I started to get seriously scared. I wasn't going fast enough to die. Hell, that would've been a relief. I'd have done a couple of back-flips on the way down. But instead, I was falling so slowly it guaranteed me crunching bones and excruciating pain.

Thankfully, just as I was about to hit, I heard them screaming out what I was supposed to do. So, actually, I landed rather gently, thank God. All I bruised was my ego.

DIRTY WORDS

JANET: There were three words I couldn't stand hearing in the house–'selling out,' 'issues,' and 'process.' And those three words came up all the time.

The word 'issue' would be used whenever a really good conversation would come up. Someone would always stop it and say, 'I don't want to make this an issue.' In other words, 'Let's not make this a topic on the show.'

As for 'selling out,' everyone was so afraid of what people might say behind their backs, particularly during the interviews. The roommates would always be accusing each other of 'selling out' one another. That was a really huge 'issue' in the house.

And we frequently used the term, 'process,' to refer to *The Real World*, as compared to the real world. That no matter how hard we tried to live a normal life, there was a 'process' at work behind the walls. There was a control room and cameras. There were people watching and listening to our every move. I used to hate it when my roommates would refer to the 'process,' because I didn't want to be reminded of it. It just made it harder to let go.

The Future
After *The Real World*

JANET: I have a year left at Northwestern. After that, I want to move to a city, either New York or San Francisco. I like the rush of New York, and the beauty of San Francisco. As for a career, I'd like to pursue some type of broadcasting. I'm not quite sure if that'll be in hard-core journalism, or lighter, entertainment stuff. Ideally, I'd either like to be the next Kurt Loder or Diane Sawyer. I can't decide which one.

I'd definitely like to get married by the time I am 35, have 1.5 kids and a couple of dogs. I can picture myself sitting on a front porch, drinking Johnnie Walker lemonades, wearing a long, flowy dress, petting my black Lab and kicking back with Lindsay talking about the good old days.

👁 Close Encounters

Whom will you stay in contact with?

JANET: I'll be in touch with **LINDSAY** twice a week. I'll probably be in touch with **DAVID** and **NATHAN** once a month. **REBECCA**, I'll speak with every six months, and **STEPHEN** a little less than that. As for **IRENE**, I'll probably never talk to her again. Or rather, I don't want to talk to her as long as she's still in the same state that she was in at the end of the show. I'm willing to talk to her after she becomes less hostile.

⬇ Predictions

STEPHEN	**5** YEARS	Launching her journalism career.
	10 YEARS	Landing her first anchor job.
	25 YEARS	Knocking Connie Chung out of commission.
LINDSAY	**5** YEARS	She'll be working hard, doing journalism.
	10 YEARS	Still working hard in journalism.
	25 YEARS	Hardly working...and enjoying her money.
NATHAN	**5** YEARS	Interning with a broadcast company.
	10 YEARS	Serving as the backup anchor at a decent-sized TV station.
	25 YEARS	The lead anchor on the network news, reporting from Bosnia with missiles soaring over her head.
DAVID	**5** YEARS	Doing some form of journalism.
	10 YEARS	A career woman with a hubby and kids.
	25 YEARS	Settling down, being a mom. She's got those instincts.
REBECCA	**5** YEARS	Working at some local affiliate in broadcasting.
	10 YEARS	Having moved on to network news.
	25 YEARS	Semiretired and married with kids.
JANET	**5** YEARS	Making $14,000 a year, smoking cigarettes, and drinking Diet Coke.
	10 YEARS	Making $16,000 a year, smoking cigarettes, and drinking Diet Coke.
	25 YEARS	Drinking martinis, smoking foreign cigarettes, and hopefully making millions.

ENCORE?

Would you do *The Real World* again?
Janet:
I'd do it again in a minute. It was truly the most awesome experience I've ever had. I learned so much about myself and about how to be more open-minded. It was also a million firsts. The first time I ever went skydiving; the first time kayaking; the first time sailing; the first time I've ever loved like this in such a short amount of time; and the first time I've ever really let go.

Lindsay

BEFORE I WENT TO SEATTLE, I prepared myself to play this by ear, to get to know my roommates and to try and have fun. And you know what? I did.

For the most part, I had a great time on the show. It was not nearly as scary as I thought it would be. I liked most of my roommates a lot. I thought the crew was awesome. And most of the time, I didn't mind the cameras being constantly in my face. I guess the biggest problem I had was using the toilets in the house.

For the life of me, I could not s**t in that house. No joke, I think I only s**t ten times in there. The rest of the time, I either went at the radio station or at the Edgewater, which was a hotel a few blocks away from the house. Man, the bathroom doors in that house were too thin. And there were just too many people around all the time, not to mention all the cameras and microphones.

But I'll tell ya, I wasn't the only one who had a hard time of it. Ask my roommates, they'll confess to ya. They all used to turn on the showers and the faucets whenever they had to go.

I also hated making personal phone calls inside that damn house. Mostly because I didn't like my roommates listening in. A couple of times Stephen commented on my conversations with my mom, which really pissed me off. So I started making all my phone calls from my favorite bathroom place, the Edgewater Hotel.

Funny thing is I began to realize the cameras never followed me into the Edgewater. Soon I was taking coffee and lunch breaks in there as well. The Edgewater became my home away from home. Ultimately, I learned the crew was actually banned from filming in there. After I heard that, I practically moved in.

In general, though, I was pretty loose about most things. I tried my best to let petty things roll off my back.

people. Well, actually, we really didn't get to know the crew personally during filming. Rather, they were just amazingly understanding and sympathetic people.

The really weird thing about *The Real World* is that you know practically nothing about the crew, yet they become your best friends. We never heard anything about their backgrounds, their sex lives, or their feelings about each other. In other words, they knew everything about us...everything that we didn't know about them.

During filming, I'd look for little signs that would help me get to know the crew better—like what made them laugh. Or, what made them upset. Oh, my God when they'd laugh with you it was just the greatest feeling. I began to figure out what made each cameraman crack up. Or what made each sound-person bust out with a smile.

I admit, I talked to the crew all the time. But they rarely ever talked back. I'd squeeze them, push them or pinch their butts to try and get a rise out of them. But their bosses will be proud to hear they remained ever the professionals. On the other hand, I ought to be charged with sexual harassment.

As for the cast, I liked everyone in the house. I got along with Nathan very well, and with David, too. I liked Stephen, though I think he has some problems he needs to work through. I liked Rebecca, but we didn't click one hundred percent. And I liked Irene, especially at the beginning when she was feeling well. But, of course, the person I clicked with the best was Janet. We just hit it off immediately.

Janet was the only roommate that I revealed my total self to. I'm just a reserved person in that way. I admit it, I'm all hyper on the outside...but I've closed off

> I tried not to second-guess myself, or judge any of the things I did. Sometimes, I felt the need to make disclaimers. I'm a pretty blunt person and I can make tasteless jokes. I might say things like 'she's a fat-a**,' which can offend some people. At first, I was constantly disclaiming, **'I'm kidding. I'm kidding.' But, eventually I was like, 'Oh, screw it! Let them see me the way I am.'**

Unlike some of my other roommates, I have very few complaints about 'The Process.' I rarely found it to be a major problem. Privacy was my biggest fear going into *The Real World*. I'm definitely a very private person who needs private time for myself. I ended up needing less of it than I thought. And the crew was incredibly understanding whenever I needed a break.

In general, I can't say enough good things about the crew. They were so supportive. So patient. So awesome. Without a doubt, they got me through this experience. People like the director, Billy Rainey, were just amazing

my inside. It's been that way ever since my father's death. I keep a lot to myself and only share it with my brother or mom. And, I'm sure you could see that when my friend Bill died, I shut down pretty quick, and pulled away from my roommates.

But on *The Real World*, I began opening up a lot more than I have since my dad died. I think Janet got to know me pretty damn well. I wanted to tell her everything. That's a pretty big deal for me and something I hope to build upon after *The Real World*.

On Lindsay

JANET: Lindsay is a five-foot two-inch bucket of energy. She's the most energetic person I've ever met. We got along so well because we have similar goals. She's very ambitious, too. We're very direct and honest people, so we never had any problems about communicating or back-stabbing. She's just very levelheaded and adorable. People are drawn to her.

But she's also a very private person. I learned more about her than the cameras did, but she still keeps a lot of things inside. She gets hurt easily, and though she may not want to show it, she's very sensitive and vulnerable. But when she loves someone, she gives herself to that person one hundred percent. She'll be a lifelong friend, I'm sure. And she'll probably be in my wedding, too.

IRENE: Lindsay: you need to learn to love like it's not going to hurt. I'm very sorry your father died. But, sweetie, you have to start going on with your life. You close yourself off. You don't let yourself get close to people. You're so scared of getting hurt that you beat them to the punch. You hurt them first. You were one of the closest I had to a friend in the house. And then you just walked away.

REBECCA: Lindsay is very flamboyant, but it's weird because she's very quiet. I mean, she stayed real closed.

NATHAN: Lindsay is fun. She's playful. I just think of her with an eternal smile.

DAVID: Lindsay is extremely hyperactive for some reason I don't understand. But she's also in extreme control at times too, like being in bed at ten o'clock every night. I don't understand how she can be manic all day...and then in bed so early. Maybe she just wears herself out. I do think she's extremely lonely right now. She's got a lot on her mind these days. Unfortunately, she keeps it all inside. I wish she'd express her feelings more, like I do.

STEPHEN: Lindsay is a cool girl, but she's probably not someone I'll talk to much again. I didn't get to know her at all. I think she didn't want me to. If she'd cared to know, she'd have let me in.

MARY-ELLIS: When Bill committed suicide, it brought out a lot of issues that Lindsay hadn't dealt with in relation to her own father's death.

JON: ...And her own fear of death. So it was very powerful.

And...

LINDSAY: What you see with Lindsay is not always what you get. I am an extrovert and I'm hyperactive. That's definitely me, but I'm also 'grandma.' Well, not really 'grandma'...but very reserved and early to bed. Personally, I think the two sides of me go together pretty well—in a funny way.

Rock & Suck

When did it ROCK?

LINDSAY: When my brother was here and we went fishing. He's my best friend in the whole world. That was the last time I saw Bill, too. Bill wasn't really himself that trip, but he was more himself that day than any other in recent memory. So, it's an important memory for me. Also, Nepal was amazing. It was one of the most incredible things I've ever done.

When did it SUCK?

LINDSAY: When Bill died, I only wanted to share it with Janet. You can't really do that in this situation. So, having to discuss it with so many people kind of sucked. I know it sounds stupid, but I'm proud of the way I handled myself. I'm proud of the way I talked about Bill's death with some of my roommates, and in front of the cameras. When my dad died, it was five years before anyone in my family started talking about it.

Pet Peeves

What annoys you the most about Lindsay?

JANET: That she went to bed too early.

NATHAN: That she's not confident in her looks.

DAVID: She could be such a bitch sometimes. Other than that, she's solid like Janet and Rebecca. When she'd scream every morning, though, it'd kill me.

REBECCA: Her loudness.

STEPHEN: The little tiger acting thing she does. And...

LINDSAY: That I'm a drama queen.

Kiss 'n' Tell

LINDSAY: I have the ugliest feet, so I made sure they never got them on film. I've run so many half marathons and played so much soccer that I have bunions. Janet has seen them, and says they're 'nasty.' I'm so embarrassed about them.

Inquiring Minds

What question would you most like to ask Lindsay?

NATHAN: How did your boobs get so much bigger while you were on the show?

LINDSAY: I had implants my second month there. No one knew about it 'cause I'm just so good at concealing things.

DAVID: Who are you?
LINDSAY: Who do you want me to be?

JANET: Do you give yourself to anyone?
LINDSAY: Yeah, it just has to be the right person.

REBECCA: Does it bother you to be closed up?
LINDSAY: I open myself to people I want to.

STEPHEN: Are you afraid of yourself?
LINDSAY: No, are you afraid of me?
And...

LINDSAY: When are you going to settle down and take a sedative?
LINDSAY: Hopefully soon.

Advice
What advice would you give to future *Real World*-ers?

LINDSAY: Stick to your guns. Make every effort to open up. And remember to masturbate in the confessional, if you have to.

Lindsay's real world

On Dad

My dad died of cancer in 1990, when I was 14. His death was by far the most traumatic thing that's ever happened to me. Everybody loved my dad. He had the most down-to-earth personality. And he was one of the most positive people I've ever met. When he was sick, you'd never know by his manner. My dad would be in the hospital on the eve of major surgery, and he'd call me, all cheerful, just to say 'Hi.'

When he was alive, he used to spoil the s**t out of us. He was the president of these health-care companies and we had the most amazing lifestyle. We'd sail every week. Fly to exotic locations. We were a very social family with lots of parties. And then he got sick, and all of that stopped. They gave him six months to live. He lasted a few years.

I remember I didn't go to soccer the day he died. Not 'cause he was sick, but because I had a cold. And there he was dying of cancer. I mean, s**t. When you're 14, you can barely tell the difference between a cold and cancer.

On Mom

She's my best friend in the world, but it took five years after my dad's death for us to get close. My whole family dealt with his death separately...not as a family. After he died, my mom started a business to take her mind off things. She'd have gone crazy if she hadn't, but she was much more wrapped up in that than us.

But now we're as close as could be, and although she's still an authority figure, we're not your normal mother-daughter relationship. I guess, we're more like sisters.

On Pouell

My brother is actually my best friend in the world, because my mother is still my mom. This kid does everything for me. I have so much respect for him. He's replaced my father in so many ways, but he's more like my right arm. I need that kid in my life 'cause he keeps me in line. He's my soul mate.

On Death

Death has played a very large place in my life. Not just my father's death, but the death of other relatives and family friends. But now when it happens, it's something I have to start dealing with right away. I can't just hide as I did when my dad died. Only when I finally started talking about his death was I finally able to get happy again. Same for the rest of my family. Unfortunately, it took several years for us to get to that point. Now that my friend, Bill, has died, I have to remind myself of that lesson all the time. I never want to isolate myself the way I did after my father's death.

October 21, 1976–Born	1981	1982	1983	1986	1988
Lindsay's 'Line' 	**First Barbie:** My brother drove nails through my Malibu Barbie's boobs.	**First love:** His name was Michael and we checked out each other's bottoms.	**First kiss:** He had red hair, just like my father. So, I kissed him.	**First chew:** My mom didn't let me chew gum until I was 10.	**First period:** 'It' happened In sixth grade. I was in my bathroom at home, thank God. It took me twenty minutes to tell my mom.

On Childhood

It was the most incredible thing. I was so innocent and didn't know anything about life. We moved every two years, but it was a nice, comfortable childhood. Idyllic, in fact, compared to my teen years.

On High School

I didn't hang out with any crowd. Actually, I totally isolated myself after my dad's death. I did my own thing. I ran an insane amount. I had friends, but I really wasn't close to any of them. It was just a really difficult time for me. All I seemed able to do was study like hell, and run.

On Eating Disorders

When I was in high school, I ran eight to ten miles a day. I was really anal about what I ate. I was an anorexic, running bitch. I knew all the tricks of the trade—all the ways of keeping weight off. I was certainly f**king up my body. At the end of junior year, I shocked myself back into reality and realized what I was doing to myself.

On the "First Time"

I was 18. It was the beginning of my senior year. My boyfriend at the time and I had been going out a few months. We decided to ditch school to have sex. We didn't know what the hell we were doing. I used this weird spermicide that lasted ten minutes. He used a condom. We were listening to the Beastie Boys in my bedroom. Basically, we were clueless. It was no fun at all. We didn't have sex again until three weeks later. But that time it was better.

On Alex

When my Dad died, Alex was the one person I let get close to me. I shut out all my friends, except for him. My mom was doing her thing, my brother his...and Alex filled the void in my life. We've been going out for four years, but we're more suited to be friends—not boyfriend/girlfriend. In fact, we're polar opposites. He's so reserved and I am so out there. Alex is the type of guy I'd tell the funniest sex story to...and he'd say, 'I can't believe you just said that!'

Basically, our romantic relationship should've ended a few years ago. But I was just too scared to let him go. It felt like he was all I had. When I was in Seattle, I finally realized I had to put an end to it. For the first time I felt strong enough to move on. And that was a really big thing for me. And a good thing for him, too, 'cause it wasn't right to hold on to him out of weakness, when we we're not right for each other.

On College

Freshman year I had a great time. But sophomore year, I started buckling down and studying my ass off. To be honest, I want to be done with college and move on with my life.

On Friendship

I make friends fast, but I tend to keep them at arm's length—except for really close friends.

On Marriage

I want to get married when I am financially stable for kids.

S T A T S	
Birthday:	October 21, 1976
Hometown:	Aspen, Colorado
Siblings:	Brother (Pouell, age 24)
Pets:	None
High School:	New Trier High School
College:	University of Michigan

F A V E S	
Band:	Booker T and the MGs
Book:	Anything with pictures.
TV Show:	Today
Movie:	Chinatown
Actor:	Jack Nicholson
Actress:	Glenn Close
Personal Motto:	Get over it. I am.
Meal:	Anything with spinach
Way to Chill Out:	To be silent
Pickup Line:	Hello.
First Date:	Get drunk, drunk, drunk.
Sleep Outfit:	Sport shorts and a T-shirt
Stuffed Animal:	Simon ("A big ol' dog that I have.")

November 1990		1994	1995	1996	1997

Father dies:
He died of cancer when I was 14.

First time:
While listening to the Beastie Boys.

Graduates high school:
From New Trier in Winnetka, Illinois.

First sex with a giant:
When I was 20, I had an affair with this six-foot seven-inch guy. I was nearly a foot and a half shorter than him.

Transferes colleges:
I transferred from USC to the U of Michigan in order to be closer to my family. Unfortunately, they moved to Aspen, and ended up being closer to USC.

Bill, Lindsay and Pouell

Losing a Friend

LINDSAY: When I got the phone call that Bill had killed himself, it felt like the worst thing that could've happened. It was like, 'S**t! When is all this death going to end?' It just seemed like Bill was beginning to get his life together. When he came out to visit with my brother, Pouell, we'd all had such a great time together. It was just so much fun.

Bill had his problems, for sure, and he suffered from depression. But it's just so hard to deal with suicide, 'cause it feels like it's being done to you. You can't help but ask questions, like, 'What could I have done? What didn't I see? How could he do this to his mom? To my brother? Or, to me?'

It's been so hard on my brother, who was Bill's best friend. Bill was practically a member of our family. And now another family member is dead. Honestly, I'm afraid to get close to someone again for fear I might lose them, too.

As for *The Real World,* I have no real problems with the way anyone—cast or crew—handled Bill's death. I yelled at Stephen for hugging me, but I explained to him later that I just needed my space. I screamed at a cameraman, too, but they were just doing their job. Fact is, maybe something good will come of having filmed this tragedy. I think people considering suicide should see what it feels like on the other end. Of course, when you're that depressed nothing seems to matter anyway, but at the very least, showing me coping might help others cope with their own loss. I know I'm still trying to deal with it. And so is my family.

JANET: I think Lindsay was a champ for the way she handled Bill's death. I know she really wanted to finish up the process without letting it affect her. I was there the day she exploded. She was just so angry afterward that she couldn't hold the pain inside until she got home.

She wanted to be around her family when she dealt with those emotions. She didn't want to be around people who had no idea of Bill's situation or her relationship to him. She didn't want people consoling her for the sake of consoling her. She wanted everybody to sit back and wait for her to come to them, which she eventually did.

That girl has loved four people in her life. The fact that two of four have died so early in life, well, that's really sad. I really feel for her.

DAVID: I don't think the cameras should've filmed Lindsay just after she got word of Bill's death. I don't think they belonged there at all. When a situation is bigger than the documentation process—like the death of a friend—you've got to show some restraint. A heartbeat was lost. A human spirit died. Someone who loved that life, who was affected by that life, deserved the space to mourn.

In a pure ideal, it could be good for people to see what that kind of loss feels like. Maybe a kid might be discouraged from killing himself by seeing the toll it takes on family and friends. But realistically, the act of filming someone grieving is just terrible. To be so detached—in the name of professionalism—is suspect. And I think it's an invasion of Lindsay's privacy to show something so personal to millions of strangers.

NATHAN: I didn't know Bill at all, but Lindsay, man, it tore her up inside. Unfortunately, she just wasn't comfortable enough with the people in the house to talk about it—not like she would be with her brother and mom. I'm sure when she got back home she was able to get it off her chest. Had she wanted to talk about it in the house, I'm sure she would've come to Janet or me.

REBECCA: It was terribly sad for Lindsay and her brother, Pouell. Lindsay, however, doesn't vocalize her worries, or her woes, as much as I do. If something bothers me, I have to talk about it with others. But for the most part, Lindsay bottled up her feelings about Bill's death. I guess she prefers not to talk about things like that.

ENCORE?

Would you do *The Real World* again?

Lindsay: I'd repeat this in a heartbeat. I learned so much about myself doing the show. I overcame so many things with Alex, with Bill, and with my fear of opening myself up to strangers. I will never, ever forget it.

 ## Close Encounters

Whom will you stay in contact with?

LINDSAY: **JANET** and I will talk all the time. I'll also be in touch with **NATHAN** and **DAVID,** although David will probably be off doing his own thing. I don't think I'll talk to the others too often. I'll see 'em when I see 'em. It's not that I didn't like them. We just didn't click.

The Future
After *The Real World*

LINDSAY: I've got one year left of college, then I'm not sure what I'm going to do. I'm a film major, but I want to go into broadcasting. I want to do something fun, where I can use my personality. I'm trying to figure all that out. I guess a perfect job for me would be something in broadcasting or entertainment. Somewhere in front of the camera. And someplace in New York or Los Angeles.

⬇ Predictions

DAVID	5 YEARS	She'll be involved in film or TV, but selling real estate on the side. She's a business-woman at heart.
	10 YEARS	Making lots of money.
	25 YEARS	Very wealthy.
JANET	5 YEARS	Starting in broadcasting, living in a small apartment.
	10 YEARS	Starring in broadcasting, living in a phat apartment.
	25 YEARS	Retired from broadcasting, drinking cognac in her New York penthouse with her phat husband.
NATHAN	5 YEARS	Bouncing off walls.
	10 YEARS	Still bouncing off walls.
	25 YEARS	Doing back flips off walls.
REBECCA	5 YEARS	Drinking a lot of coffee.
	10 YEARS	Still drinking a lot of coffee and training for a triathalon.
	25 YEARS	The 'Queen of Wall Street' and still drinking lots of coffee.
STEPHEN	5 YEARS	Working in film, and trying to make money in the stock market.
	10 YEARS	Giving up film, and focusing on business.
	25 YEARS	Going to films, but running a successful business.
LINDSAY	5 YEARS	Sweeping floors.
	10 YEARS	Polishing floors.
	25 YEARS	Sleeping on the floor.

Nathan

I WAS EXPECTING A ROLLER COASTER OF FUN.
I thought we'd get a cool place to live. Get a cool trip. And meet cool people. It turned out to be all of the above. But I just had no clue what living with those cameras would really be like. And the truth is, it's just impossible to imagine—unless you've gone through it yourself.

I mean, it's like having God standing next to you at all times. You know how people say that God is always watching over you. Well, imagine God himself, actually standing over your shoulder while you're eating. That's what it's like. You can't escape the cameras. And there's no way of ignoring them, either.

Yeah, the presence of the cameras fades in and out of your mind. Sometimes, they kind of blend into the background and you don't really care that they're around. But most of the time, you're very aware the camera is right in your face. And you're very conscious of the fact that it's there for a reason, like something serious is going on.

> **When you're in the middle of an argument with someone, you know the argument is not just between you and the other person. It's between you, the other person...and a million people watching at home. So of course, you want to come out on top. You want to be on the right side. You want to make sure your point of view is understood.**

Of course, that escalates and inflames every situation. Conversations turn into arguments because everyone becomes so hell-bent on representing their points of view to the camera. Over and over and over again people repeat their points, so the audience at home understands your side; and so the directors in the control room are sure to include your position.

There's no way of really knowing if you're up to this *Real World* challenge. During the casting semifinals, they send a camera crew out to follow you around for a few hours. But that's only for a short time. It's not 24/7, and you're not surrounded by six people who are as headstrong and controlling as you. So there's no way they can prepare you, and there's no way you can prepare yourself.

You just need to be 100 percent positive you don't care what the world sees. Whether it's your bad side, your good side, your ups, your downs, your saddest moments, or your maddest times. You just need to be secure enough to reveal your insecurities. That's what messes up most people in the house. It's just natural to freak out when they're recording something you're incredibly insecure about. Especially, those things that you don't want your best friends to know about—let alone a million strangers.

The directors constantly told us to reveal '100 percent' of ourselves. It was like their motto.

Well, nobody did completely. But I came damn close. I mean, I'm 100 percent real to the camera. But I admit, I wasn't 100 percent sure I wanted everyone to see my bad sides as well as my good.

Without question, the hardest part was being apart from Stephanie for so long. She handled the situation so well, much better than I did. If I was in her place right now, I'd have broken up with me during the show. I mean, I thought I handled it terribly on my end. Like, the way I'd get angry at her for stupid reasons. Or the jealousy I showed, thinking bad things about what she might be doing.

Before I came to Seattle, I'd never yelled at her before. It was weird. I'd look forward to talking with her on the phone each night. Then, when we'd finally speak, we'd have some big-a** fight over nothing. It was just horrible. Maybe it was because of the built-up aggression from not being together. Or my guilt about getting to have all these cool experiences, since she almost got cast. Or the resentment she had for me because I wasn't there with her. I don't know what was responsible. But I do know that she's heard enough about *The Real World* for a while.

So, now I've got to give 120 percent of myself to Stephanie. Our personalities are exactly the same. We both love to have all the attention. Well, I had it for five months in Seattle. So, now it's time to put the spotlight back on her. The only problem is that people have started coming up to me and saying, 'Are you Nathan from *The Real World*?' And that sucks when I'm with Stephanie, because she hates *The Real World*.

I'll admit, I'm a bit concerned about the reaction of viewers to the show. Like, I'm worried about meeting my next 3,000 new best friends. I'm worried about lots of people acting like they really know me now...because they do in a way. But they only know the TV me, which is not the complete Nate.

But at the same time, I'm also hopeful the show will open some doors for me. Obviously, a lot of people watch it. Hopefully, something good will come of it. Not that I'm gonna say, 'Hey, I'm Nathan from *The Real World*. Give me a job.' But, you know, having my face in the public eye might attract something. I just hope *The Real World* will be a foot in the door. And the rest is up to me.

And that's sort of what I hope to portray on the show. That a kid like me, who's had a difficult upbringing, can make their dreams come true. All you need to do is get out there...and bust your a**.

OnNathan

DAVID: Nathan is one of the strongest people I've ever met in my entire life. He's a kid who has been on his own for so long, yet he still makes it happen. He's just extremely resourceful. He'll definitely be killer successful, no matter what he does.

LINDSAY: Nathan is going to be on the cover of *BOP* magazine in a couple of years. I think all the 13 and 14-year olds that watch the show are going to love him. I like him too. He's great fun. And he can be such a Southern gentleman. I know that Nathan wants to be really successful, and I hope he gets to be.

IRENE: Nathan and I—our relationship—well, it completely ended because of the cameras. Nathan hurt my feelings. At the beginning, we were like good friends. We were kind of cohorts in crime.

　　Then if you remember, the first fight we got into was over the cameras. He got upset with me because he thought I was making him look bad in front of them and because I was looking better than him on camera. I was making people laugh more. I was, you know, beating him in those stupid little games. And if there hadn't been a camera there, I don't think Nathan would've cared.

　　It was only 'cause the cameras were there that Nathan started becoming a total d**k to me. We went from being total partners in crime, best friends...to him calling me, 'Guy-rene' on national TV. He said he had a dream about me in which I had testicles. What was I supposed to do? Call him 'Vaga-nathan,' or tell him to wax his legs? So I just withdrew. I just didn't want to speak to someone who put me down every day.

REBECCA: Nathan is a good kid. He's growing. He's learning...and he's got a lot to learn. It'll take him some time to really get things in order, but I think he will.

JANET: Nathan has been deprived of a lot of opportunities growing up. So, as a result, he's trying to make the most of everything now. He's definitely a go-getter. He'll get everything out of life he possibly can. And, he has so much love to give. He's just looking for outlets to give it to.

STEPHEN: Nathan is a cool fellow. I'd say he became a friend of mine. I'll definitely talk to him after this. He's definitely a hard worker, but he can be an arrogant a**hole a lot, too. That's just the way he is. I think he wanted to use this show to become a star. And I think he's done it. Maybe we've all done it, but for some of us, it was unconscious. For Nathan, he did it to shortcut his career. I think he had a different agenda than most of us.

MARY-ELLIS: We were sure this experience was going to be a growth one for Nathan. He hadn't been to all that many places before. He hadn't been away from Stephanie in a year and a half. So, we just knew that being in Seattle was going to test him. And it did. I think he had a lot of issues and demons that were relatable to the audience...

JON: ...demons such as jealousy, insecurity, and occasional abuse of alcohol. I think all of these demons revealed themselves to the audience during the course of the show, and I think, for the first time in his life, he began to address some of them.

And...

NATHAN: I'm as soft and comfortable as a down comforter on the inside...with rough edges on the outside. Everybody knows that I love my girlfriend, and that I'm laid-back and want to have a good time. But when a job needs to get done, I get it done.

Rock & Suck

When did it ROCK?

NATHAN: It kicked a** the whole time. Meeting Ben Harper, my favorite artist, was kick-a**. Just interviewing bands kicked a**. Having the radio show kicked a**. Going snowboarding kicked a**. Going to Nepal kicked a**. Having Stephanie come visit me kicked a**. There were definitely a lot more kick-a** experiences than there were sh**ty ones.

When did it SUCK?

NATHAN: It sucked in the beginning when I had to leave Stephanie. When I was in Seattle, it sucked having to say to her, 'Guess what we just did?' That always made her feel left out, like she wasn't a part of my life anymore. Coming back from Nepal also sucked. I mean, how can you top that experience? I was in a rut for several weeks.

Pet Peeves

What annoys you the most about Nathan?

JANET: That he was a crabby morning person.

DAVID: When he gets mad at me for using his s**t. Whenever I touch something, like his CDs, he gives me such grief. I have to beg him to borrow a shirt, when he knows he can have any shirt of mine anytime he wants. It also bothers me when he gets really drunk.

LINDSAY: When he'd get cranky about using the phone. He'd be like, 'Get off the f**king phone.' And it was always to talk to Stephanie.

REBECCA: I guess his temper.

STEPHEN: That he can be so arrogant and self-centered. That sucks.
And...

NATHAN: That sometimes I have a bad attitude.

ENCORE?

Would you do *The Real World* again?
NATHAN:
I'd only do it again if Stephanie was in the same city.

Inquiring Minds

What question would you most like to ask Nathan?

DAVID: Where do we go next?
NATHAN: Whichever way the wind blows.

REBECCA: What do you fear the most about losing Stephanie?
NATHAN: Losing our friendship.

STEPHEN: Do you admit you used this show to become a big star?
NATHAN: No, I didn't do that, I did it for the experience.

JANET: Why did you start stealing my tooth paste?
NATHAN: Because I couldn't afford to buy any of my own.

LINDSAY: Did you mind being watched while you and Stephanie had phone sex?
NATHAN: Yes, because I thought I was covering up the camera.
And...

NATHAN: Why do you make such stupid mistakes?
NATHAN: Nobody's perfect, no matter how hard I try.

Close Encounters

Whom will you stay in contact with?

NATHAN: I'll stay in contact on a regular basis with **LINDSAY, JANET, REBECCA** and, of course, **DAVID.** I'll talk to **STEPHEN** every now and then. And **IRENE,** well, if she calls me, I'll call her back. But I'm not calling her myself. Well, maybe I should. I don't know, I'm just confused. Like, which Irene is the real Irene? The one at the beginning? Or the one at the end? Because if it's Lyme disease that made her change, then I shouldn't hold it against her. So maybe I'll give her a ring in a few months and see what happens.

Kiss 'n' Tell

NATHAN:
One time, Stephanie and I were in the bedroom engaging in sexual intercourse. We had our backs to the door. Suddenly, I felt a tap on my shoulder. I looked up, and it was one of the crew telling me my interview was in five minutes. Poor Stephanie, she just pretended to be asleep.

Nathan's real world

On Mom

My parents divorced when I was four. Soon after, my mother went off to travel around the country with a country-music singer. My father wasn't having any part of that, so he took custody of me instead. During the casting process, I met my mother again for the first time in like 14 years. She's living out in a remote part of Kansas now with my stepfather and half brother, Skylar.

It was just great seeing her again. She's just a down-to-earth person, sort of like a 1960s hippie. She and her husband live off the earth. They raise their own beef. Grow their own food. They don't take things for granted the way most people do. I have no resentment toward my mom because I feel we're both responsible for being out of touch all these years. We both messed up. So, let bygones be bygones. And *carpe diem*—let's seize the day.

On Dad

My father was the coolest man in the world. He never went to college. He raised

me working at Reynold's Metal for twenty-two years. It was a tough job. Most of that time he worked on the floor of the plant with all that metallic dust and stuff. He was a single parent raising a kid on a small paycheck, but he always found a way to get me whatever I needed, no matter what. If I can be half the father my dad was, then I'll have accomplished something.

He taught me manners. He taught me everything. He was a ladies' man, too. The guy was 40 years old, but he'd be bringing home a 23-year-old hot-a** woman. All my friends wanted to come over and hang at my house when we were in high school. He'd fillet up some steaks, put some cocktail shrimps on the porch, and we'd all hang out. When he died, it left a huge void in my life.

On Childhood

I think I had an amazing childhood. But when my dad died, I had to mature right away. I was only 15. My grandmother came in and tried to change everything my dad had done. She was very religious—a born-

again Christian. She'd say, 'You're not going out at night.' Believe me, it was rough. I had to learn how to take care of myself. So, I'd have to say a part of my childhood ended with my dad's death when I was 15.

On Religion

Religion is not a bad thing, but I declare no denomination. I do believe there's a God. And I also believe that everybody is going to sin. It's just human. But as long as you honestly repent and want forgiveness, you'll be fine.

October 31, 1976–Born	1980	1981	1982	1989	1992	1993
Nathan's 'Line' 	**Parents divorce:** I was almost too young to remember.	**First bicycle:** I had this phat red and white BMX.	**Father takes custody:** When I was six, my mother wanted to travel with a country-music singer.	**First kiss:** I kissed Mandy coming back from a class biology trip to the Baltimore Aquarium.	**First love:** It was a girl I'd known since I was a kid. She was also my first sexual experience.	**First car:** A 1993 Ford Ranger.

On High School

High school was awesome. I had a great group of friends. I played all the sports. I was a class officer, and s**t like that, but sometimes it sucked a bit because all my friends had their parents...and I didn't. And 'cause my grandmother was real strict. She was real tough about letting me out of the house. I'd always have to make up a lie just to go hang out with my friends. If I told her the truth, she'd say things like, 'You're sinning,' or, 'You're sleeping around with women.' You know, the most ridiculous accusations. I was only 15. I just had learn to cope with it.

On the "First Time"

I was 16, she was 15. We'd been dating

seven months, but I'd known her since I was a little kid. We did it in her bedroom, in fact. Here's what happened: I got excited. She got excited. I got the rubber out. And I was like, 'Oh, s**t! This is better than I thought it would be.'

On VMI

VMI is a great institution. Great education. Great people. Great reputation. Tough. Hard. Definitely a more meaningful experience than *The Real World*.

When I entered VMI, I thought my s**t didn't stink. So I got my a** handed to me on a platter straight away. They'd have us doing five hundred push-ups a day. Then tell me I wasn't worth s**t. It made me rethink some of the things I'd done. And it set me straight. When I was in high school, I'd made fun of some kids. After my first year at VMI, I got in touch with some of those classmates and apologized for my behavior. VMI made me a better man.

On Stephanie

We have only been together for a little over a year and a half. But anything that makes you smile, you could call it Stephanie. I'd like to put that feeling in a jar and sell it. I'd make millions.

On Stephanie's Family

They've basically taken me in. I'm one of

their own. I've woken up in their house on Christmas morning with her grandparents, her mom, her dad, her sister, her aunts and uncles. They're just wonderful people.

On Life

My personal philosophy is to have no regrets. And live life to the fullest.

On Fame

I'd love to hit the fame, but I don't think it's going to come from *The Real World*. I think it'll come from doing other things in life.

S T A T S	
Birthday:	October 31, 1976
Hometown:	Chesterfield, Virginia
Siblings:	Half-brother, Skylar, age 8
Pets:	None ('But I'd like to get a tiger.')
High School:	Lloyd C. Bird
College:	Virginia Military Institute

F A V E S	
Band:	Ben Harper
Book:	*Celestine Prophecy* by James Redfield
TV Show:	*South Park*
Movie:	*Goonies*
Actor:	Jack Nicholson
Actress:	Meg Ryan
Personal Motto:	*Carpe diem* (seize the day).
Meal:	Anything Stephanie cooks.
Way to Chill Out:	A bottle of wine on a beach with Stephanie.
Pickup Line:	Hey, baby.
First Date:	Sex
Sleeping Outfit:	Boxers
Stuffed Animal:	Tigger

Advice

What advice would you give to future *Real World*-ers?

NATHAN: Be positive you want to be part of such a strenuous situation. Prepare yourself to have every part of your being exposed to mankind...and to yourself. Then, good luck. And have fun with it.

June 30, 1993	1994	1995	November 22, 1996	1997
Father dies: My dad died of a rare lung disease at age 44. When the doctors told him he only had 5 years to live, he never told me.	**Graduates high school:** I was the senior class treasurer and graduated with honors. I was also on the football and track teams, and got a track scholarship to VMI.	**Arrested:** At a Dave Matthews concert for public drunkenness, vandalism, and eluding arrest.	**First date with Stephanie:** I met her at my friend's birthday party.	**Reunites with Mom:** I was reunited with my mother for the first time since 1982. And I also got to meet my half brother, Skylar—for the first time ever.

Nathan & Stephanie

Nathan: Being apart from Stephanie for five months really sucked. It was pure, utter, hell.

To hear her on the phone crying, and begging me to come home, didn't sit well in my stomach. I felt responsible for her pain, and all I ever want to do is make Stephanie happy. I almost left the show twice because I couldn't stand the fact that she missed me so much. I missed her just as much, only I had so many things to distract me—like the radio station, Nepal, snowboarding, etc. She had nothing to distract her, except that jacka** that she'd been going to school with for four years.

Listen, I was a jacka** to her, too. I raised my voice at her. At times, I assumed she was doing something unfaithful, while all the time, I knew in the back of my mind she never would. I trust Stephanie 100 percent. So I feel like such an a** now for having accused her of something. She didn't deserve to be treated that way, and I can't apologize enough to her for my behavior.

Man, I cherish Stephanie so much. There's nothing in the world I wouldn't do for her. I'd give her everything, everything I own. Oh man, I can't describe the way she makes me feel, or the way I feel when I look at a picture of her. She's inside my soul, and I know we're going to be together forever. Our love is just too strong. Now, we just need to get back into the mix of things. Get *The Real World* behind us, and someday, we'll get married, for sure. I'm hoping, maybe, four or five years from now.

I feel like such an a** now for having accused her of something. She didn't deserve to be treated that way, and I can't apologize enough to her for my behavior. –Nathan

Stephanie: *Real World* relationships are put through a wringer and my advice to anyone that's got a significant other as a cast member would be to lay low while they're there and don't take anything you see too personally because it will drive you nuts.

Were you Faithful?

NATHAN:
Yes, I was faithful to Stephanie. And she was faithful to me. As far as I'm concerned, if Stephanie did something physical with another person...and didn't have feelings for him, then I can forgive her. Mistakes happen. We're young. We're all human flesh, but if she had feelings for another person, well, that's a different story. And I know she didn't.

As for me, I've got no feelings for anyone but Stephanie. Never will. If she weren't a part of my life, I don't know what I'd do. I'd never be able to feel for another woman the way I feel for Stephanie. I'd always be comparing other women to her. And they'd always fall short.

On Nathan & Stephanie

DAVID: From first-hand experience, I know this process affects relationships big-time. It can become so all consuming it takes precedence over your loved ones. I think that's happened from time to time with Nate. Stephanie would say, 'Why are you choosing that over me? *The Real World*'s only a process. I'm the one that loves you.' Ultimately, something's going to lose out if you're trying to devote 100 percent of yourself...either the person or the show. On top of that, your partner gets so conscious of being recorded, he or she begins to pull away from you.

As for Nate and Stephanie, I don't know what the future has in store for them. I hope they make it. I'm their biggest fan.

REBECCA: I hope it lasts because Stephanie is such an amazing girl. She's a real person. I just fear they might go through some rocky times ahead. He's still really young, and doesn't know where he's going right now.

STEPHEN: Honestly, I don't think Nate and Stephanie are gonna make it. If they show what I think they're going to show—or anything close to it—Stephanie's got to be real discouraged with Nate. Just the fact that he kissed another girl in Seattle is going to cause them some problems. Still, I think he remained faithful to her. As far as I know, he didn't have sex with anyone but Steph in Seattle. And he was drunk the night he kissed that girl. I'll tell you what, I really hope they make it. Stephanie is such a beautiful girl, she's so cool. They're just a pair of cool white kids.

JANET: I hope they make it, I really do. I truly don't think Nathan did anything to jeopardize their relationship. If he strayed at all, it was only because of the stress brought on by distance and this process. I think he remained mentally faithful to Stephanie, and that's what counts the most.

LINDSAY: I don't know what's going to happen to Nathan and Stephanie. I hope they end up together. He loves her so much. On top of that, her family is such a huge part of his life. Honestly, that scares me a bit. Her family is all that he's got. If he loses her, he's out on his own. That's why I want Nathan to get strong enough to be OK on his own—just in case things don't work out. That's a mind-set I'm also trying to get to myself.

The Future
After *The Real World*

NATHAN: I'll be graduating from VMI in May 1999. And then I plan to take Stephanie away on a long vacation to Europe or Australia. After that, I'll get a job and see which way the waves push me. You know, I take each day as it comes. Basically, when I grow up, I want to be happy. Professionally, I want to be a Renaissance man. I want to do a lot of things and not limit myself to any one business or profession.

↓ Predictions

LINDSAY	**5** YEARS	Cover of *BOP* magazine.
	10 YEARS	Cover of *GQ*.
	25 YEARS	Cover of *Rifle and Guns*.
REBECCA	**5** YEARS	Married to Stephanie and happy.
	10 YEARS	Married to Stephanie, happy and chasing their kids around.
	25 YEARS	Married to Stephanie, happy and chasing their grandkids around.
DAVID	**5** YEARS	Signing bands for record labels.
	10 YEARS	Working as a program director for a radio station.
	25 YEARS	Going to VMI alumni events with me...and getting old.
STEPHEN	**5** YEARS	A starving actor in Hollywood.
	10 YEARS	A fed actor in Hollywood.
	25 YEARS	A fat actor in Hollywood.
JANET	**5** YEARS	Working for a record label.
	10 YEARS	Running his own record label.
	25 YEARS	Married to some rock star signed by his record label.
NATHAN	**5** YEARS	Hopefully, married to Stephanie.
	10 YEARS	Hopefully, with at least one kid...and making my first real money.
	25 YEARS	Getting ready to retire with my lady, Stephanie, and putting my kids through college.

David

I THINK THEY NEVER SHOULD'VE CAST ME. What they really wanted was a person who was never going to stray from the house, who was going to constantly interact with his roommates and no one else, and who was going to share the details of his personal life and repeat the highlights from his casting tape. Well, bro, I was the wrong man for that job.

I thought I was prepared for this experience. I figured it was simply going to be a wild ride. Instead, I discovered I wasn't strong enough to handle it, and it brought me to my breaking point.

Going in, I knew I was going to be asked to do things I'd never done before. To put everything out there, the total opposite of what I'd been taught as a cadet at the Virginia Military Institute, and in Charlestown, Massachusetts, where I grew up.

At VMI, I was told to stay strict and disciplined. The minute I stepped out of line, I could be kicked out. So I kept quiet, studied hard and never partied.

In Charlestown, I was schooled in silence. They've got something called the 'Code of Silence,' which basically means you keep your mouth shut. Since 1974, not one murder has been solved in Charlestown. Know why? Snitches get stitches. And rats get bats. That's the way it is there, and that's the background I had coming into this thing.

position where neither of us wanted to be.

So I fell back on my defense mechanisms. I dealt with it the way I'd been taught in Charlestown—protect your loved ones before anyone else. The show had a right to my life, but not to Kira's life. It became a struggle like that, and I withdrew for about a month. The directors would say to me, 'David, it's great when you're here. But you're *present* half the time.' Well, they were right. I was present in body, but not in mind. I needed to do that to keep my sanity.

Gradually, I tried to reconnect with the show the best I could. I got busy with all sorts of things in Seattle, just the way I would if I were living in any new city. I got a second job at the Fish Market, which I really dug. I made a lot of friends around town. But then the directors accused me of leading a 'double life,' and I could sense the anger in their voices.

Well, f**k it. I was just trying to show them who I really am. I figured they chose me for the show to portray my life. Well, I'm that guy who is ambitious and would build relationships outside of the house. I'd get to any new town and throw myself into all sorts of different situations.

If that doesn't work for your documentary, is that my fault? I thought *The Real World* was supposed to show what each person is really like. Not what you want them to be like.

Listen, I don't mean to complain so much about the

> *The Real World* demanded I do the opposite of everything I'd known. I had to act out, instead of internalize. Snitch, instead of keep silent. So you might ask, 'Why the f**k did I agree to do this show?'

Well, when I went through casting, I met a few people, including Kira [see 'Romeo & Juliet'—page 38], whom I really trusted. When I spoke to them, I was able to open up in ways I'd never done before. I gave them the secrets of my heart, stuff that I'd never told to anyone—never ever. I just figured *The Real World* would be a life-altering experience...and I was strong enough to handle it.

But when I got to Seattle, I had trouble adapting, almost immediately. It was like I wanted to go one way, and the directors wanted me to go another. They kept pushing me to give more and more. They didn't seem to understand—or respect—just how difficult a thing that was for me.

Three weeks into it, my relationship with Kira became a hot issue. I'd been trying to respect her right to privacy, while also trying to respect the needs of the show and their right to my life. Well, it was hard doing both. Like, how could I talk privately to Kira, while the crew was monitoring my conversations? The directors forced me and Kira into a

show. I met some incredible people throughout this experience—both cast and crew. I know a lot of my negativity stems from my anger at the way things were handled with me and Kira. Once that happened, I started seeing things in a different light.

The directors would say to me, 'David, what happened to you? You switched all of the sudden. You never complained about the process before.' Well, I couldn't undo what had been done. I had a chip on my shoulder from what took place with Kira.

Bro, I really wanted to do justice to this experience. I felt obligated to the producers for casting me. I felt I owed it to them to be honest and give them my heart. But they had an obligation to document my life...the way I wanted to live it. Not to pressure me into staying inside the fishbowl so they could have more footage of me fighting with my roommates.

I hoped people would see David for who he really is—very human, very vulnerable and very likely to make mistakes. I'm also a kid who busts his a**, and who loves with all his soul. Hopefully, that'll come across. And if not, there's nothing I can do.

On David

NATHAN: David is a brother. I know everything you want to know about David and I'll care for him the rest of my life.

JANET: I love David. I'm attracted to passionate people and David is certainly that. Whenever he believes in something, he really believes in it. So, I loved talking to him. But that kid doesn't have a clue where he's going. He doesn't know what he wants...let alone what anybody else wants. He's just kind of going with the flow day by day.

IRENE: Yes, everybody in the house knew that David had an issue on expanding on the truth. He would often exaggerate his stories. But don't ask us if David's a liar, 'cuz he can get kicked out of the military institute for that....

One time, David got really defensive about it and got up in Rebecca's face. I was like, 'Hey David, you gotta calm down. His reaction was like, 'Shut the f**k up, bitch' and put his fist into my face. This guy's telling me to shut up with a fist in my face, and they kept filming. Nobody stopped him or said, 'This behavior is wrong.' Well, nobody has a right to put their fist into someone else. No one!

REBECCA: David is definitely a character—a very interesting one. He seems kind of like a fool, but he's smart, too. You laugh with him. And you kind of laugh at him. I know that sounds mean, but he's just funny to me.

LINDSAY: David makes me laugh my a** off. He says more random things than even I do. He's a good guy...and means well.

STEPHEN: David's a cool fellow. He has his own vibe, you know, and I can respect that. But David lived two lives completely. He hid so much from that camera. He was always doing so much stuff outside the house. I don't know what he did exactly. But he was always hiding so much.

JON: David is a charmer. I'd buy the Brooklyn Bridge from him and wouldn't begrudge him the fact that he had swindled me.

MARY-ELLIS: Yeah, he's a charmer, who completely fooled all of us. He'll probably grow up to be President.

And...

DAVID: David's a solid kid. An extremely loyal friend. He'll be there whenever you need him. But the minute you f**k with him, or someone he loves, he'll make you pay for it...and for a long time.

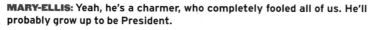

Rock & Suck

 When did it ROCK?

DAVID: It rocked when everything was working out just right, like when all the roommates were getting along. Or when everything else in my life was humming along, like in Nepal. Or sometimes when I'd go out with my roommates in Seattle, and we'd all be jamming on each other's company. The seven of us could go out from time to time and really have a great time together.

It also rocked for me at the Fish Market because that place was just mad energy. And it rocked for me when I'd come out of our weekly interviews with the directors, especially the ones I had with Billy, the director. 'Cause I really trusted him.

 When did it SUCK?

DAVID: It sucked in moments like when Lindsay's friend committed suicide. Or when they prodded me about Kira, especially after I'd just had an argument with her. All I could see then was a cameraman with a real stoic look on his face...and ambition on his mind. I understood he had a job to do, but I needed some privacy from time to time.

Inquiring Minds

What question would you most like to ask David?

REBECCA: They say you lead a 'double life.' What is it?

DAVID: I just do what I do...and it's no secret. You're welcome to see any time.

NATHAN: Why do you get naked in front of other people for no reason?

DAVID: Bro, *au naturel* is the way to go.

LINDSAY: You constantly smelled of fish. What did that remind you of?

DAVID: No comment.

JANET: Can I have my socks back?

DAVID: No, baby. Those 'tubers' are hard to find.

STEPHEN: If you don't always tell the whole truth, why do you profess that you do?

DAVID: Because I'm human, too.

And...

DAVID: Why do you think you have to keep everyone happy?

DAVID: I really don't know. I definitely ask myself that all the time.

The Future
After *The Real World*

DAVID: After Seattle, I went to Morocco for the summer to study intensive French and diplomacy on behalf of VMI and the Language Institute. It was a great experience. This fall, I'm staying in Boston for six months to be with my family. Then I'll return to VMI for my final semester, where I'll room with Nathan.

After VMI, I've thought about a number of things, including doing naval intelligence. I really don't know what I'm going to do. Eventually, I'd like to teach at the college level. Something along the lines of literature, philosophy, or comparative religion. I'd love to teach at VMI.

Pet Peeves

What annoys you the most about David?

STEPHEN: The fact that he was a pig.

LINDSAY: His schmoozy side.

NATHAN: He chews with his mouth open...and farts in his bed.

REBECCA: He smelled bad.

JANET: That he never brushed his teeth, so his breath always stank. Then he'd kiss me on the cheek and I'd have this filmy stuff on my face that smelled forever.

And...

DAVID: That I'm inconsistent and spread myself too thin. I ought to concentrate on just a few things. I'd be much stronger and effective.

Predictions

R E B E C C A	5 YEARS	He'll be living abroad and being cosmopolitan.
	10 YEARS	He'll be a used-car salesman.
	25 YEARS	He'll have switched to insurance.
L I N D S A Y	5 YEARS	Still giving advice.
	10 YEARS	Still saying, 'Shut it!'
	25 YEARS	He'll be back in Morocco, either married to Kira...or Kat.
J A N E T	5 YEARS	Either cleaning garbage cans or the CEO of a major corporation. With him, anything's possible.
	10 YEARS	Married to a foreign woman, for sure.
	25 YEARS	He'll have children, but still running around the place...completely uncommitted.
N A T H A N	5 YEARS	Still traveling the world.
	10 YEARS	Working for *National Geographic* doing wildlife refugee s**t.
	25 YEARS	Hopefully, married with two kids.
S T E P H E N	5 YEARS	Traveling for the military.
	10 YEARS	Still traveling.
	25 YEARS	Retired, I guess.
D A V I D	5 YEARS	Studying to become a professor of ethics.
	10 YEARS	Teaching at a university in Boston.
	25 YEARS	Kickin' back in St. Croix with my kids, and running a fishing business with my boys from the Pike Place Market.

Close Encounters

Whom will you stay in contact with?

DAVID: I'll be in closest touch with **NATHAN**. He and I will live together in the spring at VMI. I'll see a lot of **REBECCA**, too. I'd definitely love to stay in touch with **JANET** and **IRENE**. I don't know how often I'll see **LINDSAY**. She's a great kid, but she's going to be far away. As for **STEPHEN**, we'll check up on each other, but that's about it.

David's real world

On Father

My mother got pregnant when she was 16, and my father was just a kid, too. I knew my father off and on growing up in Charlestown. I never lived with him, but he lived nearby. It just didn't work out between my father and my mom. Frankly, she doesn't like him at all. He didn't always come through, let's put it that way.

My relationship with him was, well, not your usual father-and-son thing. One time, my father and I robbed a train shed for copper, so I could afford to go to the prom. We loaded the car with so much copper, we could barely drive away.

My father is in jail now, though I don't want to say what he did. He'll be out in three years, at least as far as I know.

On Mother

I don't know how to explain a woman like my mom. She's just so solid, that's all I can say. Picture a woman who never graduated high school', who had a kid when she was 16', who was whacked out on drugs, and beaten by her boyfriends', and then turned it all around. Who got herself sober. Got her GED. Got herself a job. She just got rid of the bad and replaced it with good. She said to herself, 'I'm doing this for my kid.' And she did! What she did was amazing. Amazing!

As mother and son, I'm not going to lie to you, we had our beefs. When I was a kid, I wouldn't listen to her. So, she had to beat the crap out of me more than a few times. Some kids need the hand. Others don't. Well, I did. I was wild. She and I got beyond that. We went to counseling together to get to know each other better, and now my mom is my girl!

On Nanna

My maternal grandmother, Nanna, raised me until my mother got her act together. I lived with Nanna in a housing project in Charlestown, which is a wild place. We were seven living in a small apartment, and my Nanna was *the* matriarch.

My mom used to come by all whacked out on drugs, looking for money. But my Nanna would be like, 'Get out of here, Karen,' and send her away. Yet my Nanna never stopped loving my mother through all of that. And, bro, my mom got herself sober just in the nick of time. 'Cause just as soon as she cleaned up her act, my Nanna got real sick with cancer. Thankfully, my mom was able to work by then, and took me and my grandmother in.

My Nanna died when I was 11. She kept our family together, man. What a woman! What a life!

On Childhood

I think I had a kick-a** childhood. I want you to know that. And I want that in the book, too. I don't think it was deprived. It was crazy. It was buck wild. There should be a movie about it, but it wasn't deprived. I'll tell you one thing, I had a great time doing it. I did whatever I wanted. I had freedom. Lots of it. I'd leave in the morning and come back at night.

I always ran around the Charlestown projects with a crew. There'd be twelve or thirteen of us. We'd cut school. Throw tiles at trucks to try and make them crash. Break into cars, too. Looking back on it, I had much too much freedom. It's a miracle I ended up alive. A few of my friends have died, and one of my best friends growing up is doing fifty in the federal pen for bank robbery and murder.

Yeah, I grew up quick. I think I'm stupid in a lot of ways because of it. I got a lot of bad habits that hinder me, but I'm conscious of them, and I'm trying to better myself every day.

On 'Zoning'

When I was 17, I worked for an escort service picking up and delivering prostitutes. It was probably the hardest thing I've ever done. I'd pick up a girl at 11 PM and take her to a customer's house. Then, I'd wait outside to make sure the girl was all right. Thank God, I never had any serious run-ins 'cause I was a scared kid.

Mind you, this was happening while I was still in high school. While my classmates would be sleeping in their beds at

August 29, 1976–Born	1982	1983	1984	1985	1988
David's 'Line' 	**First bike:** A silver BMX Bandit.	**First brake:** I broke my knuckles when I was six falling off a Jungle Gym.	**First love:** I was nuts about this girl, Erin. She was a classmate of mine at St. Catherine's in Boston.	**Favorite toy:** My pop gun. I made this gun, so I could shoot rocks with it. I'd smash windows with a quickness.	**First time:** I was only 12. Way, way too young.

night, I'd be outside a house waiting for a prostitute. I used to tell my mom I was working as a night delivery guy. I guess, in a way, I was. Man, that job was rough.

On Bulls**tting

Some people call me a bulls**tter. Well, I've been on the streets my whole life, bro, trying to get what I need. It's called hustling—making something from nothing. Let's just say that I've always had to get it on my own. I haven't had the resources most people have. For Nathan, it's been the same way. You just have to learn how to make something out of nothing. I don't like it that way, but I've had no choice.

You can call it bulls**tting, or you can call it a survival skill. Personally, it pisses me off when people give me a hard time about it. It makes me want to knock them out because they don't understand. Come down to where I'm from. You'll meet a thousand other people just like me, who could talk the pants off the Statue of Liberty or sell sand to an Arab.

On "The Code of Silence"

In Charlestown, if you saw somebody get killed, you kept your mouth shut. That's the bottom line. If you didn't, you'd get yourself killed, too. That's the way it's been since I was a little kid. And that's why the police never solve a murder there—not one since 1974. You just keep your mouth shut, bro. That's just the way it is!

On Tom

Tom Desmond rescued me! I met him at a neighborhood basketball court when I was 16. This guy just showed up in his Chuck Taylors and tube socks. I was like, 'Who's this dude with the gray hair and short shorts?' But he started shooting all these three-pointers, schooling people, and he got my attention. Turns out he'd been a point guard at the University of Massachusetts.

After the game, he asked if anyone wanted to play on a tennis team. We were like, 'Is this guy out of his mind? Only yup-pie kids play tennis.' Well, he was serious. And he kept coming back. Eventually, some of us gave it a try. First, one kid. Then, four...and so on, until we had ourselves a team.

He taught us a work ethic. That you can only get good at something by practicing. He gave us an outlet, too. Within a year, our team got pretty good. We began playing these yuppie prep schools...and beating their a**es. Well, thanks to Tom, I got good enough to play for a Division I college. What I learned from Tom—tennis and otherwise—certainly helped get me into VMI.

The best way to describe Tom is that he's a pure altruist. He simply takes pride from seeing other people transform their lives for the better. And, bro, he transformed mine.

On VMI

VMI changed my life. We're talking 360 degrees. It totally turned me around. I moved from a place in Charlestown, where I could do whatever I wanted, to a barracks at VMI, where they could make me do anything they wanted.

It's been the most challenging thing I've ever done physically, spiritually, emotionally and intellectually. It's humbled me in so many ways. I arrived a super character, saying, 'You can't tell me anything. Get out of my face!' And they were like, 'Rat, get your chin in right now, or give me fifty!' At first, I was like, 'F**k you!' They were like, 'What are we going to do with you?' But eventually, they broke me down.

VMI has taught me discipline. It's taught me to take pride in myself. And it's taught me honor. That's not just a concept anymore. It's a sensation! I've done more than any kid I know. I've studied abroad three times. I've gotten to be an editor of a college newspaper. I've gotten to play NCAA Division I tennis. And I've gotten to be on The Real World. From where I came from...and where I was headed...it's just amazing. Amazing!

Advice

What advice would you give to future *Real World*-ers?

DAVID: You can't really prepare for this thing. Know that it's going to be one of the most trying things you'll ever do, but it's also a great experience. You'll get to do some of the best things you've ever done. Just remember what your priorities are; why you're doing it; and what you want to accomplish. And don't do it if you're worried about the world seeing you in your worst light. Because, believe me, they're going to see it. So, don't fool yourself into thinking you can hide this and that. Because you can't. If you're not up to being exposed, don't do the show.

1988	1989	1989	1992	1993	1994
First time breaking nose in a fight: I was blind-sided by some Irish kid from East Boston.	**First drugs:** When I was thirteen, I tried hooch. But I didn't touch it for a long time after that. Drugs, man, nearly cost me my life.	**First arrest:** I was cuffed for stealing a portable radio from Radio Shack.	**First time watching *The Real World*:** I caught a few episodes of the New York show.	**First car:** A 1968 Dodge Dart. The color was s**t brown, but it rocked and rolled.	**Graduates high school:** From Pope John in Boston. It's a small school, and a little rugged.

'Spiritual Fish Mongers'

David: I needed some extra money and excitement, so I applied for a job at the Fish Market. Without any cameras around, I went up to talk to the guys and said, 'I want to work for you.' They said that they weren't hiring. So, I went back the next day, and the day after that. Eventually, they said they'd give me a try.

But when I arrived with the cameras in tow, they were like, 'Bro, what's going on?' Soon as I told 'em about *The Real World*, they figured I was just some wanna-be rock star, who wasn't going to work very hard. They figured I'd just last a day. But I gave my heart to that job. And busted my tail.

now'…he'd give it to me right on the spot. My bud, Justin, would take a bullet for me in a heartbeat. That's how tight we got. I was real lucky to have that experience. Those people accepted me for who I was, no matter what. That's something I couldn't say about some of the cast and crew.

The Market drew me away from the house. There was a simplicity in those guys at the Market that wasn't in the house. My roommies had problems, but they were privilege problems mostly. They'd complain about things like 'feeling confused' or 'not receiving enough affection.'

But the guys in the Market, well, their problems were basic and real. They needed money to buy their wife a birthday gift, or to put their kids through school. Problems that I

Those people accepted me for who I was. That's something I couldn't say about some of the cast and crew. –David

I wanted to learn that job, know that job, and mesh with the guys. I told 'em, 'I'm not here to f**k around.' Next thing I knew, I was moving past kids that had been working there for over two years. Soon, I was making three-something, only working a couple of days a week.

We had a cool-a** brotherhood up there, bro. I had to work my a** off to win their respect, but soon as they saw the effort, they took me in. And once you're in, they don't let you go. You know, I'll always have a job up there. We'll always have a bond, man. It's just something that cannot be touched.

If I said to Johnny, the owner, 'I need five hundred bucks right

could identify with from my own upbringing. They were like the guys I knew back home, who work hard with their hands to prov-ide for their family.

But what I liked best about the Fish Market was how much they all believed in what they were doing. I used to call them Spiritual Fish Mongers, for their devotion to their jobs. Their passion was just so inspiring, it made me want to do better. That place gave me such a lift, no matter how hard I'd worked. Nothing made me happier than the time I spent in the Market.

'Romeo & Juliet'

ACT I

DAVID
aka Romeo

I could see it coming. I just knew they were going to do some star-crossed lover, Romeo and Juliet st with me and Kira.**

Well, I guess it's a good love story. Two people meet each other; really like each other; and then get f**ked over by the people around them. It's something Shakespeare would've dug. But they never told you what really happened.

I first met Kira at open casting call in Richmond, Virginia. The minute I saw her, she struck me like a s**t-load of bricks. But when I talked to her, I was immediate-ly taken aback. She asked all sorts of direct questions, such as, 'Do you like blacks?' Well, I was like, 'Why are you so blunt, lady? I don't even know you.' Then she started asking me about my life, and I said, 'Lady, don't budge me. Get off my back.'

I don't know, bro, what it was, but there was something immediately drawing us together. I looked at her, and for the first time in my life…I wanted to tell someone what my life was all about. So I let her have it…all the details I rarely share. And she was like, 'Holy sh**, what the f**k did I just do.' Man, it was so damn powerful.

I knew Kira was something special, as I walked out that door. I told Nathan, 'Bro, I've just met a girl who I will not be able to get out of my mind.'

Well, a few weeks passed, and I still couldn't get her out of my head. From time to time she'd call about *Real World*–related business, and like neither of us could hang up the phone. I just can't explain it.

She has that effect on people, bro, just go ask the other people she's interviewed for the show. They'll tell you she gives so much of herself that it inspires you to give back. But more than anything, I could sense that Kira was just such a beautiful person….

ACT II

Throughout casting, our relationship never got physical. The business calls just got more frequent, and more lengthy. I could tell that she was fighting her feelings, and so was I. After all, there was a lot at stake–her job, and my chances of getting on the show. So we kept it as strictly professional as possible and kept each other at arm's length.

But one early Sunday morning, I awoke at VMI, just needing to call Kira. I'd just read two books by Marianne Williamson, *A Return to Love* and *A Woman's Worth*, which I wanted to recommend to her. They're powerful books that give women faith, and they reminded me of her. She told me she was really touched that a man would actually want to give a woman knowledge.

She called me up a week later and said, 'David, I don't know how to say this. But I know I'm meant to be with you. I've known it from the first time I ever saw you. I've fought it every day for the past few weeks, and I must continue to fight it. Because I can't be involved with you until this process is over. Otherwise, I risk losing my job, and I'll have to disqualify you from the show.' And I told her, 'I've felt the same way the whole time.'

Right after that, she took a step back from me and got distant. The other casting directors started calling me more than Kira, and I rarely ever heard from her. It was really hard, but I understood. This was around the casting semifinals, and she didn't want it to impact the process.

After I was cast on the show, our conversations got really intense again. We talked for four or five hours at a time, about everything in our lives. I'd send her little gifts in the mail, I just couldn't help myself.

We were never involved physically. Our affections were expressed over the phone, or through letter writing and book sending. And that was so meaningful. That we'd gotten to know each other's souls by talking and listening....

ACT III

Before I left for Seattle, Kira said to me, 'David, you've got to do what you've got to do up in Seattle. And I've got to do what I've got to do here in L.A. So now I can't talk to you again until all this is over.' I agreed.

So, we made a pact not to pursue our relationship until six months after I left Seattle. Because those were the rules governing cast-and-crew relationships, according to 'the clause.' [see page 41]

As soon as I got to Seattle, I found it unbearable to be cut off from her. I missed her so incredibly much. It was so strange, I couldn't understand it. I've never needed anyone in my life like that, except maybe my mom. Kira was pangs in my heart. Just thinking about her made me cry. She'd spoken some of the most beautiful things to my heart, and I couldn't bear not to be in contact with her.

So, I tried every way I could think of to get over her. I even tried forgetting about her by dancing with other girls, but bro, I felt like a d**khead. I couldn't disguise the fact I was missing her more than I could stand. Then, I stupidly told my roommates I was missing 'some girl.' And of course, the directors started speculating on who that 'girl' might be.

ACT IV

Well, unbeknownst to me, there were rumors in the California production office that Kira and me might be involved. I don't know how those rumors started, and honestly, I don't care now. However, what happened next changed my feelings about

The Real World beyond repair.

Two of the directors, David and Michelle, asked me to do an interview for the show. They knew I'd been sad, and they wanted to know why. In the middle of the interview, they left me sitting alone with the cameraman, and went outside to discuss something in private. When they got back, both of them had this look in their eye.

'David, why are you sad?' they asked in a way that was all evil to me. 'Who are you missing? Is it a girl? Is it a girl in L.A.? Is it Kira? Come on David, you know it is. So, tell us the truth.'

Well, I was like, 'What the f**k is going on? I did not come up here for this!' I was like, 'Shut the f**k up, or I'll kill you right here!'

I would have murdered them right on the spot, had I not left the room. I went into the bathroom to chill and started bawling. I couldn't help it, I was filled with so much rage. And at the same time, I had pangs in my heart because I missed her so much.

Man, those two crossed the line that day. I'd say that twelve times over. They shouldn't have cornered me like that. I f**king hated them for it. They should've let me come out with it when I was ready. Instead, they prodded my heart, and forced me to betray someone I loved. I'll tell you right now, they're lucky I didn't kill them that day, and that I forgave them later.

After that, I stopped trusting this 'process.' In a sense, they lost the whole me at that point, and it was really early on, like only three weeks into the show. I absolutely didn't think Kira should've lost her job. She gave so damn much to that show, it should've counted for something— f**kng 'clause' or no....

ACT V

Would I have had a relationship with Kira, if I were able to do it all over again? Absolutely, she's one of the best things that's ever happened to me. It's true love, it's something none of them could touch. This was tough on both of us, and we sacrificed a lot. But there's no question in my mind the two of us are gonna make it.

I only wish that we'd never come out with it. I should've said it's none of your business, and that would have been the end of it.

'Juliet & Romeo'

ACT I

KIRA
aka Juliet

The first thing I noticed about David when I talked to him was that he's a survivor.

He's the kind of person who has grown up with extreme obstacles, but blames none of them for his shortcomings. He takes responsibility for his mistakes, and takes on all the responsibility for his future. When you've interviewed 10,000-plus people, who blame everyone but themselves, you realize just how rare and admirable is David's perspective.

On a personal level, I found an immediate connection with David. He grew up in a dysfunctional family situation in Charlestown, as I grew up in one in Chicago. I didn't have to deal with friends getting shot like he did, but I had to deal with good friends hanging themselves. Even though the details of our childhood were quite different, our personal journeys have been very similar. He spoke a language I could understand.

ACT II

But my job was my first choice, so I wouldn't let my mind or heart go there. As far as I was concerned, my relationship with David was strictly professional. As with all the applicants I dealt with, I was just getting to know him better...and understand his essence.

As we began to speak more, however, our conversations starting getting progressively longer. And gradually, yes, our feelings for each other started straddling the so-called 'line.' I admit, I thought he was an incredibly amazing person, and knew he'd be in my life forever. We were both smitten, for sure, but I swear we weren't boyfriend and girlfriend.

ACT III

We both agreed to put any potential romantic relationship on hold until six months after filming ended in Seattle.

ACT IV

Well, three weeks into filming, the show's creators, Mary-Ellis and Jon, called me into their office. They asked me if David and I were going out, and I answered them honestly. I told them, 'No,' but I also admitted I had feelings for him. I explained that because I preferred to keep my job, I'd decided not to pursue those feelings.

I thought everything was OK. As I left their office, I assumed I'd be able to continue working there. But later that night, I got a call from a fellow staff member, who's also a good friend. She told me that 'officially' she could no longer speak with me. That I'd been deemed a part of the show, on account of my 'relationship' with David, and that I was going to be terminated by Jon and Mary-Ellis for having violated the terms of 'the clause.'

I was incredibly shocked. I'd never considered a platonic, though intimate, friendship with a cast member to be a conflict of interest. Nor had I been given the choice by them of actually choosing between my job or David. Instead, they made the choice for me...and what they chose—to suit their ratings—was David.

In the end, things turned out for the best. Yes, I gave up a job that I loved.

ACT V

But I also met the most awesome guy I've ever known in my life—my soul mate, my male version of me, my heart's desire. Until now, we haven't had the time to pursue an intimate relationship. Hopefully, this coming year, we finally will.

THE CAST-ULETS

Janet: I've always been the kind of person who follows rules. After I saw Kira and David's relationship, I realized things could be better sometimes if you broke the rules. David got to have a relationship with an awesome girl, and we got to know Kira. She's just such an awesome person.

Lindsay: I really hope things work out for Kira and David. I think Kira sacrificed so much for him. I don't know if they'll make it, though. David is such a young kid. He's just 21. Kira is a lot more mature. So, it's got to be frustrating for her to deal with him some times. After all, he's going through things now that she went through years ago.

As for their relationship affecting the house, yeah, we got closer to Kira. But she didn't turn us against the crew. She never said they were out to get us. However, she did make us aware of some things that we'd already thought about. Like that our rooms had microphones.

Nathan: David and I met Kira at an open call in Richmond. As soon as we got back from school, David said to me, 'Man, I think I'm in love.' He said, 'You remember Kira? She's hot as hell. And mentally, we connected really strong.' Well, I was like, 'Whatever!'

After all, I'd heard him say that several times before.

I knew he was actually legit when Stephanie and I went out to L.A. for the final round of auditions. I told Kira that David had a crush on her. She looked back at me with her eyes open real wide and, she said, 'Man, I think I feel it too.'

I knew about 'the clause,' and I didn't want to get Kira in trouble. To be honest, I think 'the clause' is f**king ridiculous. No show should stop the process of love. Love isn't an emotion we choose to have. It just happens, and I think you should never be punished for having it 'cause it's so hard to find.

Rebecca: I don't know if their relationship is for life or not, but as far as Kira affecting the process, any skepticism I had, I had before she came into the house.

Stephen: Personally, I thought the whole thing was weird. I'm convinced the reason David got cast was because of Kira. He was a very cool and interesting guy, but I can't see how she could've remained objective if she had those personal feelings for him.

Yeah, I think Kira influenced the process in the house. I remember her telling us things like, 'You guys are all lab rats, and they're going to f**k you over.' And I was like, 'Whoa, man! I don't want to hear this right now. I'm paranoid enough already, so don't make it worse.' I asked her to stop telling me those things.

David Park, *RW* Director: Kira was a pain in the butt. It's hard enough building a trust with the cast, without someone from the production trying to undermine that trust completely. She was always saying things to the cast that contradicted us. She constantly told them we were out to get them. Even David had to ask her to stop speaking so negatively about the process.

Billy Rainey, *RW* Director: The Boston cast was extremely open and honest. The Seattle cast was much more guarded and secretive. I think a lot of that had to do with the 'Kira incident.' I think her relationship with David broke down the so-called 'wall,' which is really important to have between the cast and crew. She made them more paranoid about the process, and this cast was already fearful of it to begin with.

Matt Kunitz, *RW* Producer: She made the crew's life miserable. She was so bitter; she tried to undermine the process entirely. She claimed to know exactly how we were going to portray each cast member, when she had absolutely no idea. She claimed to be an authority on the entire process, when she's never been involved in the production or editing of *The Real World* at all.

Mary-Ellis: During the casting process we spend hours trying to assess the characters of our applicants. Kira let us down. It was such a disappointment to learn that she had violated our trust and contract by becoming romantically involved with a cast member. It's even more disappointing that she would keep her relationship a secret from us, putting us in the position of casting someone we didn't know every-thing about. I can only hope that some good will eventually come from the enormous sacrifice we were all forced to make. Perhaps David will be the love of Kira's life, but relationships don't last when they are built on deceit.

She made the crew's life miserable. She was so bitter; she tried to undermine the process entirely. –Matt Kunitz, *RW* Producer

Jon: We tried to maintain a friendly relationship with Kira after our working relationship was no longer possible. I think Kira felt she needed to justify herself on the show by making the production the enemy. So, instead of taking responsibility for her actions, she blamed us for the way things turned out.

She began putting down *The Real World* –a show she'd been involved with for two years. One moment, she believed in everything we'd done together. The next, she was questioning everything we did. She started stirring up David and his roommates against the show. She tried making them doubt their actions and their reasons for being on *The Real World*.

The roommates gradually began to realize they had legitimate reasons for doing the show, and that Kira's issues with the show had little bearing on their own experiences. So, ultimately, they were able to take Kira's criticisms of the process with a grain of salt.

THE CLAUSE

Jon: When we first started doing *The Real World*, every crew member's contract had a 'clause' in it governing his or her relationships with the cast. In principle, it stated that 'no crew member could have an emotional and/or sexual relationship with any cast member throughout production.'

We wanted our crew members to like our cast. We wanted them to care for them, too but we did not want them becoming emotionally involved beyond the appropriate boundaries for documentarians and their subjects.

During the first season of *The Real World*, one of our directors had an affair with a cast member, Becky. Despite our warnings not to, he went ahead with it anyway. So, we had no choice but to let him go.

During the San Francisco season, our third, we were confronted with an unexpected dilemma. One member of our crew began having a relationship with a cast member, Jo. But the relationship didn't start until directly *after* filming ended.

Now, technically, there was nothing wrong with that. We'd never established any rule regarding relationships after shooting was over. But while filming was finished on the San Francisco show, the editing of it was still in progress. As long as the show was still being put together, we wanted to avoid questions about a potential conflict of interest.

So, after the San Francisco season aired, we decided to amend 'the clause.' Instead of banning relationships until the end of production, we added that no crew member could have an emotional and/or sexual relationship with a cast member *until six months after filming had ended.*

EPILOGUE

As we went to press we learned the following...

David: It's whacked. Recently, I threw out the first pitch at a Seattle Mariners baseball game and the players were coming up to me and asking, 'What's happening with you and Kira?

Well, I told them: 'You can't be Romeo and Juliet, if Romeo is in Boston and Juliet is in L.A. You gotta be realistic, bro. We're just taking it as it comes, but the show did leave a lot of scars with a lot of the relationships, not just mine. It was heartbeats and lives, bro, and it really affected all of us.'

But I want it out there: Kira is beautiful. I love her. She's just an amazing person. I know it's sentimental, but it's the truth. She's awesome. **–DAVID**

Would you do *The Real World* again?

ENCORE?

DAVID: No. Simply put, my life is mine. I want to keep it for myself and those that I love. I don't want to share it with millions of people. I don't regret doing it. I learned so much about myself. I learned so much about other people. I learned that I am not as strong as I think. That I have a lot of growing up to do. That I have to get my priorities straight. That I can't give everything to everyone. I'm grateful for the experience, but once in a lifetime is enough, for sure.

Rebecca

THIS EXPERIENCE WAS LIKE being on the Discovery Channel. I felt like a deer in a wildlife video. You know, watch the deer run, watch the deer eat, watch the deer fight, watch the deer cry, watch the deer sing, and watch the deer smile. That was me in a nutshell.

I know that's a weird analogy, but this was a weird experience. I had no idea that it was going to be anything like what it turned out to be. Of course, I knew it was a documentary and that we'd be taped a lot. I didn't realize the extremes to which it would be taken. Meaning I didn't realize *everything* was taped. When you watch the show at home, you forget cameras are filming those people *all the time*.

But you never forget the cameras when they're filming *you*. Don't believe any cast member that tells you otherwise. They're lying to you. It's like saying the emperor is wearing clothes. Listen, the emperor was naked...and the cameras were noticeable. Those two things are absolutes.

"**The show works best when the cast members live their lives in front of the camera as truthfully as they would off-camera.** I think our cast found a way to do that. I think that's why we had a successful season. Of course, it required trusting the crew and being comfortable enough with ourselves to share ourselves with others. But I won't lie to you: It was not easy for me to reach that point of comfort."

I'm a very analytical person. I need to think by myself. Well, having the cameras around all the time made it near impossible for quiet reflection. I felt like I was under constant scrutiny—like a slide under a microscope. I did not feel like I was ever allowed to think the way I prefer to think. To have the space that I require. I felt like I was constantly being invaded.

On top of that, I felt obligated to vocalize my thoughts. None of us wants to be misinterpreted. So, what do you do when a camera is taping your thinking? Especially after you've just been involved in a fight or some controversy. They haven't invented brain-cams yet. So, the only way the audience will ever know what you're truly thinking is to voice your thoughts, and that's completely unnatural for me...and unnatural for most human beings.

In general, though, I think I was as real as I could be. Or rather, as real as I could be with cameras watching me. I'm a sensitive person. I'm sure that came through. I hate fighting. I can't deal with fighting. Frankly, any type of argument to me is terrifying. I will avoid conflict at any cost.

One evening, I got into a fight with Stephen. Actually, it wasn't much of a fight, Stephen just yelled at me.

Then, he basically went around telling everyone that I was a bitch. Well, that's just one term you cannot equate with me. I am always shafting myself for other people.

So, I was hurt and started crying. Suddenly, the camera was in my face. Well, I was too upset to stop crying. So, in that way, I was as real as I could be, but, I'll tell you, I hated the process just then. After all, here was this kid being so mean to me, and the crew wasn't doing anything about it. I thought, 'Shouldn't they be coming to my defense?' If a deer is being attacked, I'm going to try and save him. Well, their excuse was they needed to remain impartial and objective. Frankly, I had a lot of trouble with that.

At home, I've got lots of people that care about and protect me. I like that protection. In the house, I felt extremely vulnerable without my defenders around, especially at stressful times like when Stephen was screaming at me. My roommates in Seattle knew me only a few months. I certainly couldn't expect any of them to be my protector.

But on that occasion, when Stephen was yelling at me, it was Irene who came to my defense. She went over to him and said, 'Don't talk to this girl like that.' And to my dying day, I'll never forget that she did that. That's why I love Irene. I knew she was a true friend that night because she was there for me when I needed her most.

Standing up for myself is something I've always had trouble doing. I've always been extremely verbal, but not always confident enough to voice my honest opinions.

When I arrived in Seattle, I wasn't secure with myself. I tolerated a lot of behavior that I really shouldn't have. I was so obsessed with my notion of perfection that I only saw my flaws, and I refused to recognize that I was making myself miserable being that way.

In Nepal, I had some major self-realizations. I realized that I would be severely misinterpreted if I didn't start speaking up for myself. The pivotal moment occurred when my roommates confronted me, saying that they thought I might be bulimic. I was shocked because nothing could've been further from the truth. The mere fact that they thought it was true was so disquieting to me. It meant that they hardly knew me at all. →

The fact that girls put themselves through hell to keep off weight goes against every belief I've ever had about femininity. Plus, imagine the skill I'd need to disguise being bulimic with a microphone on all day. I guess the fact that I'm thin, but eat so much, was responsible for their confusion. That signaled to me that I needed to be more outspoken.

So, I came back from Nepal determined to be more forceful. I realized that my insecurities were holding me back, so I started taking more risks. I recorded a song with Sir Mix-a-lot, which was a great thrill. I got up on stage and belted out a tune. I said and did things I dreamed about, but never had the confidence to do. So what if I looked like a dork. Everyone is a dork at some point or another.

I also took my new resolve into my relationship with Andrew. He's the guy I've been seeing, but the one you never saw on the show. That was mostly his choice, since he didn't want our relationship subjected to public scrutiny.

When I got back, I said to him, 'This is what I want. And what I want is you. But unless you're able to meet my needs, I have to move on and find someone else that will.' Thankfully, Andrew was totally understanding. And hopefully, we'll live happily ever after.

For me, the *Real World* experience was a gift. I went home with a fully established sense of self. I'm comfortable with who I am, and what I believe. How many people can say that? Now, I can.

OnRebecca

Inquiring Minds

What question would you most like to ask Rebecca?

DAVID: Why do you deny everything?
REBECCA: I have a difficult time with the 12-step program.

JANET: How many people have you slept with?
REBECCA: I plead the Fifth.

LINDSAY: How can you eat so many g**damn muffins?
REBECCA: When it's right, it's right.

NATHAN: When do we get to meet your boyfriend?
REBECCA: Anytime you want.

STEPHEN: In what way aren't you innocent?
REBECCA: I never claimed innocence. Sometimes I'm intentionally naïve, but it's all conscious—I know what's going on.
And...
REBECCA: Why do you make other people's problems your own?
REBECCA: I feel an obligation to be there for other people.

Close Encounters

Whom will you stay in contact with?

REBECCA: I'll probably talk to everybody in the cast, but I think I'll probably be in closest contact with IRENE. She had a tough time on the show. But deep down, she's a really genuine, good person, and extremely intelligent.

 DAVID: Rebecca is 'The Dickinsonian Glass Menagerie.' Like Emily Dickinson, she's got a real gentle sorrow in her being, and like *The Glass Menagerie* by Tennessee Williams, she's so fragile you think she's gonna break. I think Rebecca is a fragile creature. Her whole life is internal. Just shake her hand and ask her name...and you can tell everything about her is inside.

 IRENE: Rebecca was the closest thing I had to a normal friend in the house.

 NATHAN: Rebecca personifies fragile innocence.

JANET: I like Rebecca. She's an idealist who lives in a bubble...and she loves her bubble. She doesn't want to get out of it. By her bubble, I mean her family and her rock stars. I think she'll admit to that, but she's also not quite as innocent as she seems. She just likes portraying herself that way. Not that she's deceptive by any means. She's just careful and cautious about how she's portrayed.

 LINDSAY: There are certain people you click with...and certain people you don't. I guess Rebecca and me didn't really click. Not that I don't like her. I do, but we're different people. She's a romantic. I'm a realist. She's quiet. I'm far from it. I'm a drama queen.

STEPHEN: Rebecca is the sweetest girl you'll ever meet. She's as sweet and innocent as she appears. But she's not so naïve that she doesn't know about all the non-innocence in the world. She just chooses not to take part in it. She's always got the perfect shoulder to cry on, because she'll cry with you.

 JON: Rebecca was a real friend to anyone who got in trouble. Every *Real World* house needs a Rebecca in it.

 MARY-ELLIS: Rebecca is etheral, but has her own quiet strength that supports everyone around her.

And...

 REBECCA: I'm a good kid, yeah. Definitely a good kid. I'd just say that I'm very fortunate in life not to have any major regrets.

Rock & Suck

When did it ROCK?

REBECCA: In Nepal. That was the most mind-altering experience of my life. The Nepalese opened their hearts and minds to us. It's such a poor country, but so peaceful and caring. They taught us that material things matter much less than we think. That love and compassion are worth far more. I feel so fortunate to have seen their example.

When did it SUCK?

REBECCA: I'd say it sucked when I was bored, like when I didn't have something to do. We didn't have a TV, so we couldn't watch any movies. I really like classic movies, like with Buster Keaton. So I'd just walk around bored. Downtime is a killer for me, because I just start thinking way too much. I start analyzing and worrying about things that drive me crazy.

⊗ Pet Peeves

What annoys you the most about Rebecca?

STEPHEN: That she always plays the innocent. I know she's innocent. But not always.

JANET: That she played that song she made with Sir Mix-a-lot over and over again. She made everyone and their mother listen to it.

DAVID: That she denies everything.

LINDSAY: That she always needed to be in the middle of whatever was going on. Or wanted everyone to come to her. Sometimes, she should've just hung back.

NATHAN: That she's in complete denial. And...

REBECCA: That I am overly analytical.

Kiss 'n' Tell

NATHAN: Rebecca is in denial of everything at all times. She'll leave a plate in the sink, then say, 'I didn't do it.'

STEPHEN: It's crazy that Rebecca was in the most intense relationship in our house...but kept it entirely off-camera. She chose not to ruin her relationship. She's wise. But I don't think it was completely right. I think it was kind of dishonest.

The Future
After *The Real World*

REBECCA: My future plans involve having a lot of fun and being a much happier person. I've got two years to go at the University of Virginia. I'm an Echol Scholar, so I don't have to declare a major. I'm focusing mostly on English and theater studies at the moment. Ultimately, I'd like to go to grad school—maybe at Columbia—possibly, for English. I'm also sure to continue writing, including writing more songs.

↓ Predictions

DAVID	**5** YEARS	Working for some nonprofit organization and writing humanitarian pamphlets.
	10 YEARS	Married with kids and starting a family.
	25 YEARS	A cat woman wearing knits and plaids.
JANET	**5** YEARS	Still making music for Sir Mix-a-lot.
	10 YEARS	Bearing Sir Mix-a-lot's children.
	25 YEARS	Divorcing Sir Mix-a-lot, and running off with his millions.
LINDSAY	**5** YEARS	Eating lots of muffins.
	10 YEARS	Baking muffins.
	25 YEARS	Burning muffins.
NATHAN	**5** YEARS	Pursuing a singing career.
	10 YEARS	Definitely married, and still pursuing a singing career.
	25 YEARS	With three children...and still singing.
STEPHEN	**5** YEARS	Married with one child. Teaching English or writing books.
	10 YEARS	Happily married with two children.
	25 YEARS	Still happily married, putting her kids through college and writing bestsellers on romance.
REBECCA	**5** YEARS	Seeking some form of higher education.
	10 YEARS	With husband and child, and living in bliss.
	25 YEARS	Continuing blissful living.

Rebecca's real world

On the First Kiss

Well, it was really just a peck. I was 14. It was with this older musician guy, whom I had a crush on in high school. I think he felt sorry for me. He knew I had a crush on him, so he took pity on me.

On the Identity of Her Crush

How embarrassing. I can't tell you that. All right then, but my friends had a big crush on him, too. It was...Dave Matthews. When I was 14, I went to one of his concerts. One of my friends tried to meet him by sneaking backstage. Well, just as we were figuring out a way to get in, he spotted us and came over. Of course, we got all excited. We acted so dumb and stupid. Anyway, he was real cute about it, and gave me my first peck. I thought I was in love with him for the next couple of years. I went to about six billion concerts after that.

On Feelings for Dave Now

No, I don't like him at all anymore. Not at all. No, I'm not the slightest bit attracted to him any longer.

On Love

I want perfect love, with no compromises. I want a love that's so strong it's almost painful, horrible love. A love that's almost torturous. I think a lot of people compromise and settle for something too safe.

On Mother

She's an amazingly beautiful, selfless woman. She's a fourth-grade teacher and an artist. She's sugar and spice and everything nice. She's also my best friend.

On Father

My father's a complex individual. He's very kindhearted. But he's a strange bird. The best way to describe my dad is that he's like the absent-minded professor.

On Childhood

I don't really remember my childhood all that well. I think I watched too much TV. Basically, I had a relatively normal childhood. It had ups, and it had downs.

On Revealing Rebecca

I guess I only give glimpses of myself for other people to see. Glimpses of what I think is right or what they want to see. But I'm trying to do less of that because I think it prevents me from being whole.

On High School

I thought I didn't like high school, but my mom seems to think differently. All I remember is that I went through a series of major changes during high school, mostly adolescent stuff. I acted like a full-out dork for a couple of those years. I was an athlete, on the varsity soccer team all four years. When I was a freshman, I hung out with the seniors. I guess I was kind of popular, I mean, I had friends. I never partied, ever. Basically, I thought high school was arduous. It just seemed boring to me. It's not that I had a horrible time, I was just anxious to get on with it.

July 7, 1978–Born	1982	1983	1987	1988	1989	1991
Rebecca's 'Line' 	**Moves:** From Ohio to Richmond, Virginia.	**Devours competition:** I won the ice cream-eating contest at the Fourth of July Fair in Thornston, Maine.	**First tragedy:** My puppy, Snowy, got run over by a car. It was devastating.	**Singing debut:** I had my first solo in our fifth grade play, *Wynken, Blynken, and Nod.*	**First political stand:** I gave speeches to my class about the mistreatment of elephants at the Barnum & Bailey Circus.	**First bra:** I got my first bra in eighth grade.

On Innocence

Everyone seems to think that I'm an innocent, and I guess that's partly true. I know there's a Victorian thing about me. I'm into the idea of a lady...and what a lady is supposed to be. I'm also not as innocent as people seem to think, nor as naïve. I know things that I don't say. I see things that I just choose to ignore. Like, I can see things about a person that are really negative, but I choose to ignore them because

it would make me too miserable to deal with them. I'm like that a lot. Some things would just drive me insane if I thought about them too much.

On Guys

I used to fear guys, but I've changed my mind about that. I fear people in a position where they can hurt me. I can feel terribly vulnerable. So, I try to protect myself from getting hurt. I'm terrified of getting hurt. I guess I'm very sensitive. Equivalent things seem to hurt me much more deeply than they hurt somebody else. So I'll be flirtatious with guys, but I'll keep them at a distance.

On Boyfriend Andrew

I've known him a year and half, but we started dating last October. Yeah, I think about him a lot. He's always in my head. I'm a total romantic. So, of course, that concept of fated love is always a component of my thoughts. I'm pretty picky. Actually, ridiculously picky. So, I'm going to be pretty bummed if Andrew and I don't work out. Because it'll take me a while to find somebody else that compares.

On Christian Science

Yeah, I'm a Christian Scientist, but I don't think I'm a good example of a Christian Scientist at all. I don't study the religion. I don't really go to church, but I do think I'm a spiritual person.

On Music

You know, I didn't realize I had these desires to create music. Before the show, music had just been my outlet. It's always been incredibly important to me. After recording with Sir Mix-a-lot, I realized that music was where my passion lies. So I will probably pursue something in that direction.

On Rock Stars

I'm not into meeting rock stars. I used to be when I was in high school. At this point, I would prefer to meet real people, not demagogues.

On Fame

I don't seek it. I don't want it, and I really don't want to think about it.

On the Future

I dream to be happy. I dream to be fulfilled. I dream to be a mother. And I dream to have a career, where I can create beautiful things—probably as a writer.

S T A T S	
Birthday:	July 7, 1978
Hometown:	Richmond, Virginia
Siblings:	Two brothers, one sister (I'm the youngest.)
Pets:	None (My dog, Jessie, died last year at the age of 14.)
High School:	Godwin High School
College:	University of Virginia
F A V E S	
Band:	The Rolling Stones
Book:	*The Fountainhead* by Ayn Rand
TV Show:	*The Simpsons*
Movie:	*The Godfather*
Actor:	Orson Welles
Actress:	Audrey Hepburn
Personal Motto:	To thine own self be true.
Meal:	Phad thai
Way to Chill Out:	Popcorn in bed
Pickup Line:	If I wrote the alphabet, I'd put U and I together.
First Date:	Dinner and a walk in a park.
Sleeping Outfit:	Oversized men's pajamas
Stuffed Animal:	A gorilla named 'Ty.'

Advice

What advice would you give to future *Real World*-ers?

REBECCA: Really consider whether or not you want to do it. But I know you'll do it anyway.

ENCORE?

Would you do *The Real World* again?

Rebecca:
Yes, I'd do it once more. I learned so much doing it the first time. I took away so much more than I ever thought I would. It wasn't always easy for me, but I'd definitely do it again.

1992	1992	1993	1994	1996	1998
First kiss: It was more of a peck.	**First period:** Walking home from school in ninth grade. I'd say it was a welcome relief, because I was relatively old. I thought there might be something wrong with me.	**First season watching *The Real World*:** The L.A. show. My favorite cast member was Jon, the country music guy.	**Wins state championship:** My tennis team won the Virginia state championships my sophomore year. And we repeated senior year as well.	**Graduates high school:** From Godwin High School in Richmond, Virginia.	**First love:** My boyfriend, Andrew.

Irene

IT WAS LIKE THIS STUDY WHERE they put rats into a tub full of water, and all the rats find a way to swim. But then they cut off the rats' whiskers and put them back in the water...and suddenly all the rats drown. That's what it was like in Seattle. It was like my whiskers were cut off.

"Riding the roller coaster. That's what Seattle was. I was emotionally on an island that had a roller coaster on it. I was on the island myself the whole time.

The Seattle *Real World* was a nightmare... I felt like puking the whole time. "

Although I did get physically ill, the root of my physical illness was my emotional distress, not my Lyme disease. Since I've been home, I've been considerably healthier physically. Since I removed myself from that situation where I was literally judged and analyzed all the time, I've felt 30,000 times healthier emotionally.

I do have Lyme disease. I can't deny that. But as far as things go, my fatigue was all the result of *The Real World-Seattle*. Since I returned, I've gotten all my energy back. I've started to run again. I've picked up my life again. I think the reason I had so little energy there was because I was so emotionally drained all the time.

The root of my headaches and fatigue was my overall feeling of isolation in that house. From the first day I walked into that place until the day I left, I felt completely isolated. It's almost impossible to be good friends with somebody in that house because of the weekly interviews. They're just like going to jail. You know how they seclude people when they get arrested and ask them, 'Who did it?' Somebody always rats. Well, that's what happens on *The Real World*. Whenever my roommates would come back from one of those interviews, you'd see the face of a sellout.

You know, it was ridiculous. I was treated with no respect during those interviews. It was like, 'What's the point of talking?' I was completely defensive. They were not a good time. Besides, interviews are contrived. In real life, people aren't interviewed.

Nobody's real on camera. Get that through your head! Meaning: when you have a conversation on the phone or on a street corner...and there are cameras around...nobody's real. There's nothing real about it.

I couldn't take that. I'm a very real person. I think I'm the first truly real person they've ever had on their show. My bulls**t meter was going off from the moment I woke up until I went to bed. It was distressing.

The producers really think they're capturing a person. Well, I think they're really misguided. And I think they need to be made aware of that.

The problem with the show is that you only get to see people two-dimensionally. There's a lot more to the person than what the show portrays. It only shows what a person is like living under those extreme conditions.

From the moment I walked into the house, emotionally I was on a different level than I've ever been before. The first month and a half I had fun. I think you saw that on the show.

I was good with my roommates. I was going out, being a 'rock star.' I was running. I was healthy.

Then I realized how the process was affecting me, and I became less and less real. I wasn't myself. I was unhappy. I felt attacked in my interviews. I felt attacked by my housemates. If you feel attacked, you either withdraw...or attack back. And I just withdrew.

Leaving the house was always on my mind. But you need to understand there were lots of reasons why I stayed as long as I did. One: I needed to stick around to get paid. I was paying for my health insurance, so I needed the money. Two: I'd already committed to taking a semester off from college, so where was I gonna go? And three: I didn't want to appear like a quitter on TV.

I'm not a person that quits. Quite the contrary. But since I did leave early, I see myself as a g**damned champion. I see myself as a moron for not having left sooner.

Was I upset the whole nation saw me sick with Lyme disease? Yes, because Lyme disease is a functioning disease. Rarely do I get that ill for such an extended period. That's part of the reason I was so upset. I felt the way I was being portrayed was a very poor reflection of my disease. The good reflection was me snowboarding, working out, having fun and laughing. That's also what it's like to have Lyme disease. That needs to be clear...

I'm not a sick person. I'm a person living with a disease that most people wouldn't know about, except that the entire nation knows about it now 'cause I'm on the show. Yes, I have bad days, but it rarely infringes on my life. I'm upset that I ever said I was 'sick.' I'm not that way anymore. It was situational. That experience was so stressful it caused me to relapse. But now I'm feeling much better and I can go on with my life.

Th Departur

David: It's in Irene's nature to be hyper-conscious of every-thing that's going on. In Seattle, she was constantly monitoring the entire process. Constantly disagreeing with the way the directors were doing things. On top of that, her Lyme disease made things worse for her, I'm sure. So, things just began to build up inside of her.

She started getting in arguments with her roommates, espe-cially the girls. She began blaming the crew for every conflict that happened. She felt the directors were trying to turn her against her roommates, that whenever they sensed conflict, they tried to

capitalize on it. Clearly, she and some of the girls weren't getting along. So basically, Irene had to leave. Those last three weeks would've felt like an eternity if she hadn't and I respect her for doing so. It made it easier for everyone, most importantly Irene.

know what was happening to her. It was as if Irene was desperate-ly trying to dig herself out of a hole she'd dug herself into.

Lindsay: What happened to Irene? I think it was a combi-nation of things. I definitely think it had something to do with her Lyme disease. I have no idea, and I'm sure stress played a part. But the truth is, we didn't know Irene all that well. We only knew her for a month and a half before all this started happening.

I really liked her at first, so it frustrated me when she started to change. Suddenly she was a different person. I'd ask, 'How can I help? What can I do?' But eventually, I'd stop trying. Especially when she'd turn on me. She was out of control at times, and she didn't seem to be trying to help herself. So, how the hell was any of us going to help her?

Nathan: Irene was a really cool person for about the first month and a half. We were like brother and sis-ter, and then she just snapped, man. She did a complete three-sixty personality-wise. She went from the Irene you see on the casting special—funny and laid back—to a person who felt she was almost godlike. She believed that everything she said was the only truth. That she was the only person who truly listened to anyone in the house. She started throwing out opinions left and right. Yelling at people without realizing she was yelling. Just a completely different person.

Does she have Lyme disease? Yes. And Lyme disease can affect your nervous system and your mentality, but there are a hun-dred different strains of Lyme dis-ease across the United States. Personally, I think it was the stress of the *Real World* experience. She was against the process the whole time. From the first week, she was flipping out over it. In the back of my mind, I was like, 'Irene, what did you sign a contract for? Why are you here if you're so against it?'

"She got to a point where she was absolutely miserable. There was no need for her to continue to be on The Real World. It just meant unnecessary pain for her." –Rebecca

Janet: This process is strenuous enough that if you are any-where close to the edge, it will definitely push you over. Irene dreaded interviews—but I looked forward to them. Those two hours with Billy (Rainey-*RW* director) each week were kind of my release. It was the only time you could say exactly what you need-ed to say about everything going on. It was almost therapeutic. I don't think everything Irene did was because of the process, but I think it stimulated whatever stuff was already there. What that is, I'm not certain. I know she has Lyme disease. We had an expert come in and tell us that Lyme disease was capable of making her feel that way. But who's to say if that was the reason why she did?

In general, it was just a bad situation all around. Most of all, I feel terrible for her. It was like she had no control. Like she didn't

She made it hard on the crew. It's not easy working 24/7, and having someone bitch and complain the entire time. Irene was constantly throwing her hand in front of the camera. Frankly, I think the crew went out of their way to please Irene. None of us were supposed to go home during the five months we were in Seattle. But they suggested she go home for a week to cool off and relieve the stress, but she refused.

Personally, I think the directors did everything for that girl. They had special meetings with her off-camera to help her out. Each of us did interviews once a week. Irene said they weren't healthy for her. So she quit doing them. They went out on a limb for that girl, and she did nothing but jerk them around. There was no other alternative. She just had to leave.

Rebecca: She really couldn't take the process. It was just too difficult for her. I can't say exactly why, because I don't think anyone knows—including Irene. But she got to a point where she was absolutely miserable. There was no need for her to continue to be on *The Real World*. It just meant unnecessary pain for her. At the end, the only way she could've dealt with the process was if everyone put down the cameras and started hanging out.

She wasn't happy in the house, for sure. She's a good person deep down. She just had a hard time, that's all.

Stephen: She just couldn't take it. From the first day, she was always so funny, always telling jokes, always perfect, but I kept thinking to myself, 'What's wrong? Where's the rest of her?' She has a fear of herself. She wasn't, and isn't, comfortable with herself. I could see that the first day. Ask any of my roommates. I said, 'I won't be comfortable with Irene because she's not whole.'

*   *   *

Billy Rainey *RW* **Director:** It is true that Irene was obsessed with the process from the start. Even during the casting process, she had a zillion questions about the process, and virtually none about the experience itself. That probably should have been a red flag for us that things might be problematic down the line. But she was just so funny and compelling that we cast her anyway.

Mary-Ellis: I'm not a medical expert, so I can't tell you the exact reason why Irene's behavior changed so much. I do know that Irene told her roommates she'd had a reccurrence of Lyme disease and, in her own words, she'd told them the disease had affected her 'severely' in the past. Now, we know Lyme disease can produce nerve damage and that, in some cases, it can alter your brain chemistry. So, when her behavior became so aberrant, even Irene thought it might be attributable to the disease.

But Irene somehow adopted the point of view that her erratic actions had nothing to do with the Lyme disease, that her change in behavior was the result of stress brought on by the production.

Well, her roommates didn't know what to say. The angrier and more unstable she became, the tougher it got for them to remain sympathetic to her condition. In particular, Stephen had the most difficulty. But Stephen's behavior wasn't so sterling, either. The two of them had a couple of very serious moments that I'm sure they both regret.

Jon: When Pedro was sick with AIDS during our San Francisco season, we made it clear to him his health was far more important to us than the show. We told him that if he needed to leave *The Real World* because of his illness—even for just a few weeks' break—he was welcome to do so. But Pedro decided not to leave.

We said the same thing to Irene. Our producer told her, 'If you need to take a break from the show because of your Lyme disease, than feel free to go home...without the cameras.' She's an adult, so the decision was up to her, and she told us she didn't want to leave.

But things got so bad with her roommates that Irene lost all of their support. She finally decided she needed to leave—and permanently. She claimed her illness had nothing to do with why she was leaving, and that the stress of *The Real World* was actually the culprit. Whatever her reason for leaving, we wish her nothing but the best.

On Irene

DAVID: Irene is solid. She's just a dynamic, unbelievable personality. Her personality was so intense it made people step back for a moment. She's very strong-willed and full of pride, but she's also a prudent woman and made a good decision by leaving.

JANET: I won't deny that I didn't like dealing with Irene at the end. That she was difficult to be around. That she was constantly slandering people. That she was angry, defensive and aggressive. But I also really liked Irene the first few months I lived with her. She was the funniest person I've ever met. No one had ever made me laugh as much in my entire life. She could floor people for hours.

LINDSAY: I hope she works everything out—for her sake most of all.

NATHAN: Which Irene? The Irene we first met? The one that was really laid-back, laughed at any situation, and never got mad? Or the Irene that left us and quit the show? And I emphasize 'Quit!' That was nuts. At the end, she thought she was godly. She thought that she was the genius of the world. She wasn't! But I still wish her the best of luck in whatever the hell she does.

REBECCA: Irene is a good person and extremely intelligent. She saw a lot of negativity in the process and couldn't deal with it.

STEPHEN: When I think of Irene, I think,'Sad, man. Sad.' The situation with her was very sad. And what happened between us on the show sucked for her...and for me.

MARY-ELLIS: Irene was too curious about the process from the start. It should've been a signal to us that she was never going to be comfortable with it.

JON: I'm no doctor, but I think Irene wouldn't have had such a hard time if she hadn't had the relapse of the Lyme disease. I think she would've ridden through the storm and been fine.

And...

IRENE: Irene knows who she is. She knows what she likes.

Irene on Lyme Disease

I never fully had a way of talking about my Lyme disease on the show. So, to set the record straight:

I got diagnosed right before my sophomore year in college. What happened was I'd gone to the doctor—five, six times that year, different doctors even, and no one knew what was wrong with me. One night, I began to complain of fatigue, nausea and a backache. I didn't know what was going on.

So, I went to the hospital at 3 A.M. and the doctor checked me out. He kinda held my hand and said, 'We're gonna check you out for mono, and we're gonna give you a Lyme disease test. But, we think you're pregnant!' I just lost it, cuz I'm a virgin. I thought I was Mary. I was like, 'Oh, my God! Jesus is inside of Irene.'

I left the place crying, while the whole office had a big laugh. But two days later, I got a phone call saying I had Lyme disease. Well, I had no idea what Lyme disease was. Fact is, I had no idea what it was like not to feel good. And the person said to me, 'You need to seek treatment immediately. You're really ill.' So, I immediately went on an IV, which lasted nearly three weeks.

Soon as I finished with the IV, I went out for the soccer team at Georgetown. Now I know a rational person coming off an IV treatment for several weeks should not play on a Division I soccer team. But I'm not that rational. I thought I could conquer anything....

Well, by the second semester, I was still fainting. I looked like I was stoned all the time. I'd just pass out for hours on end. Still, Lyme disease is a functioning disease, so it would not appear to people that I had it. I could maintain an active life. But my sleeping was affected. And the lack of sleep affected my recovery and my anxiety level....

I take this medicine now, called Ameletripoline. Some people take it for depression, too. And bed wetters as well. My doctor is trying to wean me off of it, but I still have to take it. I have no choice. I've been on it for almost a year now, and I rarely mess around with it. Because if I don't take it, I wouldn't sleep at night. And I do not want to be the way I was when I didn't sleep.

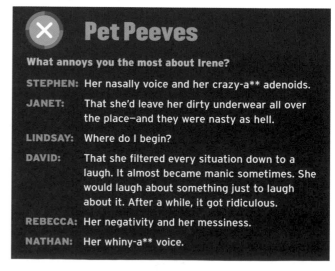

⊗ Pet Peeves

What annoys you the most about Irene?

STEPHEN: Her nasally voice and her crazy-a** adenoids.

JANET: That she'd leave her dirty underwear all over the place—and they were nasty as hell.

LINDSAY: Where do I begin?

DAVID: That she filtered every situation down to a laugh. It almost became manic sometimes. She would laugh about something just to laugh about it. After a while, it got ridiculous.

REBECCA: Her negativity and her messiness.

NATHAN: Her whiny-a** voice.

Since this medicine is associated with depression, some people react badly when they hear I'm taking it, so I don't talk about it much because things like that are handled so poorly within our society. You know what I mean? I wish I could make it so people would understand that others need to take those things. We live in a society where it's 'Buck up.' Well, some people can't just 'buck up.' Nor can they f**k up.

The stress of being on the show definitely caused my Lyme disease to relapse. In fact, it caused symptoms I've never even had before. I got migraine headaches, which I'd never gotten from my Lyme disease. My hands started turning black and blue. My legs and feet would fall asleep all the time. A doctor in Seattle told me I developed peripheral neuropathy—nerve damage—which is extremely rare in cases of Lyme disease. That was pretty traumatic news to get. I was always the healthy one.

But I can handle it. Since the show, I've sort of become the poster child for Lyme disease.

Lyme Disease: The ABC's

Brief History: Lyme disease was discovered in the U.S. in 1975, after a mysterious outbreak of arthritis near Lyme, Connecticut.

Number of Cases: More than 112,000 cases of Lyme disease have been reported in the U.S.

How Do You Get It?: Lyme disease is spread by the bites of ticks infected with a bacteria. People are most commonly exposed to ticks by brushing against vegetation with a tick attached.

Where Do You Get It?: In the U.S., the highest incidence occur in the Northeast (from Massachusetts to Maryland), the north-central states (especially Wisconsin and Minnesota), and the West Coast (particularly northern California.)

Symptoms: The early stages of the disease are usually marked by one or more of the following symptoms: fatigue, chills and fever, headache, muscle and joint pain, swollen lymph nodes, and/or a red, circular skin rash appearing at the site of the tick bite.

Diagnosis: Blood tests are used to determine if a patient is infected with Lyme disease.

Treatment and Prognosis: Lyme disease is treated with antibiotics under the supervision of a physician.

Prevention: Avoid tick-infested areas, especially in May, June, and July. Spray insect repellent containing Deet on clothes, and on exposed skin other than the face. Walk in the center of trails to avoid grass and brush. And wear a hat and a long-sleeved shirt for added protection.

Courtesy of:
Centers for Disease Control and Prevention
National Center for Infectious Diseases
Division of Vector-Borne Infectious Diseases
Atlanta, Georgia 30333

For further information, contact the CDC Voice Information System at (404) 332-4555, your physician, www.lyme.org, or your local health department

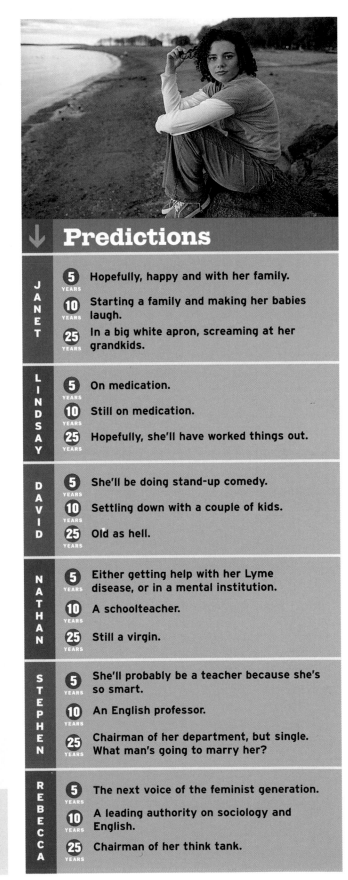

↓ Predictions

JANET
- **5 YEARS** Hopefully, happy and with her family.
- **10 YEARS** Starting a family and making her babies laugh.
- **25 YEARS** In a big white apron, screaming at her grandkids.

LINDSAY
- **5 YEARS** On medication.
- **10 YEARS** Still on medication.
- **25 YEARS** Hopefully, she'll have worked things out.

DAVID
- **5 YEARS** She'll be doing stand-up comedy.
- **10 YEARS** Settling down with a couple of kids.
- **25 YEARS** Old as hell.

NATHAN
- **5 YEARS** Either getting help with her Lyme disease, or in a mental institution.
- **10 YEARS** A schoolteacher.
- **25 YEARS** Still a virgin.

STEPHEN
- **5 YEARS** She'll probably be a teacher because she's so smart.
- **10 YEARS** An English professor.
- **25 YEARS** Chairman of her department, but single. What man's going to marry her?

REBECCA
- **5 YEARS** The next voice of the feminist generation.
- **10 YEARS** A leading authority on sociology and English.
- **25 YEARS** Chairman of her think tank.

Stephen

I REMEMBER UNPACKING THE SECOND DAY, having just watched the first few reactions of my roommates to the cameras. I saw how they'd become really loud and animated whenever the cameras were around. I didn't even know my roommates yet, but I could already tell this situation was going to be too much for any human being. As I was putting my mirror out on the dresser, I remember thinking, 'This is going to be weird.' I'm glad I did it.

"**But _The Real World_ is not for real people. This show is for people who have the ability to put on a facade and play someone else, or play just one part of themselves. And that's what most of my roommates did—most, but not all—and that sucks, because I didn't get to meet real people, at least on camera. I found out so much more about people off-camera, than I did on.**"

Take David, for example. He was just a total facade. He gave them whatever he thought they wanted. Like that journal entry he supposedly left out by mistake. You know the one where he got mad that other people had read it. First of all, why would you ever rip out a journal entry? Then he referred to it as a note. A note is addressed to someone. And it was left in the middle of the floor. That was a total setup, man. He wanted to create drama in the house. That's not a real person. That's not reality. That doesn't happen. David just wanted to get himself a half hour of the show.

So much happened like that—so many people acted for the cameras. I didn't think you could possibly put on a facade for five months. I'm too much of a real person to do that. You figure eventually they'll have to let their guard down. Well, hell, I saw people 'playing' from start to finish. And I'm talking more than half my roommates.

But not all of them were like that. Janet was really true to herself throughout the entire thing. She went through all the emotions like I did, and that's why we connected so well in the end.

Some of the others, man, I just wanted to call them out. Back home, I'm used to calling people out if they are lying to me, but you don't want to embarrass someone on national TV. So, you don't say things that could totally ruin them, like, 'You're a bulls**tter. You're a liar. Why don't you just admit it?' I just had to laugh to myself and think, 'This ain't real.'

But eventually, I'd felt compelled to speak up and call someone out. Like I was the only one who actually had the gall to say to Irene, 'You're tripping out. Why don't you calm down? You're acting like a bitch.' Everyone else was quiet and stood back, just so they wouldn't look like an a**hole on national TV. That was Nathan's thing. He was always very conscious of not looking like an a**hole on national TV.

I was like, 'Bro, I'm living my life here. I cannot hold back my feelings in any way, shape, or form. If I feel it, I'm going to act it. I have continuity in myself, which means my inside connects with the outside. What I'm thinking in my head, I'm gonna do with my body. I can't pretend to be something I'm not. If I need to cry, I will. I'll laugh like hell, too. And sometimes, I'll get mad as well.

Still, I was so upset with myself for slapping Irene. Mainly, I was so embarrassed for me. Of course, I was pissed at Irene, too. She planned what she did, and was so conscious of it going on national TV. I was like, 'Steve, this girl just planned an attack against you. She tried to insult your manhood in front of the world.' Even though I knew intellectually what she was doing, I still snapped, but right after my hand left her face, I felt like crap.

I've always prided myself on being a cool head. On being someone that people could talk to when they were angry or having problems. With Irene, I freaked out. I imploded. Now, I fear, I'll be seen as this 'angry black man,' and that's the kind of stereotype I've worked against my entire life.

My mom molded me in a way not to be anyone's stereotype. If someone stereotyped me as a dumb-a** n*gg*r, then I showed them how intelligent I was. If they thought I was angry, then I showed them how cool a head I had. Now, here I was on national TV succumbing to the stereotype of the 'angry black man.' I felt like s**t.

Thankfully, things began to settle down soon after Irene left the house. All of the roommates started to become a lot closer. I think we'd all been through a lot with Irene, and her leaving was a relief. My roommates knew me well enough to know that I wasn't the 'angry black man.'

Yeah, I have some anger issues, but I'm a lot more than that. I'm also a fun-loving fellow, who's always looking for something cool to do. I'm intelligent and have things to say. I'm gentle and compassionate, too. Yes, sometimes, I'm a jacka** as well, but basically, I'm just trying to be a whole person...and I'm also still a kid.

You know, I expected to have a whole lot of fun on _The Real World_. I expected to live in a cool house, have a cool job, get to go somewhere cool and meet some cool people. I thought the entire experience would be phat. Well, I got a cool house, cool job, and cool trip...but it turned out to be a phat recorded lesson on life.

I was ready to quit several times, especially after the incident with Irene, and that scared me because I'm not a quitter. So, I'm very proud of myself for hanging in there. I've grown a lot 'cause of this experience—about five years' worth of knowledge packed into five months. And although it was hell going through the _Real World_ experience, I'm very glad I did it.

On Stephen

Pet Peeves

What annoys you the most about Stephen?

DAVID: When he shoots his mouth off. He always has something to say and sometimes it's real hurtful.

REBECCA: That he can be overly self-absorbed.

JANET: His temper.

LINDSAY: His temper.

NATHAN: Oh, man. Where do I begin? And...

STEPHEN: That I can get annoyed too easily.

 REBECCA: Stephen was pretty open. In fact, I think he revealed as much of himself as anyone in the house. He was fully himself. He'd really react honestly to every situation. He definitely didn't hold back his anger, that's for sure, but I think Stephen is a good kid.

 JANET: Stephen doesn't want to be angry at the world. He'd much rather express his love, but sometimes he can't bottle up his anger and it just comes out. Then, it's too late. He's burned his bridges with the people who might've been able to receive his love.

 IRENE: I tried to get Stephen voted out numerous times in the beginning. He has a problem with women. He'd repeatedly swear at Janet, at Rebecca, at Lindsay, and at me, too. The kid has severe issues. They should've had his a** out of the house, but I couldn't get the house to vote him out. That's because he's like a little devil. Like if the devil had horns and tail we'd know he was the devil. But Stephen doesn't look that bad. He's really manipulative, though. That needs to be recognized.

 DAVID: Stephen is really eclectic and there's a lot to him. At times it was extremely difficult getting along with him. On the other hand, he wrote a lot of beautiful poetry and he could really be in tune with people's emotions. He's a strange kid. He'd be there for you, one moment. Then, react violently and vindictively the next. I think he hurt the girls—emotionally, not physically—especially Janet and Rebecca. He tried to hurt Irene as well, but she just left and got him last. I'd say I had a tough time getting to know Stephen. To really know Stephen, you've got to be really tolerant and patient.

 LINDSAY: I hope good things happen for Stephen. He just needs to learn how to control his temper. I think it stems from his past history and I think the therapy he's been getting will help him deal with it. But for the most part, Stephen has such a winning personality, and can be a wonderful guy.

 NATHAN: I think Stephen is uncertain and immature, and for that reason, he just doesn't know how to handle situations.

 JON: Stephen is still very much in that age where he blames others for anything bad that happens to him. I think a large part of what he learned from *The Real World* experience is that some things you just can't blame on others.

Certainly, the Irene incident was a big lesson in that. Because even if Irene provoked him, it still didn't justify Stephen laying a hand on her. He needed to see that he was ultimately responsible for his actions and that's something he's begun to come to terms with. If he can take that away from this experience, he'll be all the better for it.

 MARY-ELLIS: Stephen is so bright and articulate. He's capable of having an amazing future. Hopefully, what he learned from his roommates, from his experiences, and from anger management will help him to realize his great potential.

And...

 STEPHEN: I'm just a guy that thinks too much sometimes. I'm cool, fun and understanding. I always, always try to be understanding. And I'm very much an intellectual, or at least, I try to be. Someday, I'll hang my card out and it'll say, 'Intellectual.' I won't be making any money as one, but it'll make me happy.

Rock & Suck

👍 When did it ROCK?

STEPHEN: It rocked in Nepal. It rocked at the radio station. It rocked meeting all those bands. It rocked many more times than it sucked.

👎 When did it SUCK?

STEPHEN: It really sucked for me during and after the incident with Irene. It also sucked when we'd be harassed in Seattle. It sucked a lot then, because the girls were scared. They'd come home crying 'cause things had been thrown at them. Sometimes, they were scared to go out, and I felt like I needed to protect them.

Inquiring Minds

What question would you most like to ask Stephen?

REBECCA: What was it like not having a male figure in your life?
STEPHEN: It forced me to look elsewhere for male role models—everyone from Bill Cosby to W.E.B. DuBois.

DAVID: What's going on inside your head?
STEPHEN: Many, many different things. At root, I'm a person who thinks all the time.

LINDSAY: Why did you leave your hairs in the sink whenever you shaved your head?
STEPHEN: Those weren't my head hairs.

JANET: Do you really like your *fast food*—a.k.a. one-night stands?
STEPHEN: One-night stands are less maintenance than relationships, so I love my *fast food*.

NATHAN: Have you ever heard of sit-ups?
STEPHEN: I'm too preoccupied with matters of the mind.
And...

STEPHEN: Why the hell did you do this show?
STEPHEN: I don't know.

Kiss 'n' Tell

JANET:

Everyone in the house thought Stephen menstruated 'cause he'd PMS every month, like clockwork. By the third month, all the girls in the house were on the same clock, and Stephen always seemed to have his period about a week before us.

👁 Close Encounters

Whom will you stay in contact with?

STEPHEN: I'll be in touch with **REBECCA** and **JANET**. I won't be in touch with **LINDSAY, DAVID,** or **IRENE.** Irene needs to settle something with herself. And I won't be in contact with **NATHAN,** unless he needs me for something.

The Future
After *The Real World*

STEPHEN: I've got several more years to go at Berkeley before I graduate. After that, I'm considering a career in investment banking. I definitely plan to pursue something in business—something that requires leadership, because I have that ability. But I'd also like to go to grad school, possibly in communications and possibly at Columbia. I wanted to be a broadcast journalist, but that was before I realized how lucrative a business career could be.

↓ Predictions

R E B E C C A	**5** YEARS	Modeling for Hugo Boss.
	10 YEARS	Modeling for Pierre Cardin.
	25 YEARS	Retired and drinking Absolut Citron in Tahiti.
D A V I D	**5** YEARS	He's real business-oriented, so he'll be working at some company.
	10 YEARS	Running his own business.
	25 YEARS	Living his distorted, wacked-out American Dream.
J A N E T	**5** YEARS	Still in Berkeley.
	10 YEARS	Married to either gender.
	25 YEARS	Writing some deep philosophical book on his life's journey.
L I N D S A Y	**5** YEARS	Looking in the mirror.
	10 YEARS	Looking at his wife in the mirror.
	25 YEARS	Having a good time.
N A T H A N	**5** YEARS	Living in Los Angeles, and making money in business.
	10 YEARS	A big-time business exec.
	25 YEARS	In jail for a white-collar crime.
S T E P H E N	**5** YEARS	In investment banking or working for a big corporation.
	10 YEARS	Owning my own very successful business, probably in venture capital.
	25 YEARS	Still single. I don't believe in marriage. And I'll be living in Seattle.

Stephen's real world

On Mom

It was hard growing up because she was always working really hard to feed three kids, while going to school at the same time, and I resented her for never being around. But we're rather like the same person, so we clash in a lot of places. She's awesome; she's the most amazing woman I know because she's gone through so much. Somehow, she's managed to raise great kids and provide them with great futures.

On Mom's Opinion of *The Real World*

She didn't want me to do the show because I'm such a real person. She just knew it wouldn't work out. I should've listened to my mom.

On Dad

My daddy is married to a white woman right now and living in Orlando. He's got a little son, Jordan. He's a Captain in the Navy; a traveling man. I've only seen him twice. Once, I visited him. The other time he visited me to drop off some 'Daddy Money.' He knows we'll never really have

the relationship we'd like to have. But he came back into my life, and, at least, he's a presence.

On 7 Step-Fathers

These guys, you know, they just came in and out of my life. Sometimes, I barely noticed. My mom would just get tired of the guy and let him go—even if she had a kid with him. She just doesn't believe in staying with a man, just 'cause they've got a child together. At the same time, she also doesn't believe in being with a man for too long, unless he's going to

marry her. So, I've had six stepfathers, and I'm on my seventh right now.

On Marriage

I've seen a lot go down, and a lot of marriages go away. I just don't think it takes a ring and a big ceremony to make things meaningful.

On Being Married

I just don't believe I could be with one person for my entire life. I just know the way I am. I get tired of chicks after a while. Sometimes they get tired of me first.

On High School

I was always kind of a loner in high school, but I had a few friends and we were really close. I went to private school for two years. I kept busy in clubs, in leadership roles, but high school was definitely painful, because I was really fat. I know it's hard to believe now, but I was five foot ten and 275 pounds. I was quite a big guy.

On Losing the Weight

I lost the weight when I started lifting weights and I did have problems eating—complications, if you will. For a while, I had a hard time with food, but eventually, I got over that and started working out.

On "Fuses"

Oh, I definitely have a short fuse but the thing is, I've known that since I was about 14. My mama is the exact same way. But

April 26, 1978–Born	1982	1988	1989	1993	1994
Stephen's 'Line' 	**First Big Wheel:** It was awesome. I cruised for little chicks in it.	**First kiss:** In my mom's garage. The girl's name was Cassidy, and I was 10.	**First broken bone:** My wrist when I was 11. I got run over by a ten-speed. A hit-and-run by a bike. Can you believe that?	**First love:** Lisa, and she went to Crawford High in San Diego.	**Arrested:** For fighting with someone. But they let us go.

I've been able to control my temper, for the most part. Before I came to *The Real World*, I hadn't gotten in a fight in three and a half years and that only happened because some guy jumped me first.

Man, I hate fighting because I don't want something happening to my face. I've always been the guy in my college fraternity who says, 'No fighting in my house!' I just don't want be forced to jump in, and accidentally get a fist in my face.

On College

Berkeley has been the best experience of my life. Everyone is so smart. My teachers are so interactive. I've just learned so much being there. I love it. Berkeley is the best thing that's ever happened to me.

On Judaism

When I was growing up, my mom wasn't around much. So, I stayed with a Jewish family, and fell in love with their religion. So, when I was 14, I decided to convert. Before then, I didn't know what my religion was. My mother was a black Muslim, but she was the worst black Muslim. She never went to church, and never observed anything of her religion. The only thing I got from her black Muslim friends was what and who not to like.

My conversion to Judaism was cool. It's been a cool force in my life because at Berkeley a lot of my friends are Jewish. It's just a real welcoming community. Jews are like, real people. They've been through a lot, like African-Americans. Struggle is struggle, man. We'd all understand each other better if we embraced that.

My friend's parents were Orthodox. So, at first, I was an Orthodox Jew, but when I went back home, I couldn't control what my mom did in our house. So, I had to keep kosher myself, and that was hard. So, I'm now a Reformed Jew, which is a less strict way of living. Which is why I wasn't very observant in Seattle. Rituals are cool and symbolic but God realizes what's in my heart.

On Being African-American and Jewish

Yeah, a lot of African-Americans and Jews are surprised I can be both. Some are even bothered by it. Look, both groups have struggled. Both have been persecuted. There's a lot to learn from one another. But a lot of African-Americans and Jews are very rigid and full of pride, and that pride blinds people sometimes. Well, if the two groups could put down their pride more, they might go, 'Hey, we've got a lot in common.' It's just so crazy how parallel our histories have been, but no one sees it because of their pride.

On Affirmative Action

People say, 'Oh, it's not needed anymore.' Well, they ought to remember people like myself, who've gone to inner-city schools with one computer for two hundred students. It's impossible to compete with kids that have one computer in their bedroom and one for them at school. That's why we need Affirmative Action. It's about creating a cohesive America. All it takes is a bit of common sense and compassion to realize that we need to level the playing field.

On the Dream Job

I'd like to have Peter Jennings' career. I'd love to be an anchor. I reckon he has enough money as an anchor to start his own business. I'd love to start my own business and write books, too. That would be awesome. I'd publish an African-American-male anthology of poetry. I'd like to do that in the next few years. An anthology of strong African-American male writers between the ages of 18 and 25.

S T A T S	
Birthday:	April 26, 1978
Hometown:	San Diego, California
Siblings:	Four (I'm the middle one.)
Pets:	Dog 'Smokey'
High School:	San Diego High School
College:	University of California at Berkeley

F A V E S	
Band:	Matchbox 20
Book:	*My Bondage, My Freedom* by Frederick Douglass
TV Show:	*Politically Incorrect*
Movie:	*The Color Purple*
Actor:	Morgan Freeman
Actress:	Angela Bassett
Personal Motto:	Compassion manifests good karma.
Meal	Anything at Tup Tim Thai in Seattle.
Way to Chill Out:	Hanging out with close friends. No TV. No radio.
Pickup Line:	Baby, I got to pull this stop sign you're standing on.
First Date:	Dinner
Sleeping Outfit:	Naked
Stuffed Animal:	A little brown bear.

Advice

What advice would you give to future *Real World*-ers?

STEPHEN: Really check this out before you commit to it. Personally, if I were you, I wouldn't do it. But if you really want to, remember it's going to be hard. You're bound to be pissed off at some of your roommates. Or pissed off at the way you're being portrayed. Either way, you're going to be pissed off.

1995	1996	1996	1998
First time: It was her first time, too. I'd known her for a year and a half. It was great. It was awesome. It was cool. It was funny.	**Graduates high school:** From San Diego High School.	**First time meeting his father:** It was during my first year at Berkeley. Yeah, I was nervous. Who wouldn't be?	**First time appearing on *The Real World*:** And it'll be the last!

The 'Incident'

The Slap

STEPHEN: In my mind, there's no question Irene intentionally provoked me in order to embarrass me on national TV. Just look at the way she planned it.

As she was leaving, she told me she had a gift for me, but she said it really loudly, as a call to the camera. Everyone knew that whenever you'd say something really loudly in that house, the cameras would come rushing toward you. Irene even waited for the camera guy to reach us before she continued talking.

I expected Irene to say something like, 'Steve, we've gone through some crap together, but now that I'm leaving, let's wish each other well.' But instead, she looked me right in the eye and said, 'You remember how we talked about getting married. Well, we're not getting married, Steve, because you're a homosexual.'

I went and threw her little stuffed animal into the ocean and that's where I should've stopped. Unfortunately, my anger got the better of me.

I began to think of what she'd just done. I thought to myself, 'Man, this bitch just planned an attack on you in front of the world. She's just made you look like a fool.' And so, I snapped. I freaked out. I ran back to her cab, and slapped her across her face. It was a moment of anger. A moment of heat. A moment I'll regret the rest of my life.

Immediately, I knew what I'd done was wrong, but I had no idea it would turn into such a big deal. Part of the reason was because it was caught on video. I'd gotten so caught up in the moment I forgot the cameras were there. Had I known, I probably wouldn't have slapped her. I also didn't know there was a clause in our contract protecting us from acts of violence.

The next few days turned into a sort of living hell. The most agonizing part was waiting to hear if the roommates had

entirety of you.' And I thought to myself, 'He's right. I'm not going to quit like Irene. If they give me another chance, I'm going to see this thing out and redeem myself.'

IRENE: I came into the house a lady, I was leaving the house a lady. There is no person—not MTV, the creators Bunim/Murray or my housemates—that could make me compromise me. So, in the face of all these people that betrayed me, that made me feel isolated...still, I left a present for every one of them as I was leaving. I left a present from my Nana for Janet because she and I had bonded over our grandmothers. Basically, I gave everyone some small, personal thing.

But as I'm walking out, I was like, 'Whatever! I'm not gonna lie.' You know, there are some times in your life you wanna know, 'Can I be a bitch?' Well, hell yeah... So, I was walking to the car and I thought to myself, 'Forget it.'

So, I said to Stephen, 'You know I jerked you around that you had such good domestic skills I was gonna marry you...

Straight out, I didn't get angry at Irene because of what she said. A remark like that would never piss me off. Hell, I heard that kind of s**t before in high school. Besides, there's just no way I'm gay.

That girl was just looking to get laid. She probably had animosity towards me

voted me in...or out. Man, I didn't know what to do with myself. I talked and talked with Craig Borders, the director, about the pain and guilt I felt. And I waited...and waited. It took almost five hours before I heard their decision and the longer I waited, the more I lost faith in my roommates.

well, we both know that would never work out.' And he was like, 'No?' And I was like, 'You know—'cuz you're a homosexual.' Then I just walked away.

Listen, I do admit my behavior was uncalled for. You do not treat another person that way. It was uncalled for. But then he proved everything I said. I turn around and he's throwing my stuffed animal off the pier. Then, he starts swearing at me. And finally, he runs up to my car, and whaps me across my face. I just remember like holding my face and bawling. I had his palm print across my face. A six-foot, two-inch man hit me. There's something wrong with that.

So now I don't feel so bad about what I said to Stephen. That kid is the walking devil. So all I did was stick my tongue out at the devil. And you can't hurt the devil by sticking your tongue out at him.

I do admit my behavior was uncalled for. You do not treat another person that way. It was uncalled for. But then he proved everything I said. I turn around and he's throwing my stuffed animal off the pier. –Irene

for not hooking her up. Well, Irene, I didn't hook you up because I don't have sex with ugly women...not 'cause I'm gay.

At first, I reacted to Irene's comment with an insult response. I just kind of gave her a jackoff motion and thought, 'Well, you're a bitch, Irene. I'm out of here.' Then

As time passed, I told Craig that I wanted to leave the show right then and there—regardless of the vote. So, he sat me down and said, 'If you leave right now, you'll have no chance for redemption. You'll have no chance to prove who you really are. To prove that this incident is not the

The Vote

DAVID: The vote was unanimous in favor of keeping Stephen and I'm glad it was. We didn't get to have closure with Irene. So personally, I wanted to have closure with Stephen. I was willing to forgive, and give the kid another chance. Yeah, I disagreed with a lot of what he did. The boy has some issues he needs to sort out—like controlling his anger for one, but he deserved to stay.

JANET: I never considered kicking Stephen out of the house, and I think he argued with me more than anyone else in the house. If I'd ever felt fearful, it should've been earlier on when we were fighting the most, but he didn't hit me then, so I didn't fear he'd hit me after he slapped Irene. Yes, it was really wrong to hit her, but I don't think any of us felt we had the right to kick him out. And everybody had their gripes with Stephen. So, to our credit, I think we handled it maturely because all it would've taken was one vote to kick him out.

and she executed it to perfection. Calling Stephen a homosexual was the worst thing you could ever say to that kid.

As for kicking Stephen out of the house, I felt I personally couldn't make that important a decision on his life. So I left it in the hands of my roommates, but said I thought he should stay. I just wouldn't want anybody else kicking me out of the house under any circumstance.

REBECCA:
I think we made the right choice in not kicking Stephen out. He's a good kid, but also very young and emotional. Sometimes, he would react like a child, which was exactly what he did in this instance. I

do so after Stephen slapped Irene, and that decision was directly influenced by a similar incident, which occurred in Los Angeles during our second season.

During *The Real World-L.A.,* a cast member named David was voted out of

Prior to the slap, we'd never shown the cast video of themselves until after they moved out of the house. We just felt it would make them much too self-conscious. In effect, our policy became a so-called 'line,' between the cast and crew. –Mary-Ellis Bunim

the house by his roommates. In short, David had wrestled a blanket off one of his roommates, Tami, while she was dressed only in her underwear—even though she'd repeatedly told him to stop. Several members of that house, particularly the females, felt that David had committed an act of violence against Tami. One of them even likened what he'd done to rape.

Before they voted on his fate, David

LINDSAY: I'm glad we voted to keep Stephen in the house, but I definitely thought he needed to go through some kind of rage therapy. I was never frightened of him, but he definitely had a horrible temper. I don't think he even realized how monstrous he could be. Honestly, I'd never met anyone capable of saying such things.

NATHAN: Stephen blamed himself for the incident with Irene, and he certainly deserved a lot of the blame. I lost a lot of respect for him for doing such a d**k, cowardly thing. You can be sure he'd never try slapping someone like me.

But he also reacted just the way Irene wanted. He should've known she was intentionally pushing his buttons, and she got just what she wanted. She made him look like a complete a** on national television. That was her plan the whole time

figured he deserved another chance, and we ought to give him it to him.

CRAIG BORDERS, *RW Director:*
Not kicking Stephen out was the best choice made all season. For the cast. For the crew. And for Stephen, especially.

'The Line'

MARY-ELLIS: The Stephen and Irene 'incident' created a first in the history of *The Real World.* Prior to the slap, we'd never shown the cast video of themselves until after they moved out of the house. We just felt that if our cast saw footage of themselves—while we were still filming them—it would make them much too self-conscious. In effect, our policy became a so-called 'line,' between the cast and crew.

But for the first time ever on *The Real World,* we crossed that line. We decided to

begged us to show his roommates the video we'd shot of that incident. Since not all of them had been witnesses, he wanted the rest to see what he'd actually done—not what the rumor mill had spread. He wanted them to see that she'd been laughing throughout the incident, but we decided against showing them the videotape. We felt that it was something the roommates should work out on their own, as though we weren't there.

In the years hence, we've grappled with that decision. At the time, the women in the L.A. house were angry at David for prior indiscretions. I believe they let that anger affect their judgment of what David did to Tami. Had we shown them the actual video footage, they might've seen the David incident more objectively. And probably, they might've voted to keep David in the house, instead of kicking him out.

JON: Being kicked out of the L.A. house was very hard on David. He was forced to live with the stigma of being 'the guy that got kicked off the show.' And frankly, we were never convinced his roommates' decision was fair to him. So we wanted to make sure it was fair to Stephen.

Also, none of Stephen's roommates had actually seen the slap itself. Or, in fact, the events leading up to it. So, how could they vote objectively on Stephen without having seen what transpired between him and Irene? Well, we believed they couldn't. So, that's why we broke with precedent and showed them the footage.

MARY-ELLIS: We've always said we wouldn't intrude upon the process…unless the roommates felt unsafe. Well, how could they determine their safety without actually seeing the incident for themselves? So, we let them view it to make their own determination.

JON: We showed the roommates a few minutes of videotape relating to 'the slap.'

unfortunate event, and end up turning it into a very positive experience.

Yes, viewers would see the violent side of Stephen, but they'd also get to see how far he could go from there. He wouldn't only be seen as 'the guy that slapped the girl in Seattle.' Instead, he'd be seen as 'the person who took that experience and made something positive out of it.' That's a much better place for him to be post-*Real World*. It's certainly a better place to be than being remembered as 'the one that got kicked off the show.'

Listen, I've always been reluctant to intrude on the documentary process that's the lifeblood of this show. But I'd rather intrude on the process if it'll make people the best they can be, and if some documentarian is upset with me for crossing 'the line,' then it's fine with me.

I think the *Real World* setting puts so much pressure on these people, and I'd rather afford them the opportunity to grow from the experience, than to suffer interminably from their mistakes.

verbally abusive—behavior he had to change.

Otherwise, we felt he was a risk to his roommates, and we couldn't let him stay in the house.

JON: I think any time someone lays a hand on another person, they're out of control. And as the people in charge, we have to make sure that we're not putting the production and ourselves in a liability situation. Say, we didn't do anything. Then, God forbid, the cast member takes it to the next step. Everyone would turn around and say, 'Why didn't you intervene?'

MARY-ELLIS: And Stephen had already subjected his roomates to a number of instances of really horrible verbal abuse. Several cast members had left confessionals for us regarding Stephen's temper. Some said how horrified they were that we hadn't intervened or stopped Stephen when he was in the midst of one of his tirades. Rebecca was particularly bothered by Stephen's tantrums, and horrified the production didn't confront him.

TCR 19:20.26:01   TCR 19:20.26:21   TCR 19:20.27:07   TCR 19:20.27:26

The footage featured the actual slap as well as the events leading directly up to and after that incident. The directors set up a monitor in the house to screen the tape for the roommates. Neither Irene, who was on her way back home, nor Stephen, who was getting a tattoo, were present at the time.

We showed the cast the footage but we still left the decision on Stephen in their hands. We felt it was necessary for the cast to have all the information but also essential for them to be the ultimate decision makers.

To be perfectly honest, both Mary-Ellis and I had hoped the roommates would vote to keep Stephen in the house. Partly because of the stigma that had affected David years after the L.A. show. But also because we believed there was an opportunity for Stephen to learn from this

MARY-ELLIS: In addition to showing the roommates, we also decided to show Stephen the footage along with several additional instances where his anger had become out of control. Again, this was unprecedented for *The Real World*.

But we showed some to Stephen for everyone's sake. For his sake, because he

was having so much trouble controlling himself. But principally, for the sake of the roommates, because if we allowed him to stay—provided the roommates voted that way—we wanted Stephen to see what sort of out-of-control—mostly

Until we showed Stephen those scenes of him out of control, he hadn't taken the subject of his anger very seriously. But after we played them for him, he took it much more seriously.

In addition to showing Stephen the video, we also wanted to provide him with an effective solution for addressing his

Several cast members had left confessionals for us regarding Stephen's temper. Some said how horrified they were that we hadn't intervened or stopped Stephen when he was in the midst of one of his tirades. –Mary-Ellis

anger problems. Given the short-term nature of our show, we looked for something that might have more immediate results. We wanted a place that might immediately give some tools for dealing with his anger ideally, so that Stephen could have an opportunity to redeem himself on the show.

JON: We solicited recommendations from a number of sources, including the Seattle police. We were told that similar

'Shouldn't you take some responsibility for inciting Irene with the cameras? You're sending me to Anger Management, when my anger was brought on by something manifested by you.' –Steven

instances of domestic violence, like Stephen slapping Irene, usually resulted in the aggressor being sentenced to anger management counseling.

So, that's how the idea of anger management counseling came into play. We decided to make it a condition for allowing Stephen to stay in the house. We saw it as an appropriate penalty for slapping Irene, but more importantly, a means of protecting Stephen's roommates, while giving him a productive means of dealing with his violent side.

then I'll do it, but I'm just going through the motions with it.'

The first day I went to Anger Management was hilarious. They sent me with Craig, the director, and we just laughed and laughed. The anger management department was located in the psychiatric part of the hospital. As soon as we entered the ward, there was this lady pinned against the wall with her eyes wide open. Then, we saw this table with a huge puzzle laid out on top of it. And we're like, 'Oh, s**t! We've entered the nut house.'

Then, my doctor came out and he looked just like Dr. Katz from the comedy show. And I was thinking, 'Oh, my God. This is going to be a long one.'

Well, as soon as he said my living situa-

after all. In fact, the stuff I learned would be good for everyone. It would be good for every single person in the house, and the world. Because we're all human beings. We all get dissatisfied with the way we react to things, and finding better ways to react is what Anger Management is all about.

Honestly, I'd never do this *Real World* bulls**t again. Hell no. It was a very weird situation, and very compromising for me, but I came out of it grateful that I'd learned some things about myself—and a lot of those things I learned in anger management counseling.

The Reaction

DAVID: Knowing how skeptical he was of counseling, I'm glad it worked out for him.

JANET: In the beginning, Stephen was embarrassed about the anger management class. He didn't want his friends back home thinking he needed such a thing. So he tried to make a joke out of it. Later on, he actually realized he does

The Anger

STEPHEN: The production made me go to anger management counseling as a condition for my staying in the house. Honestly, I was insulted when they told me I had to go. I was insulted they were making me take the entire blame for the slapping incident. I was willing to take one hundred percent responsibility for my actions. No, I shouldn't have slapped Irene, but surely Irene was responsible for some of what happened.

And what about the X-factor? What about the responsibility of *The Real World?* I was like, 'Shouldn't you take some responsibility for inciting Irene with the cameras? You're sending me to Anger Management, when my anger was brought on by something manifested by you.' I was pissed. I was like, 'Hey, if that's what it's going to take for me to stay in the house,

tion was f**ked up, I was like, 'Man, this guy gets it.' And ever since that moment, Dr. Maiuro became like my closest friend.

I felt like I could talk to him about anything in my life. We spent a lot of time going over the Irene incident. He gave me something called a 'feelings checklist,' where I indicated my exact emotions at the time. But basically, Dr. Maiuro, my hero, gave me some ways to deal with any problems that could come my way.

He showed me how to take a step back in a heated moment. He taught me how to accept responsibility for my actions. He taught me that apologies don't take any of your pride away. An apology is a simple package that says, 'Look, I understand your frustrations with my actions. And I'm taking the steps to mend that with you.'

And you know what? Anger Management turned out to be not such a bad idea

have an anger problem and that the counseling was helping him deal with it.

There were days when I'd see him get pissed off, and he'd start counting to himself, one through ten. I'd ask him what he was doing and he'd say it's what the counselor told him to do when he got mad.

After he started counseling, he definitely became more tolerant of his roommates. I could tell he was trying so hard.

LINDSAY: I could sense a change, too. I never got to be great friends with Stephen, but I thought he had a really charming side. More of that side came out after he learned how to manage his angry side.

NATHAN: Yeah, the anger management calmed him down. He needed it. But I saw more sulking out of him than anything else.

REBECCA: Listen, I think Stephen was fine before he came to Seattle. But if those classes helped, I'm glad for him.

S-e-x in the House

NATHAN: 'Our house was one big hormone pumping all over the place. We were just a bunch of 20-somethings with sex drives on full f**king charge.'

REBECCA: I'd say the girls experienced some definite sexual repression. We coped by complaining—and a lot of exercise. As for the guys, I don't know how much sex they were having, but they certainly weren't as sexually vocal as the girls. Well, on second thought, they all talked a lot about sex, too.

DAVID: Sex was the subject of a lot of conversations in the house, but Nathan was the only person that got laid in the house and that was with his girlfriend, Stephanie. On the other hand, I was super-celibate. I just couldn't get my mind off of Kira. I found that priorities change when you start to love someone. The things that you used to crave, you no longer crave in the same way anymore. Like, for example, getting it any way you can.

JANET: Yes, there was an extreme amount of sexual energy in the house. Our whole group was very touchy-feely with each other. David and Nathan were constantly in the girls' beds, but I think we all just needed constant affection. It wasn't a sexual thing. We were just affection-starved people.

STEPHEN: Oh, man, there was so much sexual tension in that house. Everyone talked about sex night and day. It was always, 'Sex, sex, sex, sex, sex—24/7.' But what do you expect? We're all between the ages of 19 and 22.

LINDSAY: The first two weeks, all I ever talked about was sex, but it wasn't because I was a walking hormone. I was just being funny about it. Gradually, I cooled down on the subject. You know, I'm just the type of person who goes through certain stages. I'll talk about sex forever, then fixate on something else.

Virtual Sex

NATHAN: Phone sex kicks a**, especially when your girlfriend is several thousand miles away, but TV phone sex takes it to another dimension. Stephanie and I had a great time with the videophone they installed in the house. We'd get really into it late at night when my roommates were asleep.

But I didn't know they were able to film us talking on the videophone. I had no idea until after the show was over, and one of the directors told me. Honestly, it really pissed me off they didn't warn me beforehand. It pissed off Stephanie even more than me. Before the show, she told me she was going to cut off my d**k if they ever filmed us having phone sex. I told her, 'No way. They wouldn't do that.' Luckily, she holds them responsible and not me, so I survived with my d**k intact.

Was there any hooking up within the house?

JANET: It's just too hard having a romance within the house. You hit that brother-sister stage so quickly, like within a couple of weeks. You live together, play together, and work together. It's way too stressful to have any sort of relationship. I don't know how other *Real World* casts have done it.

You know, it really surprised me that they made it look like Nathan and I were having a flirtation at the beginning of the show. I've always had lots of guy friends, who'd take care of me like an older brother would. Well, Nathan was that way with me, and David was, too.

DAVID: No one hooked up, but look at the intensity of our existence. Imagine what would've happened if, say, me and Lindsay started going out. Yeah, we liked each other at first, but if we started dating, then the entire house would've been internalizing our goods.

I think it's virtually impossible to hook up with someone in your *Real World* house. Like, what happens if you hook up and it doesn't work out? Then, you have to look that person in the eye every day walking down the hall, or sharing a bathroom. Basically, you just want to keep things as simple as possible with your roommates on *The Real World*.

STEPHEN: The only single people in the house were Janet, Irene, and me. Irene had really gross habits, so much so that I couldn't see any guy dating her. Janet, well, she didn't come on to any of the guys in the house—which was kind of weird. As for me, I only date black chicks, 'cause that's what I like. No discrimination. That's just what I'm attracted to and there were no black girls living in the house.

REBECCA: Even if I hadn't had a boyfriend, no one in the house was really my type. I mean, can you really see me with any of those guys?

LINDSAY: Yeah, in the beginning I had a flirtation with David. I thought he was a good-looking guy. But our flirtation didn't last very long. Listen, flirting is real fun, but acting on it is a whole other story. I admit, I'm the biggest flirt in the whole world, but I don't take phone numbers, and I won't put out unless I'm with someone I care about. I'm just no random hookup girl, that's all. I went through that stage a while back, but who hasn't? And I don't do that any longer.

NATHAN: All of us roommates were straight, as far as I know. But none of us were ever like, 'Man, we're gonna hook up.' We just had our share of good ol' flirtatious fun.

First of all, David had a girlfriend. I had a girlfriend. Rebecca had a boyfriend. Lindsay kind of had a boyfriend. Stephen, well, I don't think anyone found him attractive. I mean, he's an attractive guy... but he has unattractive personality traits. And Irene—well, to me, she was just one of the guys.

I know that's a bad thing to say about a woman, so I hope she doesn't take it the wrong way, but that's just how I felt. The first month and a half Irene and I hung out together all the time, but it was just to sit and laugh and burp together, that's all.

"The 8th Roommate"

David: The '8th Roommate' is my penis. I wouldn't say it's an 8th wonder of the world, but I was blessed with a large penis. I presented it as a cordial present to my roommates. Actually, Lindsay wanted to see my schlong, so I obliged. She asked how it got so big. I told her, 'Perhaps because

I haven't worn underwear since the first grade.'

Janet: David has a beautiful body, by far the most beautiful body I've ever seen on a guy, and boy is he proud of it, and proud of his penis, too. Yeah, it's large, but it's not Peter North-like-skin-flick-large.

Lindsay: I'd say David's penis is as big as Stephen's snowboard.

Nathan: Give me a break, the kid's d**k is the same size as mine. But I just don't go flashing it all over the place. Man, what's with that? If that kid's d**k is the '8th Roommate,' then mine is the 9th, and Stephen's the 10th. I mean, we're both pretty hung guys. But, Stephen and I don't fling it onto the table and say, 'Hey girls, look at this!' David just wanted the girls to talk about him. That's why he showed it to them the first week we arrived.

Stephan: He's got a big d**k. So what? I'm not so small myself.

Rebecca: Thank goodness I missed all of that business. So, I have no idea how big it is, and frankly, I don't care.

RACE in the House

Rebecca: Race had absolutely no role, period!

Lindsay: We had a Korean-American and an African-American in the house. Janet has never been gung-ho on racial issues, and Stephen didn't make a big deal about it, either. I don't know where Stephen stood with race, as with a lot of things.

Janet: I felt no effect as the only Asian in the house. Actually, that's not totally true. It bothers me whenever I read the media's description of the show. They always say something like, 'Janet is a young ambitious woman, who's *Korean-American*.'. I know that was a major reason why I was cast on the show and I completely accept that.

Nathan: It had zero effect. We never talked about anything political in the house. No presidential politics. No Bosnia. No abortion. Nothing.

David: Race was a nonissue in the house.

Stephen: The race issue rarely came up. Nathan was the only person in the house whom I had some issues with over color. Nate told me that he'd gotten into a fight, and the guy was running away, so he called him the N-word to try and stop him. But I was like, 'Nate, to even think such a word is floating around in your head, just disgusts me beyond belief.'

I'm certainly not an angry person on the topic, like some people I know. I just think the only one to blame for racism is ignorance itself. So, I try to educate people by speaking up on issues, like affirmative action, and by using my life as an example.

Friend or Foe?

JANET: The reports of Seattle hating us were greatly exaggerated but yes, there were some hostile people around town. And I'd be lying to you if I didn't say it bothered me. It was hard enough dealing with the *Real World* process to have to deal with that. And nobody likes to get their coffee in the morning and have some 35-year-old woman tell you to f**k off, which happened to me.

I'd say most of the hostile comments were directed at MTV. The Seattle underground scene is very anticorporate. They'd say things to us like, 'Nothing personal, but we just don't like your network.'

Just a small part of Seattle was anti-*Real World* or anti-MTV. For the most part, the people of Seattle were real welcoming and warm.

DAVID: I'd say the people of Seattle were more friend than foe, but at certain venues, some of the locals were pretty hostile—especially the scenesters and hipsters. Norman Mailer would've been proud of those kids. They'd be smoking cigarettes and yelling, '*The Real World* sucks.' They were total posers, self-proclaimed barometers of coolness. I don't know, maybe they're just guilt-ridden 'cause they made millions with the grunge scene. I just laughed at them.

Seattle thinks:
THE REAL WORLD SUCKS!

T-shirt for sale in a Seattle bar.

ter to do. In fact, I wonder what they're doing now that we're gone—probably boycotting Planet Hollywood or something else really inspired.

REBECCA: For the most part, everyone in Seattle loved us. But young Seattle also prides itself on being an alternative city. So if you live there, you have to be against conformity, and MTV qualifies as conformist. At the beginning, I was offended by every negative comment. But it got to the point where I began to find it comical.

STEPHEN: The older the person, the less likely they were to give us a hard time. It was the twenty-somethings who were down on *The Real World*. Personally, I just figured it was jealousy. It made me want to write a big fat note

"Norman Mailer would've been proud of those kids. They'd be smoking cigarettes and yelling, '*The Real World* sucks'."—DAVID

For the most part, the people of Seattle were real receptive and cool—especially around the Fish Market. I got to know a lot of locals working there, and those people are now friends.

LINDSAY: Generally, the people of Seattle were really nice to us, but some of them were a little hostile, especially at first. It was scary when those guys jumped Irene at the OK Hotel bar. That was horrible because she could've gotten hurt; but after a while in Seattle, that sort of stuff died down.

NATHAN: The city was friendly for the most part. I'd say there were only about 15 hostile people, the rest were real cool, and those 15 just had nothing bet-

to all those jealous people, saying, 'What the hell are you so jealous about? Being on *The Real World* ain't so great!'

BILLY RAINEY, *RW* **Director:** In San Francisco, we just said we were shooting a documentary and they believed us. Now you walk through town with seven reasonably telegenic people and it's like, 'Duck, *The Real World* is in town.'

MATT KUNITZ, *RW* **Producer:** There's no question it was harder shooting in Seattle than, say, Miami, where the entire community rolled out the red carpet for us. Seattle scene-sters made it difficult for us a number of times. For the most part, however, the people of Seattle were just great.

DAVID AND NATHAN
WAS IT FAIR?

DAVID:

Yeah it was fair. I mean, s**t , bro. Everyone needs change. The old formula was getting tired. I know the fact that Nate and I knew each other coming into this bothered Stephen, especially at first. But he's a whiny kid anyway. I think everyone else thought it was wonderful.

JANET:

I loved it. I thought it was a nice twist. The rest of the cast has no history together beyond these five months. So it's nice to see the effect of this process on two people who've known each other much longer. The fact that David and Nathan are completely different people made it less of an 'us-against-them' situation.

LINDSAY:

Yeah, it was fair. In fact, it was cool. They get along, but they're different people. Initially, I think some of us thought they might hang out together a lot more than they actually did. I know Stephen was upset because he felt like the odd man out. But I think he got to be pretty good friends with both guys.

NATHAN:

Before we left for the show, David and I talked about making an effort not to alienate ourselves from anyone in the house. We wanted to give 100 percent to our roommates. So we were careful not to let our friendship freeze the others out. Still, Stephen complained about being alienat-ed. Personally, I think Stephen found ways to alienate himself even without our help.

So, yeah, it was fair. I don't think it would've been fair to eliminate one of us just because we knew each other.

REBECCA:

I thought it was fine. But I do think it was unfortunate for Stephen, in the sense that he felt left out. It didn't bother me at all. Actually, I'd have loved to go through this experience with a friend from home.

STEPHEN:

No, I don't think it was fair at all because David and Nate clicked a lot. I was expecting to hang with the guys in the house, but they mostly hung out together. Whenever they'd start telling their VMI stories, I'd just up and leave the room. But I found my own set of guy-friends outside the house. So I just hung with them.

IRENE:

They took two people that traveled the country and internationally together before the show. And once they got to the house, they stopped speaking. You saw a split between them. Something is going on there, you know.

*   *   *

MARY-ELLIS:

We'd long toyed with the idea of putting twins together on the show, or a brother and sister, or even a couple, like Nathan and Stephanie. I think it worked out great this time, but I don't think we'll do it again next season. The general premise is still 'seven strangers living together.'

JON:

I think it worked out fine, too. Nathan and David are so different from each other.

Strangers No More

The Original Opening

This is the true story...of seven strangers...picked to live in a loft... have their lives taped...to find out what happens...when people stop being polite ... and start getting real... The Real World.
-The Real World-New York (1992)

The New Opening

This is the true story...of seven people...picked to live on a pier... and work together ...and have their lives taped... to find out what happens... when people stop being polite ...and start getting real... The Real World.
-The Real World-Seattle (1998)

"DEAD AIR"

JANET: It was an ideal job. We were working in the No. 13 market, at the No. 3 station in that market. That's an awesome opportunity! We had awesome bosses. Phil and Tony were the best bosses I've ever had. We got to do things we'd normally never get to do, like meeting all those bands. Oh, my God, we met so many great people.

I also think we put together a pretty decent, relatable show. If I were scanning the radio dial at that time of the night, I'd have definitely tuned in to our show. Of course, we weren't the most accomplished radio people, but I think listeners could certainly tell we were having a good time.

NATHAN: Working at the radio station was a blast! The best part was being on the air, and also interviewing bands. I'd never done anything like that before. The first person I got to interview was Peter Buck from R.E.M. After I spoke with him, he was like, 'Damn, Nathan! Do you do this a lot? Man, we've been interviewed a thousand times, and this is one of the best interviews we've ever had.' That felt really great. I also got to meet Ben Harper, which is my favorite band. So that was really cool, too.

REBECCA: It was a really interesting experience. I got to produce the show and run the board. I'm a music fanatic, so working at a radio station was a fantasy job for me.

KNDD 107.7 THE END

DAVID: I had a nice time working at The End radio station. Without a doubt, the best part of it had to be interviewing the bands. I got to do an interview with Bad Religion, which I think has some of the most brilliant musicians in the past 20 years. The worst part of the radio job was kissing a** as a moderator. I felt that my intelligence was being insulted. Nevertheless, I ate humble pie, and took it like a man, bro.

Truthfully, the radio station wasn't my first-priority job. Maybe it should've been, but I preferred to work at the Fish Market. If I could've worked at the Market full-time, I would've done so in a heartbeat.

I think the best part of it was getting to be surrounded by music all the time. I really liked that. I really liked sitting in on music meetings, learning how music actually got on the air and selecting different types of music to play, and of course, getting to hear the music played live really rocked.

The worst part of the experience? Starting at midnight. I'm an early bird, so the late nights took some getting used to. I was so tired sometimes, I'd screw up when I was running the board.

STEPHEN: It was a great experience. I loved it. I met some awesome people there. We got to be on the air, have our own show. Our two girls were so sexy. I could see little 15-year-old boys getting off listening to them.

*   *   *

LINDSAY: I loved working at The End. It was a fantasy job. I mean, Seattle is a big-time market. And here we were, getting to go on the air. It's hard to beat that. You know, we thought nobody would listen to our show, "Dead Air," but people actually enjoyed our shows. Not just teenagers, either, but 28- and 29-year-olds. We didn't even let on with our listeners that we were from *The Real World*. Working at The End made my experience in Seattle so much better.

MARY-ELLIS: *The Real World-Boston* made us believers in having a unifying activity for the entire cast outside of the house—whether that be working at the After School Program or some other communal enterprise. We first tried doing that in Miami with a business start-up, which was less successful—though full of drama. Given the city of Seattle's connection to music, we thought working at a radio station was an ideal job for the cast.

JON: It was also more of a fantasy job for the *Real World* age group than either the After School Program or the business start-up. The Seattle cast seemed to take the radio station more seriously than the Boston or Miami casts had taken their responsibilities, and I suspect that was because it was something they really wanted to do. Most of them were really into it from the start. By contrast, the Boston cast took a long time to bond with the kids at the After School Program. That was more of an altruistic activity, and I'm not so sure people at that age are always ready to be altruistic.

Girl Power
Why did the girls rock 'n' roll over the boys?

DAVID: The girls did better because they were the most dedicated. Everyone had an equal chance of being talented at that job. So, it simply came down to work ethic. I was simply not motivated enough. I had another job going on, plus I was balancing a f**king intense relationship with this brilliant woman, Kira. That was a brain-picker.

A little more was happening in my life each day than in the girls' lives, so they had more time to focus on their radio work. The radio station was a good time, but bro, it took a back seat on my priority list. Sorry, Phil. Listen, I know it was a great opportunity, but that's just the way it came down.

LINDSAY: Why did the girls do better at The End? Easy. The girls busted a**, and the guys slacked off. Either they had girlfriends in town, or other interests—like David having a second job. I guess we led more boring lives, but I don't think that was it. We just kicked a**.

JANET: I think the girls did better than the boys because of our work ethic. And I think our work ethic was partly driven by competitiveness. Girls, in general, are a lot more competitive than guys are. The competition aspect, however, was also the worst part of the radio experience. It created a lot of tension in the house.

REBECCA: The girls just worked a lot harder for the DJ spots. They came into the station a lot more, and put in a lot more effort.

STEPHEN: I don't know why the girls rocked over the guys. I thought I worked just as hard. At first, I was really disappointed when I wasn't picked to go on-air. I felt like I deserved to be chosen. But the boss made the selection, and I ended up loving what I did. It was so much easier and less stressful interviewing bands instead, and so much more fun. When the show was on the air at night, I'd just go out drinking with my boys, and listen to it in a bar.

Fab 5 FAVORITE CDS

DAVID	**10,000 Maniacs** *Our Time in Eden*	**Rolling Stones** *Sticky Fingers*	**Cat Stevens** *Greatest Hits*	**Enya** *Shepherd Moons*	**Frank Sinatra** "Any CD will do"
	I think Natalie Merchant is wonderful.	I grew up on Mick.	Cat sings to my heart.	Really soothing and inspiring.	I got nothing but love for Old Blue Eyes.
LINDSAY	**James Brown** *Greatest Hits*	**Miles Davis** *Kind of Blue*	**Beck** *Odelay*	*The Big Chill* *Movie Soundtrack*	**Beethoven** "Any symphony is fine"
	It pumps me up.	It relaxes me.	It's pure fun.	It reminds me of being back home.	It reminds me of my dad.
JANET	**Van Morrison** *Moondance*	**Tracy Chapman** *New Beginnings*	**Dave Matthews Band** *Live at Red Rocks*	**Frank Sinatra and Dean Martin** *Best of Frank and Dean*	*Dirty Dancing* *Movie Soundtrack*
	I just like his sound.	She has a lot of depth to her music.	I love the group.	I dig their swing.	I've always liked dancing to it.
NATHAN	**Ben Harper** *Fight for Your Mind.*	**Dave Matthews Band** *Live at Red Rocks*	**Digable Planets** *Blowout Comb*	**Beastie Boys** *Licensed to III*	**Bob Marley** The box set
	Ben Harper is the Bob Marley of our generation.	Dave Matthews is the Pearl Jam of Richmond.	It has a lot of relaxing jazz.	It's the first tape I ever bought.	He could do just about anything.
REBECCA	**Rolling Stones** *Sticky Fingers*	**Bob Dylan** *Highway 61 Revisited*	**Billie Holiday** *Greatest Hits*	**Sinead O'Connor** *I Do Not Want What I Haven't Got*	**Louis Armstrong** *What a Wonderful World*
	They are the quintessential rock band.	He's a poet.	She's so soulful and passionate.	An amazing album. My music is influenced by her.	He's such a love of mine.
STEPHEN	**Matchbox 20** *Yourself or Someone Like You*	**Ben Harper** *The Will to Live*	**Various Artists** *City of Angels Soundtrack*	**Blink 182** *Dude Ranch*	**Erykah Badu** *Baduism*
	A great album.	He's an excellent artist.	Especially the song "Iris," by the Goo Goo Dolls.	Their sound is really cool.	It's a really relaxing CD and she's awesome.

Zip Off

Dueling Tubes

The Aqua Games

The Real World-Seattle vs. *Road Rules-Australia*

What did you think of *Road Rules*?

DAVID:
I thought they were good kids, very reserved, though. They seemed like a bunch of everyday Joes. I'd have gotten along with them just fine, if I'd been cast with them. But then again, I think I can get along with anyone.

NATHAN:
They were definitely cool kids, but we tore their s**t up.

REBECCA:
I got so excited during the competition. I'm a very reserved person, but sometimes, especially in competition, I get real intense and obnoxious. I'll even trash talk, too. I'm just very competitive when it comes to sports. I'm obsessed with sports.

So, I was totally into it against *Road Rules.* I even sacrificed myself for the team. I went up against this much bigger guy from *Road Rules,* and ended up with a huge raspberry on the back of my head. But it was worth it in the end 'cause we kicked their butts.

JANET:
I liked them a lot, but I think they thought we were really spoiled on our show. They kept on calling themselves the 'bastard children of MTV' because they had to start their days at 7A.M., while we could sleep until noon. They also traveled around in a Winnebago and we got this phat house. You know what? They were right. We were pretty damn spoiled.

STEPHEN:
I thought they were really cool. Christina would've been a nice addition to our cast. She was pretty disco. She had a lot of soul, and she's a Gemini, too.

LINDSAY:
We only got to hang out with them for a short time, but they seemed pretty nice. More importantly, I'm sure as hell happy we won. I had phone bills to pay.

Blindfolded Canoe

Raft-O-Rama

Extreme Fishing

Beach Bungee Bull

Would you have preferred to do *Road Rules* or *Real World*?

JANET:
If I had to choose, I'd pick *Real World*. It's just a longer, more intense experience, but I'd love to do *Road Rules*, too.

NATHAN:
I originally wanted to do *Road Rules*. Until the final round of casting *Real World*, I thought I was actually being considered for the other show.

DAVID:
Definitely, *Real World*. I would never have gotten to meet all the great people I did, if I hadn't done this show, and I would've missed out on some incredible experiences, like going to Nepal.

REBECCA:
I definitely thought they had cool people in their cast, but I preferred our group over theirs.

LINDSAY:
Originally, I wanted to do *Road Rules* because it was shorter. I just wanted to be nearer to my mom. But I'm sure as hell happy I did *Real World*. It's just a more intense, more interesting situation because you're in it twice as long. I'm much prouder of myself for getting through this experience, than I would've been had I done *Road Rules*.

STEPHEN:
Man, I can't imagine being trapped in a Winnebago with four other people for 10 weeks. I'd lose my mind. So, no question. *Real World* over *Road Rules*.

STEPHEN:
Going to Nepal was the greatest experience of my life. I haven't traveled much, and to get to take a helicopter ride to Mount Everest, ride elephants, and see rhinos—man, that was unbelievable.

DAVID:
Our trip to Nepal was one of the greatest things I've ever done in my entire life. Everest, trekking, elephant rides, rhino, river rafting. Oh, my God, being on the back of an elephant and watching a rhino go between my legs. Amazing! My only regret was that I wished we hadn't been accompanied by all the hoopla.

LINDSAY:
It was incredible. The things we got to do—see Mount Everest, ride an elephant, go white-water rafting. The people were so simple, so happy, and so warm. Everything about that trip just took us away from our reality and opened our eyes.

IRENE:
I was very upset in Nepal. I shouldn't have had to be the one to explain culture in Nepal to my housemates. Nathan shouldn't have been handing out money left and right to the people there. It was like someone jetting into the suburbs and handing out $20 bills. The producers just sent a bunch of people into a country without teaching them about it. So these kids went around saying the most ignorant things I've heard in my entire life. I felt fried by the end.

JANET:
The trip was truly unbelievable. I went from city girl to jungle bitch. The closest I'd ever been to camping before was sleeping on an air mattress in the middle of the woods, but I really got into it in Nepal.
   The Nepalese we met were just incredible. They were so warmhearted toward us. Even the most selfish on our trip were turned into considerate people. You'd look at how they treated each other and you wanted to be more like them.

REBECCA:
Nepal was fantastic! It was one of the most vital experiences of my life. I learned so much about myself, and how I would hope to live. The Sherpas were so nonmaterialistic. You'd give them a simple pair of gloves and they'd treat it like it was the biggest deal in the world. The Nepalese were so beautiful and so genuine. I feel so fortunate to have seen that.

NATHAN:
I just kept thinking to myself, 'How lucky am I to be here? I'm only 21 years old and I'm getting to do such a thing at my age. I'm so privileged.'

David:
Eating water buffalo. It tasted like a hockey puck.
Nathan:
Yak jerky. It tastes just like it sounds—like a**...complete a**.
Janet:
Water buffalo. I'd say it tastes like chewy beef jerky. Thankfully, we covered it in so much barbecue sauce we couldn't taste the meat.
Rebecca:
Dal with curried chicken. Personally, I loved the food in Nepal. Everyone else hated it. I ate so much there, I think I literally gained 15 pounds.
Lindsay:
Water buffalo. I won't be ordering that in a restaurant anytime soon!
Stephen:
Water buffalo shish kebabs, for sure. They were tough and kind of gross.

RUSTY, Tour Leader:

I think the trip to Nepal exceeded the cast's expectations, and my expectations as well. Most people who go to Nepal go there by choice. This cast, like all other *Real World* casts, had their vacation selected for them. Nepal is a rugged place to travel around, especially if you're not mentally prepared. I think this group pulled together extremely well, and got the most out of their experience.

I've been traveling to Nepal just about every year since 1978. And like everyone who ever visits there, the 'Sacred Seven'—my pet name for the cast—was in awe of Nepal's physical splendor. Of the fourteen highest mountain peaks in the world, Nepal has ten of them. In addition, it's got the largest canyons in the world; it's got some of the wildest rivers; and it's literally got lions, tigers, and bears.

I know each of the group was struck by the kindness, the gentleness, and the general happiness of their Nepalese hosts. Most of those qualities are attributable to two major 'isms': Hinduism and isolationism.

The Hindu religion, which is practiced by the majority of Nepalese, has made the locals more accepting of their fate.

Hindus believe in reincarnation, so basically, circumstance in this life is predetermined by your actions in an earlier life. It's almost as if their attitude is, 'There's nothing I can do about it now. So why worry myself to death?' *-Rusty, tour leader*

Certainly more than any Westerner would be. That's because the Hindus believe in reincarnation, so basically, circumstance in this life is predetermined by your actions in an earlier life. It's almost as if their attitude is, 'There's nothing I can do about it now. So why worry myself to death?'

Nepal is also a physically isolated country, so most of the Nepalese just don't know how poor they are. Few ever leave their country, so they never see how much better the rest of the world

Nepal is also one of the poorest countries in the world. The average worker makes only $225 per year. I don't even think of Nepal as a Third World country. It belongs more to the Fifth World. The 'Sacred Seven' visited Nepalese families that owned only four pieces of metal—a plow pick, a spoon, and a couple of pots. The rest of their possessions were made of wood, bone, and stone.

The Nepalese also march to a different drummer, so to speak. Their whole notion of time is different than ours. There is no rush hour in Nepal, because there is nowhere to rush to. Most of the watches worn by the Nepalese are purely decorative, and don't even work. Most of Nepal actually seems locked in a time warp, stuck somewhere in the 1700s.

lives. Luckily, Nepal is a completely self-sufficient farming society, so starvation is not a problem, unlike in neighboring India.

But in spite of the major cultural differences, the 'Sacred Seven' realized just how universal is the human condition. They discovered the Nepalese are in many ways no different from them. They have wants and desires, too, and possess the same bottom-line needs: to get enough to eat, to raise healthy children, to spoil their grandchildren, and to get along with their neighbors.

Culture Clash?

DAVID:
My favorite culture clash moment was watching Stephen treat a Sherpa like a New York City cabdriver.

JANET:
The fact that they s**t on the side of the road was strange. It was funny when Lindsay fell in it. I was dying of laughter.

LINDSAY:
The lives of the people we met seemed so simple. Yet, what we brought in equipment and attitude was so complicated and warped.

NATHAN:
It was extraordinary to see a funeral procession, where they carry the exposed body over their heads. They brought the body to be cremated, and we watched it start to burn. I thought, 'What if that was me? I wouldn't want all these foreigners looking at my funeral. Let's get the hell out of here.'

REBECCA:
The time when the woman in the village wrapped the sari around me was such a special moment. I can't explain why, but I just felt this real connection to her.

STEPHEN:
My favorite cultural moment happened in Thailand. I went in the hotel pool in my underwear. The bartender told me no one in Thailand ever swims in their underwear. I thought that was funny.

*   *   *

MATT KUNITZ, RW Producer:
The production worked with REI to plan a trip that would be exciting, educational and enlightening. We worked closely with local Sherpas, guides, and government liaisons to make sure the trip ran smoothly, and would in no way exploit the country or people of Nepal.

Nepalese No-Nos

Before leaving for Nepal, I gave the cast a few cultural tips to avoid offending the Nepalese:

✘ Use your right hand in social situations, never your left—customarily the left hand is reserved for bathroom activities.

✘ Women should never wear shorts, it's considered extremely disrespectful. Men may wear shorts, but it signifies a lower caste or class.

✘ Men and women should never touch or show any physical affection towards each other. However, men can hold hands with each other at all times—and many do. (It does not indicate sexual preference.)

✘ Don't ever put paper into a person's fireplace. It's considered unholy and extremely offensive. You may only put holy sanctioned wood or cow dung into a Nepalese person's hearth.

✘ Never touch an adult on top of the head. It's considered disrespectful.

✘ Don't point the bottom of your feet at a Nepalese person, or step over them. The bottom of your feet are considered the part of your body unseen by God.

Phat-est Part?

David: The phat-est part definitely had to be checking out Everest at 12,000 feet. It was awesome to see the snow blowing off of it.

Janet: On Mount Everest, for sure. We were at this little inn, staring out at the mountain. Lindsay and I just gave each other this kind of look—a look of complete 100 percent contentment.

Lindsay: I'll never forget getting off the helicopter at base camp, and looking up at one of the peaks of Everest. That was unbelievable.

Nathan: Hiking on Mount Everest. You're at a spot only a few people can say they've ever been. It just made me reflect upon life and death.

Everybody knows life is short, and that's such a cliché. But it really is true. So, carpe diem, man. Seize the day!

Rebecca: I loved riding the elephants, which is pretty ironic, considering I used to protest the mistreatment of elephants at the circus when I was a kid.

Stephen: Seeing Mount Everest was probably the single highlight, but experiencing the people of Kathmandu was right up there. They are by far the most peaceful and beautiful people I've ever seen. They're so intense, so positive, and so spiritual that they're inspiring.

Nepal Numbers

Number of days the *Real World* cast and crew visited Nepal	8
Number of cast and crew on the trip	23
Number of cast and crew that got sick at some point on the trip	12
Number of cast and crew that got seriously sick on the trip	2
Number of hours (including layovers) it took to fly to Nepal	29.5
Number of bags and cases transported by the cast and crew	93
Number of items lost on the way	0
The year Nepal first became a unified kingdom	1769
The year Nepal first opened to outsiders	1951
The year Nepal was first overrun by *The Real World–Seattle*	1998
The highest elevation (in feet) of Seattle's Mount Rainier	14,410
The highest elevation (in feet) of Mount Everest	29,028
The elevation (in feet) the cast helicoptered to on Mount Everest	12,700
Number of minutes Janet blacked out from lack of oyxgen	2
Number of crew members filming from one elephant	3
Number of cast members dunked in the river by their elephants	6
Number of water buffalo eaten by the cast and crew	.25
Number of Power Bars brought to Nepal by the cast and crew	200

Favorite Souvenir?

DAVID: I got two swords in Nepal that could hack a hole through anything.

JANET: By far, my walking stick. We went on a tiger ride through the jungle, and the guides had sticks to ward off tigers. Which is pretty ridiculous, if you think about it. Anyway, one of the guides was telling us about these tigers and bears he'd fought off with his favorite stick. So I asked him if I could get one to give to my grandfather back home. Well, he just gave me his stick right then and there. It was just so incredibly nice. My grandfather now has it hanging up on his wall.

NATHAN: I brought back a big black and white picture of a Tibetan guy with dreads down to his ass, and I got Stephanie some really nice handmade jewelry.

REBECCA: The beautiful sari the Nepalese woman wrapped around me.

STEPHEN: I brought back a prayer ring that I really like.

LINDSAY: My favorite souvenir? My memories of the trip.

Janet's Mishap

JANET: I didn't want to look out of shape on camera. So I kept it to myself that I was having trouble on the mountain...until it was too late. After all, everyone else seemed to be doing just fine. When I passed out, it was because I let the cameras affect my better judgment.

To tell you the truth, I was scared s**tless out there. The minute we got off the helicopter at Everest, I didn't acclimatize very well. I was having a really hard time breathing. As we started hiking, I started to black out. Initially, I just thought I was in a little danger. I'm hypoglycemic, so I know what if feels like when I'm about to pass out, and I could feel a blackout on its way.

When I awoke from passing out, I had no idea where I was. I was so disoriented, I didn't know what continent I was on. I wish the cameras hadn't been around to record that moment. I could've been drooling or pissing in my pants. Honestly, I wasn't sure what bodily functions were getting out.

LINDSAY: When I first saw Janet pass out, I was really concerned. One moment she was standing, and the next moment—*boom*! They'd told us that people can die from altitude sickness. So, since I'm such a drama queen, I figured Janet was in mortal danger.

NATHAN: David and I were sitting on a peak facing the other way. Suddenly, we heard this commotion, and saw people running towards Janet. We were like, 'Oh, s**t! Somethings wrong!' Especially, when you see Sherpas start flipping out. But our Janet hung in there all right.

STEPHEN: At first, I was very worried. I rushed over to Janet and gave her my hat, as if that was going to help. She was like, 'I'm all right. Leave me alone.' So I did. What happened to Janet was probably the most real thing that happened all year on *The Real World*.

*   *   *

MATT KUNITZ, *RW* Producer: We were pretty worried, no question about it, but thankfully, Janet woke up fairly quickly.

SHERPAS!

Sherpa is the actual name of an ethnic group of Tibetan origin. The Sherpas live in the mountains, in close proximity to Mount Everest. As a result, they are extraordinary climbers, and served as trekking guides for the cast and crew.

Green Apple Splatters*

DAVID:
Yeah, I had the muds. But not half as bad as some of the others.

JANET:
Oh, my God. When I got back from Nepal, it was just so embarrassing. I couldn't keep anything inside of me for five days. I spent the entire time either in bed, on the toilet, or running in between.

LINDSAY:
I exploded once or twice.

NATHAN:
I blew mud with a quickness.

REBECCA:
My stomach was fine in Nepal. I got a bit sick when I came home, but basically I didn't have any repercussions.

STEPHEN:
I was the only one that left Nepal unscathed. I have this huge immune system, so I didn't have any diarrhea. Maybe, it's because I grew up with spicy African-American food.

*We called it green apple splatters because it came out looking like green apples...and it splattered.
–anonymous crew member

Most Mystical Moment?

DAVID: The most mystical moment for me was seeing the Himalayas when I woke up.

JANET: We camped along the river for several days. One night, everybody was dancing and having a good time. People were coming from miles and miles to join in. They had torches, so you could see this stream of light coming down from both sides of the hill. It was just incredible. I decided to step away from the group, so I could take in the whole scene.

Well, this girl my age came over and sat down next to me. She patted me on my shoulder, and started speaking to me in Nepalese. Of course, I didn't know what she was saying. She kept smiling and laughing and repeating the same phrase over and over again. She also kept putting her hand to my heart. She did this for about fifteen minutes. After a while, I got one of the guides to come over and translate for me. It turned out she was asking me if I would be her soul mate. It was one of the most touching moments of my life.

REBECCA: The first day we were in the Himalayas, we visited this Buddhist temple. We watched the sun rise, and it was just so serene and beautiful. I thought to myself, 'Now, this must be heaven.'

NATHAN: One night, we were sitting around a campfire surrounded by Nepalese villagers. Most of them had never seen a Westerner before. So they'd all turned out to greet us. Then, they started performing their village dance. They couldn't understand a word we said, but they were so welcoming and warm.

LINDSAY: I'm not really mystical, so I couldn't tell you.

STEPHEN: We were at this monkey temple in Nepal, and it started to rain really hard. The monks were chanting. There were monkeys all over and I just ran around in the rain spinning prayer wheels, situated around this huge tower with a Buddha on top. It was such a blissful day. I'm a very spiritual person, so that day was very meaningful to me.

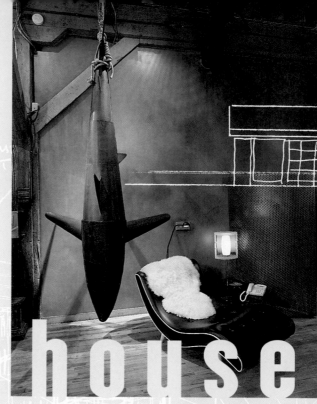

in the house

What did you think of the house?

DAVID:
That was one *phat* pad. Wish they had dorms like that at VMI.

IRENE:
That place was nothing more than a studio. It was horrendous.

JANET:
Oh, my God. It was beautiful! I could not have asked for anything better. The place was a museum. It had a rock-climbing wall, a hot tub, an $8,000 pool table, and the most beautiful bathroom I've ever seen.

The only problem was going to the bathroom in that place. The first three weeks I literally couldn't go 'cause I was just so self-conscious about it. I literally held it in that entire time. I've had problems like this before, but this was extreme, even for me. Finally, I was like, 'Ah, forget this. I'm starting to feel more comfortable in the house. It's time to go.'

Well, obviously it was going to be a huge poop, 'cause I'd held it in for three weeks. I asked Lindsay to stand guard for me outside the toilet door, and I yelled out to her, 'Oh, my God. Lindsay, I just laid a bomb. Light a match. It stinks in here!' Well, guess who was standing right outside the door? Naturally, a camera crew, who were both shaking and grimacing from laughter and from the smell. I was never so embarrassed in my entire life.

LINDSAY:
It was amazing, except for the fried chicken in the hot tub.

NATHAN:
Everyone says *The Real World* isn't real. Well, the interactions were. The conflicts were. The missing Stephanie was. The house and the trip to Nepal were the only unreal aspects of the show. That house was a fantasy. It was like Disneyworld. It had everything I could've wanted. Just amazing.

STEPHEN:
The house was awesome. It was the best house in the world and the best house *The Real World* ever had. But I agree with Janet about using the bathrooms. The first few weeks we'd turn all the faucets and showers on to cover our sounds. It's not something you want to end up on national TV, but after a while, we were like, 'Who cares? This is our house. We'd better get used to it.' And we didn't worry anymore.

REBECCA:
Walking into the house felt like I was walking into a movie set. I felt like Alice moving into Wonderland.

Favorite Room?

NATHAN:
The bathroom 'cause it was so neat and weird. The sinks shot up through the floor with copper pipes. The bathroom doors slid open. I felt like I was in a Japanese dojo. I expected Jean-Claude van Damme to do back flips out of the wall.

JANET:
I dug the living room with the hot tub, the pool table, and the view of the water and mountains.

DAVID:
The bathroom. It was really cool.

STEPHEN:
The bathroom was dope. It had the sinks that came out of the ground like fountains. I liked that a lot.

LINDSAY:
The kitchen. I liked the refrigerator.

REBECCA:
My bedroom. It was comforting and dark.

Favorite Thing?

DAVID:
The rock-climbing wall because I could hang up there like a monkey. I hung out on jungle gyms my whole life as a kid. So it took me back to my childhood.

JANET:
My favorite part of the house was the garage door, right near the hot tub. It was just so nice. I've never had an opportunity to live near the water, so each morning I'd grab a huge cup of coffee, slide open the garage door and gaze out onto the water and the Olympic Mountains.

LINDSAY:
The sliding garage door beside the hot tub. You could open it and see the world.

NATHAN:
My bed was my favorite thing because it was so damn comfortable, and that's where Stephanie and I spent most of our time together.

REBECCA:
The fireplace. I've always been very temperature sensitive, and that fireplace kept me cooked.

STEPHEN:
The computer was my baby. I'm a 'Berkeley techie-geek,' so I was always e-mailing or hanging out on the Internet.

What did you do in the hot tub?

DAVID:
I gave Rebecca a foot massage, I peed in it, and I jumped stark naked into it while drinking a beer.

JANET:
I never used the hot tub for more than just soaking. I just couldn't imagine getting intimate with someone in there with a camera crew around you.

LINDSAY:
I only went in there twice, both times fully clothed. No, I never peed in the hot tub, but other people did.

NATHAN:
I used it for relaxation purposes. I used it for some sexual healing with Stephanie—massages and stuff, but we never actually had sex in there because there was that damn camera overhead. One time, Stephanie and I were going to get up at 5 A.M. while

everybody was asleep inside the house and control room, but we slept through it ourselves.

REBECCA:
I didn't spend much time in the hot tub. It was so nice when you got in, but so cold when you got out. So I preferred to sit around the fireplace and stay dry.

STEPHEN:
I had a lot of chicks in that hot tub, and lots of hot times.

What did you use the Confessional for?

DAVID:
Occasionally, I did confessions. But mostly I masturbated in there. Yeah, frequent masturbations. That was the only room in the house where we could control the cameras and mics. And I also went in there to read a lot. I read *Sheltering Sky* inside there during one five hour sitting.

REBECCA:
Random confessing and frequent chilling out.

STEPHEN:
To confess, mostly. Yeah, I brought a chick in there once or twice. But no, I didn't masturbate in there, unlike David.

JANET:
Mostly confessionals. Sometimes the girls would go in there to smoke. It was filled with butts. Or, we'd have private conversations in there because the crews' cameras couldn't go inside. The guys masturbated in there all the time. And Irene would go in there every time she had to pass gas. The place was just disgusting.

LINDSAY:
I used it to confess. I'm not like David. I didn't masturbate in there.

NATHAN:
Not for confessionals, that's for sure. I probably did a total of four or five the whole time I was in Seattle, but I didn't spank rope in there, either. That was David's routine. I saved that for my bedroom or the shower.

However, Stephanie and I did have sex in the confessional because it had no cameras in the ceilings. We also had sex in the showers, my bed, and the bedroom floor, too. Hell, we'd have christened the whole house—the bar, the pool

table...everything man— if there hadn't been any cameras.

What did you break?

DAVID:
Nothing that I can remember.

JANET:
I broke a shower rod, but I didn't tell the crew until way after I'd done it. You know those shower gel containers? Well, sometimes they have a hook on it so you can hang them onto your shower for easier access. I decided it was a really cute gadget, and wanted to hang it on the shower rod. Unfortunately, the whole thing came crashing down. I finally bribed David to put it back up for me.

LINDSAY:
Nothing.

NATHAN:
I broke a lamp. A few of us were wrestling around and the next thing I knew...CRASH! I figured, 'No big deal. That's a $40 lamp'. Well, the next day I got a phone call from the producer, saying, 'Nathan, last night you broke a $500 lamp'. I said, 'Are you kidding me? Give me the $500. I'll get you a better replacement...and pocket the change'.

REBECCA:
Perhaps a glass.

STEPHEN:
I broke a glass, but Irene broke like five glasses and plates.

What did you swipe?

DAVID:
Books. Lots of books. I took C.S. Lewis' *Chronicles*. I swiped *The Iliad*, Dante's *Inferno*—hardcovers, mostly. You know, the expensive stuff.

LINDSAY:
Just the fruit flies that snuck into my suitcase.

REBECCA:
I took my duvet *cover*, but Janet took her whole duvet.

JANET:
I couldn't leave without my comforter. Also, I swiped a couple of vases and a picture frame.

NATHAN:
Three egg candles, two books, a few trinkets, and the little black telescope.

STEPHEN:
I swiped one of the wooden canisters, about four or five books, and a picture frame.

How did you wipe?

DAVID:
Everyone in the house was too cheap to buy toilet paper, especially the girls who used up the most. The girls used calendars to wipe their asses. The strangest thing I used was

a towel. It might've been Nathan's, but I was in a desperate situation.

JANET:
We used everything from socks to the tissue paper you get in shoe boxes. I think David used the socks.

LINDSAY:
On occasion, I used either a calendar, notebook paper, or cotton swabs.

REBECCA:
I never used the calendar. I just went into the arcade next to our house, and used their bathroom whenever we ran out.

NATHAN:
Well, you know, guys don't have to wipe when they piss. So it was the girls that were going through the toilet paper like wildfire. So whenever I got a hold of some toilet paper, I hid it under my bed. Listen, it wasn't just me. All the guys kept a stash in their room. Thankfully, the girls never found out. Whenever we heard

them screaming for something to wipe with, we'd just sit back and laugh.

STEPHEN:
Yeah, I hid rolls from the girls too, but one time I got stuck, so I had to use a damn calendar myself.

10 Questions with *The Real World—Seattle* house designer Dominick Montalbano

1. How did you get the gig?

The *Real World* producers approached four art directors—all Seattle locals—to apply for the job. I think they felt that a local design firm would give the house a more authentic Seattle feel. Each of us was asked us to create a 1,000-square-foot living area with a fish tank and a pool table inside.

The set decorator, Nina Fleebe, and I submitted five large presentation boards with 3-D computer renderings featuring our conceptual house— a renovated industrial loft very similar to the house on the show. We sent our boards to the producers' office wrapped in white fur and held together with two black leather belts. It was a very cool presentation.

2. Have you ever designed a house for a show like *The Real World*?

Not really, has anyone? My company, Two Downtown Inc., usually creates 'environ-ments' for both private and commercial clients. We design and build exhibits, sets, interiors, etc., but historically we are best known for our special event designs.

3. Why did you pick Pier 70 as the location for the house?

Originally, the producers were going to use a large Victorian house on Queen Anne Hill, which is an elevated historic part of Seattle, but we weren't really happy with the layout, so we decided to look for an industrial space on our own. Then our executive vice-president, Howard Weiner, found this space at Pier 70, which was right on the water and fit our original concept perfectly.

4. So, what did you want the house to look like?

We wanted it to have a relaxed and eclec-tic atmosphere that reflects Seattle's youth culture. We wanted it to reflect the Northwest to some extent. We thought that was important for the show, but we also didn't want it to become a caricature of the Northwest region, so it was a fine line. We used some Northwestern Native American art, and some Northwestern icons like the climbing wall, but we tried not to overdo it.

We tried to use local artists' work as much as possible to give them exposure, and we got trade-outs (items in exchange for screen credit) from local companies for things like lighting, statuary, books, etc. It allowed us to put much higher qual-ity pieces in the house than the budget would otherwise allow.

But in general, we chose to give the house the feel of an old industrial reno-vated warehouse. For example, one of the first things you see as you walk in through the steel front doors is a fish cannery mural above the kitchen. It looks like it was left by the previous tenant.

5. What kind of construction did the house require?

There were three commercial spaces that

had occupied the part of the pier we used. So, when we arrived the space was already full of walls and decks. Our construction company took out 70 tons worth of demo material in three days. It was amazing. The whole process, from the time we got the space to when the kids moved in, took ten weeks and three

wanted this house to be about the architecture and the 'space' itself. More relaxed and casual, yet still funky.

This was also the first house that was completely 'camera-ready.' In other words, we built the house from a completely gutted box. They've never done that before. Everything we designed was

limited-edition desktop with a flattened body, which you see in the main living area. And, of course, there were other trade-outs from a number of companies.

8. Did the cast trash the place?

Actually, no. The kids were very respectful of the space, the art, and the furniture. Hardly anything was damaged.

I think it's most important to try to enhance the inherent character of your space. A lot of people try to mask what they're starting with, but that can become really expensive, and the results usually aren't very good

days. Actual construction took about eight weeks. The technical people, who rigged the house, arrived pretty early on and stayed until shortly before the cast arrived.

6. How does the Seattle house compare to previous *Real World* houses?

We intentionally tried to make it very different, so that it stood apart from the other houses and seemed fresh. Most of the other *Real World* houses have been very much about the furnishings. We

to allow the cameras to follow the cast easily, and create interesting camera compositions and camera angles.

For example, we designed the sinks in the middle of the bathroom, almost like fountains. You could have three kids at three different sinks in close proximity to each other, and the cameramen could still move a full 360 degrees around them, and the hallways were much wider than usual, so the crew could move around easily without banging their equipment.

7. Where did you get all the goodies to put inside?

We bought or rented most of the pieces at local furniture stores. Some of the things we built ourselves. Nina's husband built the bed that lowers over the pool table. The producers had wanted an extra bed in the house in case someone stayed over.

Of course, we put in a lot of Ikea stuff, which has become a mainstay of *The Real World*, but since Ikea products have been used so much in the other houses, we tried to avoid using them in the main living area. We put them mostly in the kitchen and bedrooms, and tried to alter them whenever we used them.

The upside-down fish and barking dog door signal came from a local artist named Peter Reiquam. A local company, AquaQuip Spa, loaned us the hot tub. The climbing wall was built by a local climbing gym, Vertical World, and paid for by R.E.I. Most of the 2,000 books and the Internet computer in the library came from Amazon.com, but some came from Simon & Schuster as well. Apple Computer loaned us a special anniversary,

9. What happened to the house after the cast left?

Like the cast, all of the furniture is gone, except for the mechanical dog. The pier is privately owned and the owner plans to turn it into a cafe or restaurant.

10. How much would the house have sold for, if it were put on the market as it appeared on the show?

I'd assume easily in the millions because of the size, the location and stuff inside.

Extra Credit: Do you have any design tips for people designing on a budget?

I think it's most important to try to enhance the inherent character of your space. A lot of people try to mask what they're starting with, but that can become really expensive, and the results usually aren't very good. So, that's what we did with the *Real World* house. We left its inherent character intact as an industrial loft.

Neat Freaks vs. Slobs

BEFORE

AFTER

David:
Nathan was the neatest and I was in second place. The slobbiest was Rebecca, and Irene came in second. Their room was atrocious!

Nathan:
Lindsay and I were the neatest. David was somewhat neat, too, but he'd cook salmon and leave it in the oven, and let the plates stack up in the sink for weeks afterward. Rebecca was a slob. Irene was dirty. Stephen claimed to be clean, but he'd leave a bowl of rice on the stove for weeks straight.

Lindsay:
I was a lot cleaner than my room-mate, Janet, but I still got pretty damn messy. Nathan was meticulous. As for the slobs, Irene was a slob. Rebecca was a slob. And David was a slob, too.

Janet:
Nate would be the closest to a neat person, and Lindsay was pretty neat, too. Everyone else was a slob, partic-ularly Irene and David. I was a neat slob, though. A neat slob is someone who's a slob, but only takes a minute to pick up her things.

Rebecca:
I'd say that Nate was neat and every-body else was messy. But I'm not real-ly slobby. I was just like, 'forget it, let it be messy.'

Stephen:
Nate and I were definitely the neat guys. We're both really organized, kind of like control organized. David is sloppy, he's gross. He doesn't even wash his fish clothes after he gets back from work. He washed one load of laundry the entire time we were in Seattle. He was always borrowing our clothes, which was gross, and he fart-ed everywhere.

SEATTLE SPEAK

Ever wonder what the Seattle cast was really saying? Here's a translation:

Bad Breath Troll	Morning breath (as in, see David).
Banging You Out	Knocking someone out (as in, 'Shut it, or I will *bang you out*')!
Batting for the Yankees	Being gay (as in, David wondered if his friend Harry was *batting for the Yankees*).
Blowing Mud	Taking a s**t.
Cheesy	When something is really lame, but the person thinks it's really cool.
Chew-Screw	Eating quickly.
Cigabutts	Cigarettes.
Desert Fox	The cast's code name for *RW* Director Craig Borders.
Desert Storm	The cast's code name for *RW* Director Drew Hoegl.
Diesel	Awesome.
Disco	Even more awesome.
Eat It and Beat It	Getting food.
Face Off	Male masturbation (as in, what the guys did in the confessional.)
Fast Food	A one-night stand.
Getting the Shaft	Getting dissed.
Getting Your Groove	Getting sexually satisfied.
Goat Herder	A redneck.
Hella Phat	Very good (as in, 'Super Deluxe is *hella phat!*').
Kid	The universal first name (as in, what David calls everyone).
Legit	Someone or something that's real
Merkin	A toupee for a bald pubic region (as in, 'To avoid friction burns get a *merkin*').
Mikey	The nickname for Rebecca (because she eats everything like Mikey from the cereal commercials).
Much Murray	When you're afraid.
OK, Good	1. Good. 2. Bad. (Basically, its used whenever you have nothing else to say.)
Padoodle	Lindsay's term for farting.
Rock Star	Someone who stays out until 5 A.M. and sleeps until noon.
Sex Pot	Janet's sex appeal (as in, 'Janet is a legit *sex pot*').
Smuck & Futhered	Really drunk.
Shut It	A call for peace and tranquility (as in 'Stephen and Irene, *shut it*').
Silent P.	The nickname for Janet because she thought she had pneumonia. But her roommates accused her of being a hypochondriac.
Stealth	Keeping a low profile (as in, 'Stephen went *stealth* after slapping Irene').
Wicked Pissah	Really good (but must be said with David's heavy Boston accent).
With a Quickness	Quick and with authority (as in, 'I'll bang you out *with a quickness*').

'REAL' NUMBERS

Number of people who applied to be on *RW-Seattle*	11,535
Number of people cast to be on *RW-Seattle*	7
Number of crew that worked on *RW-Seattle*	108
Average age of the *RW-Seattle* cast	20.57
Average age of the *RW-Seattle* crew	28.22
Number of the pier where the *RW-Seattle* house was located	70
Number of days the cast lived in the *RW-Seattle* house (Jan. 19-May 25)	126
Number of square feet in the *RW-Seattle* house	4,500
Number of man hours it took to construct the *RW-Seattle* house	840
Number of dollars it cost the production to rent the space each month	7,500
Number of original pieces of art in the *RW-Seattle* house	67
Number of books in the *RW-Seattle* house	2,000+
Number of surveillance cameras in the *RW-Seattle* house	12
Number of lights in the *RW-Seattle* house	226
Number of TV monitors in the control room tracking the cast	15
Number of minutes of video shot on the *RW-Seattle* cast	132,120
Number of countries in which *RW-Seattle* will be seen	41

To Grunge or Not to Grunge?

DAVID: 'Not to grunge.' Grunge is dead. Now all you've got is a bunch of disgruntled hipster swingers in Seattle.

JANET: 'Not to grunge.' Grunge is old. Grunge is lame. Grunge is dirty.

LINDSAY: 'Not to grunge.' Actually, do whatever the hell you like.

NATHAN: Grunge is gone. If you want to get off on the wrong foot with a person from Seattle, ask them, 'Hey man, where's all the grunge at?' I guarantee you'll get your a** kicked.

REBECCA: Definitely 'not to grunge!'

STEPHEN: It's not possible to grunge anymore. Grunge is dead. But I definitely rocked.

TALE OF TWO CITIES
A HOUSE DIVIDED—ONE TO LIVE; ONE TO WORK

THE LIGHTING ROOM
All lighting within the house is controlled by the crew. Four times a day, the lighting is adjusted to match outside lighting conditions. Before bedtime, the cast has to ask the crew to turn off the lights in their own bedrooms.

THE VIDEO PHONE
Video phones are placed inside the homes of the cast members' parents and significant others to gather footage of everything from late-night bull sessions to mushy phone calls.

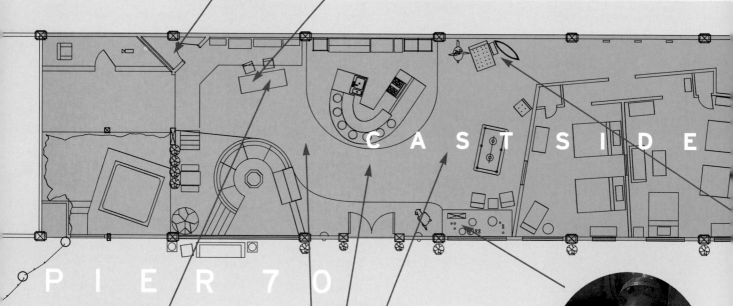

CASTSIDE

PIER 70

LIPSTICK CAMERA
Tiny cameras are aimed at the telephones for filming conversations. This particular one is tucked inside the paper tray beside the phone.

VIDEO LIGHTS
Thousands of dollars' worth of television lighting is installed in the house. In the early days of *The Real World*, the lighting raised the temperature level in the house 20 degrees. But these state-of-the-art lights are as cool as Sir Mix-a-lot.

SURVEILLANCE CAMERA
Tucked among the piping are 12 security-type cameras used to monitor the cast's movements inside the house. Each camera is hooked up to a monitor within the control room, so the directors can know what the cast members are up to at all times.

THE DOOR

A door with a combination lock is all that separated the cast's residence from the crew's control room. Only the crew knew the combination, which is changed on a regular basis.

SOUND MIXER

The directors in the control room are able to monitor up to 64-channels of sound.

EQUIPMENT ROOM

This functions as the supply and repair center for all the state-of-the-art video and audio equipment. On average, filming takes place 20 hours a day (from 8 A.M. until 4 A.M. the following day.) So, the equipment is in constant use and consistent need of repair.

C R E W S I D E

THE "BAT PHONE"

"Bat Phones" serve as the main direct link between the cast and crew. A phone is placed within the house and control room; the directors or producers are the only crew members permitted to answer it. Prior to leaving the house, the cast member rings the control room on the "Bat Phone" to update the directors on his or her plans.

CONTROL ROOM

The epicenter for *The Real World -Seattle* house is loaded with 15 monitors, multiple high-end computers, and four caffeinated directors. The directors monitor the cast from inside the control room and determine which of the seven they should film with their two crews. (The three-person film crews are on a staggered schedule throughout the twenty-four-hour day, but no more than two crews are ever on duty at one time.)

THE REAL WORLD
FASHION ACCESSORIES
(ONE SIZE FITS ALL)

Mono Earpiece
Enables the director to monitor the sound being recorded by the sound mixer without the cast members hearing. (Available for pierced ears, too.) $7.99.

Director's Notebook
A 3" x 4" notebook for the director to record what the cast is doing each day. (Ideal for personal notes and noting bad behavior.) $5.

Lectrosonic Receiver
Receives the sound directly from the camera and transmits it into the director's earpiece. (Perfect for evenings and eavesdropping.) $1,200.

Nikon TI-28
A high-end "point and shoot" camera for capturing still images of the cast and crew. (Handy at birthdays or breakups.)$1,150.

Motorola Nextel Cellular Phone and Walkie-Talkie
A digital phone that doubles as a walkie-talkie with a range of 1,500 miles. Keeps the director in constant contact with his crew and base camp. (Beats two cans connected with string.) $325.

Director's Denim (ripped Armani)—A must for maximum styling. (Can be worn at informal occasions or in the field.) $85.

Microwave Transmitter
Transmits images from the camera to the monitors inside the control room, when filming inside the house. (The microwave transmits at a range of 200 yards, but does not pop popcorn.) $10,000.

Camera Mic
Records sound only in cases where the sound mixer is unable to hear something with the "boom." $70,000.

Anton Bauer "Brick"
The battery that powers the camera. (Duration: 90 minutes. Number used per day: five. Weight: six pounds.) $500.

Sony Camera Lens
Wide-angle zoom lens. Manual focus. Auto/manual zoom. (For shooting up close or in your face.) $20,000.

Mono Earpiece
Enables the camera operator to hear what sound is being recorded by the sound mixer. (Available in flesh tones.) $7.99.

Moore Breastplate Walkie-Talkie Holder
Makes it easier for the camera operator to reach his walkie-talkie, instead of having to reach for his belt. (Also protects against charging cast members.) $35.

Sony Beta BVWD-600 Camera
Top-grade video camera used for capturing the cast. Weighs 28-pounds with battery. Designed to look through with your right eye. $70,000.

Director Billy – aka The Director

D.P. John – aka The Director of Photography

Opposite page, left: Going mobile; the crew keeping up with the *Real World* cast. *Opposite right*: D.P. John changes filters for an interview with Lindsay. *Left*: Directors Billy and David in the control room, checking on events in the house. *Center*: audio gear accessories. *Right*: Audio mixers Aaron and Martin.

All prices are based on approximate retail cost.
Source: Tracy Chaplin, *RW* Technical Coordinator

Motorola Earpiece
Permits the camera assistant to hear instructions from the director and camera operator without the cast overhearing. $49.95.

Anton Bauer Battery Belt
Energy source for Lowell Pro-Sungun (see below) Weight: 15 pounds. $700.

SKYTEL 2-Way Pager
Allows the crew to receive and send pages and e-mails. (Cast members were only permitted one-way pagers, so they couldn't communicate with each other without the crew knowing.) $500.

Motorola GP-300 Radius Walkie-Talkie
Enables the camera assistant to communicate with the camera operator and director. Mostly used to ask for a new videotape or battery. $850.

Fuji 30-minute Beta-SP Tape
Broadcast-quality beta tape used by *The Real World*. Approximately 31 tapes are shot each day, or 6,510 minutes each week. At $14 per tape, that's $61,656 per season.

Lowell Pro-Sungun
A 300-watt light used for dark settings, particularly for illuminating the cast in the street at night. Weight: three pounds. $500.

Sennheiser MKH-60 Microphone with Rykote Softie Windscreen
(Translation: The thingamajig that records sound.) $1,650.

"The Boom"
Eight-feet long. Four pounds in weight. Can rest on your head. Or take to bed. (Also known as the "big phallic thing." Used for difficult shooting situations. Or lonely nights.) $500.

Sony Headphones MBR-7506
Enables the sound mixer to monitor the four channels of sound being recorded. (Also can be used as an ear-warmer.) $120

Audio "Guns"
The biceps an audio mixer gets from holding "the boom" above her head each day. Equivalent workout with personal trainer: $125 per hour.

M4a+ Audio Mixer
The high-tech rig for mixing all sound in the field. Controls decibels (not screaming roommates). $41,000.

Sennheiser Receiver
Picks up the sound from four separate microphones—three wireless and one boom. Allows the mixer to hear several cast members at a time (or none if she desires). $6,000.

A.C. Andre – aka The Camera Assistant

Audio Libby – aka The Audio Mixer

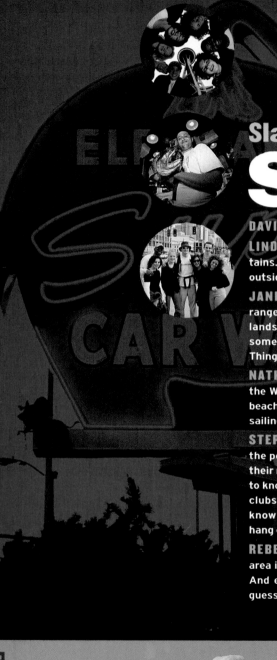

Slacking in
Seattle

DAVID: I absolutely loved the city. I had some great days in that f**king place.

LINDSAY: I'd never been to Seattle before. I loved the water. I loved the mountains. But it's a tough city, especially the music scene. They don't seem to like outsiders very much.

JANET: I liked Seattle a lot. You get all the benefits of nature—the mountain ranges and Puget Sound—while also living in a city. I'm used to living on flatlands in the Midwest. All I have there is Indiana, Dayton, and Milwaukee—for some beer. In Seattle, I got to do so many things—like kayaking and sailing. Things that I'd never, ever done before.

NATHAN: I loved Seattle. It was the first time I'd ever spent any real time on the West Coast. It's a beautiful city. It reminded me of Virginia—an hour to the beach, an hour to the mountains. It was cool living on the water. One day, I went sailing and saw a killer whale. You can't beat that.

STEPHEN: Seattle took some getting used to because it rains there a lot, and the people are very different. They're very protective of their city, especially their music scene. A lot of the people I met in the clubs were rude, but after I got to know a few people in town, the city opened up to me and I started hitting the clubs. There are definitely some excellent clubs in Seattle. You've just got to know where to go, and only the locals seem to know where the best clubs to hang out.

REBECCA: I thought Seattle was fine, just a bit small and constrained. The area is very compact, just a few blocks long. So you can walk the city in a day. And everyone knows everyone else there, so I always felt like an outsider. I guess Seattle was just a little too enclosed for my tastes.

CITY TIMELINE

1850

1851
The city is founded.

1852
Seattle is named after Chief Sealth, head of the Suquamish and Duwamish tribes.

1875

1878
Seattle creates its first microbrewery.

1889
The Great Seattle Fire destroys 30 city blocks.

1900

1907
America's first gas station opens in Seattle.

1908
William Boeing moves to Seattle and makes it the home of his Boeing Co., of airplane fame.

1915
Seattle's Jefferson Park becomes the site of the nation's first public golf course.

1925

1926
Seattle elects Bertha Landes as the first female mayor of a major U.S. city.

1931
A Seattle music teacher creates the first electric guitar.

The Cast's Favorites

Record Store

David
Orpheum
618 Broadway

They have a huge selection of old-school records and eight-tracks.

Nathan/Lindsay/Janet
107.7 The End
1100 Olive Way, Suite 1500 (Kim's private stash)

Nathan: The prize closet at the radio station had the best for the least. That's where we all stocked up.
Lindsay: Without a doubt. Their shelves were stacked with CDs.
Janet: If Kim and Rose will let you inside, it's the place to be.

Rebecca
Tower Records
500 Mercer Street

It has a great selection.

Stephen
Cellophane Square
The "U" District (University of Washington)

It's got an excellent mix of stuff.

Orpheum

Breakfast Hangout

David
Café Minnie's
1st Avenue and Denny Way

It's open twenty-four-hours a day. They have the best Italian potatoes west of the Mississippi, and a real eclectic menu. Their brunches kick a**.

Lindsay
The Edgewater (Hotel)
2411 Alaskan Way Downtown Waterfront

It has a beautiful view, lots of coffee, and a cheap breakfast. I recommend bagels with cream cheese...and lots of coffee.

Nathan
The Hurricane Café
2230 7th Avenue Belltown

It slaps up good ol' greasy, country breakfasts, and they're served to you by somebody with 18 piercings, a bunch of tattoos, and a cigarette hanging out of her mouth. I recommend the biscuits and gravy.

Janet/Rebecca/Stephen
CJ's Eatery
2619 1st Avenue

Janet: Good food. Cheap prices. I recommend the fruit plate.
Rebecca: It's really cheap and really satisfying.
Stephen: Excellent service. Excellent food. And a lot of it. I recommend the early bird combo—two scrambled eggs, hash browns, and some meat. Awesome!

The Crocodile Café

Dinner Place

David
Beppo's (Buca de Beppo)
701 9th Avenue North

It's family-style Italian. The atmosphere is unbelievable. Everyone there is screaming crazy and the food is served in huge quantities.

Janet
The Garlic Tree Restaurant
94 Stewart Downtown

Oh, man. Lindsay and I used to go there all the time. Really good pan-Asian-style food. I recommend their *mandus*, which are Korean fried dumplings.

Lindsay
Under My Bed (literally)
Pier 70 (private restaurant)

My favorite dinner was the box of crackers under my bed. I eat a lot, but I have to eat in little bits because I have an ulcer.

Nathan
The Palisades
2601 West Marina Place Elliott Bay Marina

It's expensive, but pretty cool. You can sit overlooking Puget Sound and watch the sunsets. Underneath my table was a stream and I could reach down and grab a salmon the size of a leg. I recommend having the salmon.

Rebecca
Kiku Tempura House
5018 University Way NE The "U" District

I liked the chicken yakisoba, and the muffins, too.

Stephen
Chandler's Crabhouse
901 Fairview Avenue North

Expensive, but really good seafood, large portions, and excellent service. The Dungeness crabs are great.

1943
The city of Seattle orders a vice cleanup.

1948
A teenage Ray Charles begins playing the Seattle music circuit. A young Quincy Jones makes the rounds as a trumpeter at the same time.

1949
The worst earthquake in Seattle history registers 7.1 on the Richter scale and causes eight deaths.

1950
Seattle's Northgate Mall becomes America's first covered shopping center.

1950

1955
Seattle passes New York as the pleasure craft capital of the world with 60,000 boats.

1952
Panty raids at the University of Washington spark riots on Greek Row.

1960

1961
A local paper reports that nearly 10,000 Seattle women have a drinking problem.

1962
Seattle hosts the World's Fair, featuring the recently completed 607-foot-high Space Needle.

Place to Take a Date

David
The Capitol Club
414 E. Pine Street
Capitol Hill

I didn't date in Seattle 'cause of Kira, but I took my roommates out on fake dates. Janet and I went to the Capitol Club a couple of times. It was awesome. An unbelievable atmosphere...good bistro...great chairs, and the patio was spanking.

Janet
Alki Beach Park
Alki Avenue SW

It's a really romantic spot, where you can look out on the water.

Lindsay
The Edgewater (Hotel)
2411 Alaskan Way
Downtown Waterfront

Get acquainted in the bar...then get a room later.

Nathan/Rebecca
Space Needle
Seattle Center

Nathan: The first time Stephanie came to visit, I took

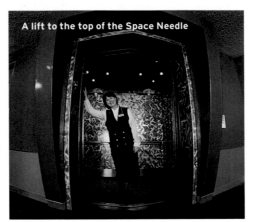
A lift to the top of the Space Needle

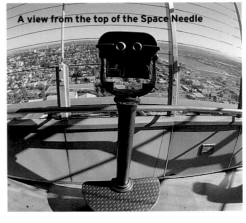
A view from the top of the Space Needle

her to the fountain over by the Space Needle. We hadn't seen each other for about a month. So, we just talked for hours and watched these kids run around and get soaking wet. We talked about our future together and about having a family someday. That whole day was perfect.
Rebecca: I know it's cheesy to say the Space Needle, but the views of Seattle from up there are so beautiful.

Mama's Mexican Kitchen

Stephen
Mama's Mexican Kitchen
2234 2nd Avenue
Belltown

It's dark and filled with candles. I like that on dates.

Chillin' Spot

David
Sara's Deck (private)
Above Pike Pace Market

My favorite spot was my friend Sara's deck, overlooking the harbor and Mount Rainier. It was right above Pike Place Market. I'd walk up there after work. We'd eat some smoked salmon. Drink some wine. Smoke some butts. And I'd grab my sack and chill.

Lindsay
Real World House garage door
Pier 70

The garage door next to the hot tub. It had a view of Puget Sound and the mountains.

Nathan
Nite Rite
2nd Avenue and Virginia

It's a great, seedy spot. The bar has been open for 90 years and it seems like a number of their original customers are still there. The guys behind the bar appear to be about 80.

Rebecca/Janet
The Palisades
Elliott Bay Marina

Rebecca: I liked hanging out there and looking at the boats.
Janet: It's just a great place to cool out.

Speakeasy Café

Stephen
Speakeasy Café
2304 2nd Avenue

It's always a great place to chill. It's also got computers, so you can tap the Internet.

1965
Namu, the killer whale, becomes the feature attraction at the Seattle Marine Aquarium.

1969
Seattle lands its first Major League baseball team, the Seattle Pilots. Shortly after, the team moves to Minnesota and is renamed the Twins.

1971
A coffee company is founded in Seattle and named after the coffee-drinking first mate in *Moby Dick*, Starbucks.

1973
Martial arts expert and Seattle native Bruce Lee dies of a cerebral hemorrhage and is buried in local Lake View Cemetery.

1967
Seattle PR-man David Stern creates the yellow smiling "Happy Face" cartoon for a local bank ad.

1970
Seattle-born rock star James M. "Jimi" Hendrix dies and is buried in the local Greenwood Memorial Park.

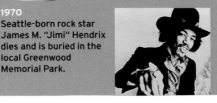

Live Music Joint
David/Nathan/Lindsay/Janet
The Crocodile Café
2200 2nd Avenue

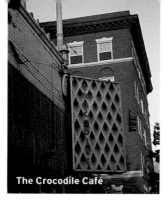
The Crocodile Café

David: It's got the best acoustics in town. The crowds are wonderful. The coolest f**king people in Seattle and they book the best bands. Plus, they got the best mashed potatoes this side of the Mississippi. It's just a cool venue. A concert hall in one place and a lounge and café in the back.

Nathan: Theres so much history at that place. So many big bands got their starts at the 'Croc.'

Lindsay: The 'Croc' always has good acts playing there.

Janet: The 'Croc' has all you need—good shows, good food, and good atmosphere.

Rebecca
Paramount Theater
911 Pine Street

I saw a lot of great bands there. It's a refurbished old 1920s movie theater. It's a grand setting. Really classy—and really intimate, too.

Stephen
Showbox
1426 1st Avenue

I caught some good music at Showbox. Plus, you could smoke there.

The Showbox

Coffee Drink
Lindsay
Tall Coffee
with lots of cream and sugar

I'm a very simple girl, and easy to please.

David
Double Tall Latte
(with one Sweet 'N Low)

Legitly Latte.

Janet
Triple Caramel Macchiato
(nonfat)

Awesome!

Nathan
Frozen Mocha Latte

Best on warm days.

Rebecca
Hot Cocoa

I don't drink coffee.

Stephen
Double Latte

Seattle was the first time I'd ever had a latte before. They're awesome.

Pickup Joint
Stephen
Fraternity Parties
"U. Dub" (Univ. of Washington)

Any frat party will do, and most won't cost you a cent.

The Pike Place Market

David/Janet
Pike Place Market
Downtown Seattle

Janet: It's just beautiful. There are huge fruit and flower stands —and lots of friendly people.
David: I used to like picking up the bums at the Market— literally picking them up.

Nathan
The U District
University Avenue—"U. Dub" (Univerity of Washington)

That was one big pickup scene.

Lindsay/Rebecca
None

Lindsay: I didn't have one. I didn't meet any guys in Seattle.
Rebecca: I didn't do any of that stuff either.

1975
Harper's magazine names Seattle the nation's most livable city.

1976
Seattle opens Kingdome Stadium, the enclosed home of the football Seahawks and baseball Mariners.

1976
The Seattle-area-based Microsoft company is founded by Bill Gates and Paul Allen.

1979
The Seattle SuperSonics basketball team wins the NBA championship, Seattle's first and only major sports title.

1980
Mount Saint Helens erupts 100 miles south of Seattle, sprinkling the city with ash.

1981
A resident of Carmel, California, wins cash and prizes for coming up with "The Emerald City" as Seattle's new city motto.

1982
Seattle's Dr. Barney Clark survives 112 days after becoming the nation's first artificial-heart recipient.

1983
WarGames is shot in Seattle, starring Matthew Broderick and Ally Sheedy,

Dance Club

David
ARO.space
925 E. Pike Street

The crowd is pretty hip.

Lindsay
Neighbours
1509 Broadway

It's primarily a gay dance club. I only went there once, but I'd have to say it had the best dance music.

Nathan/Stephen/Rebecca/Janet
Art Bar
1516 2nd Avenue
Belltown

Nathan: On Sunday night, it has the best dance music I heard in Seattle. Old-school, hip-hop stuff I like.
Stephen: On Saturday and Sunday nights the place rocks.

Rebecca: The music is great, but I have to admit, I'm not much of a dancer.
Janet: It reminded me a lot of Chicago—small, classy, dark, and a lot of different music.

Neighbours

ARO.space

Coffee Bar

David
Uptown Espresso
525 Queen Anne North

They make lattes there that'll make you orgasm.

Lindsay
The Edgewater (Hotel)
2411 Alaskan Way
Downtown Waterfront

That place was my hideaway, and I liked their coffee, too.

Nathan/Janet
Tully's Coffee
1st Avenue and Virginia Street

Nathan: They have a wall of every magazine in print. You can just grab one, sit down, and read to your heart's content while you drink.

Janet: The huge rack of magazines was awesome. Lindsay and I would spend full days there reading magazines and writing letters.

Stephen
Bauhaus Books and Coffee
301 E. Pine
Capitol Hill

I used to go there all the time. That place is really cool.

Rebecca
Bell Street Deli and Grocery
2215 Alaskan Way
Waterfront

I don't drink coffee, only hot cocoa, and their hot cocoa was excellent.

Lunch Spot

David
Queen Anne Health and Fitness
330 2nd Avenue West
Queen Anne

My health club had the best lunches in town. Great sandwiches and Korean chicken. Nothing could touch it.

Janet
Belltown Pub
2322 1st Avenue

It had really good food, and good water, too. I recommend the chicken sandwich and soup.

Lindsay
Larry's Market
100 Mercer Avenue
Lower Queen Anne

It's cheap, which is good 'cause we didn't have any money when we were in Seattle. I'd stock up on apples, a lot of bananas, and a lot of French bread.

Nathan
The Crocodile Café
2200 2nd Avenue

Great food and great garlic mashed potatoes; and at night, the place rocks.

PICTIONARY

1986
Bruce Pavitt and Jonathan Poneman start Seattle's Sub Pop Records, producing such bands as Green River, Soundgarden, and Nirvana.

1990
The Hand that Rocks the Cradle is filmed throughout Seattle starring Rebecca DeMornay and Annabella Sciorra.

1991
Plaid shirts and cutoff denim become the nationwide rage as grunge begins descending from Seattle.

1985

1990

1984
A couple of Seattle café waiters develop the first game of Pictionary.

1985
Seattle is picked as the nation's top recreational city for the fourth year in a row by Rand McNally's *Vacation Places Rated Almanac*.

1989
Seattle elects its first African-American mayor, Norm Rice, despite the city being only 10 percent African-American.

1991
The band Mookie Blaylock (named after the basketball star) debuts at the Seattle club, Off Ramp. The band later changes its name to Pearl Jam.

Rebecca/Stephen
Tup Tim Thai
118 West Mercer Avenue
Queen Anne

Rebecca: Kudos to the chef. Great food. I recommend the No. 6: phad thai.
Stephen: I recommend the cashew chicken.

Seattle Band

David
Modest Mouse

They have the best trailer-park rock sound I've ever heard.

Janet
Ben Harper

He's not from Seattle, but he's the best act I saw in Seattle. He's got an intense presence on stage.

Lindsay
Tuatara

They play wonderful instrumental music.

Nathan/Rebecca
Pearl Jam

Nathan: I saw them play a secret show at ARO.space with only 200 people, and it was only $5 a ticket. The *Real World* crew wanted to film me at the concert. But I said, "There's no way Pearl Jam is going to let you in. They hate MTV. Leave the cameras in the car and come inside." But the crew wouldn't, because they were working.
Rebecca: I like Pearl Jam, too.

Stephen
Severna Park

Awesome!

Tourist Spot

David/Stephen/Lindsay/ Rebecca/Janet
The Pike Place Market
Downtown Seattle

David: It's a great tourist spot, and it's also my joint.
Stephan: There's always cool stuff going on there, particularly on the walkways where you can buy all kinds of s**t.
Lindsay: I'd recommend any place near the water, but I really liked walking through the Pike Place Market.
Rebecca: It's a great place to see all the cultures of Seattle intertwined. Plus, it's got interesting shops and food.
Janet: There's so much activity. I'd recommend it to anyone.

Nathan
The Waterfront Area (Alaskan Way)
Downtown Seattle

Up and down the waterfront area is so beautiful. On a clear day, you can see huge, cascading mountains all around.

The Pike Place Market

The Pike Place Market

Celebrity Sighting

David

Carl Weathers, who played Apollo Creed in *Rocky*. He used to come by the Fish Market a lot.

Nathan

Pearl Jam. Well, I didn't actually get to meet them, but I saw them on stage and they rocked!

Janet

Adam Duritz of Counting Crows. I met him at a Matchbox 20 concert.

Lindsay

Steve Wilson, from the comedy show, *Almost Live*. He's a hilarious guy. Check out his show this fall. I hear it's going national.

Stephen

Lenny Kravitz, who I got to meet him at a Virgin Records listening party. He's pretty phat.

Rebecca

Sir Mix-a-lot, who I got to record with. That was definitely a highlight of my time in Seattle.

1994
Nirvana's Kurt Cobain commits suicide in his Seattle home. Fearing a mob scene, a Seattle cemetery rejects Cobain's ashes, so instead Courtney Love buries him at a Buddhist monastery in upstate New York.

1995
Time magazine names Seattle-area resident Bill Gates the world's richest man.

1998
Real World 7 arrives in Seattle.

1993
Movie star Brandon Lee is accidentally killed on a movie set and is buried beside his father, the legendary Bruce Lee.

1993
Sleepless in Seattle, starring Tom Hanks and Meg Ryan, is filmed at locations across Seattle.

1994
Hole bassist Kristin Pfaff dies in Seattle of an overdose.

1996
Ken Griffey signs an $8.5 million contract, the largest contract in baseball history, at the time.

B E S T +

		DRESSED	HYGIENE	COOK	TABLE MANNERS	
DAVID	BEST ▶	Janet She has a funky diva style.	Nathan He's almost neurotic about hygiene.	Me I am.	Janet Her Korean upbringing taught her well.	
DAVID	WORST ▶	Me I am a very sloppy dresser.	Me I'm a slob.	Irene She can't cook toast and butter.	Rebecca She's always nibbling wherever she goes.	
JANET	BEST ▶	David He has a great body and his clothes hang well on him.	Lindsay She's afraid of germs.	David He knows his food and knows his taste.	Me My dad owns a restaurant and made me learn that stuff.	
JANET	WORST ▶	Stephen He gets a little flashy with his clothing.	David He loves germs.	The Girls None of us ever cooked.	David He ate everything with his fingers.	
LINDSAY	BEST ▶	Janet She knows her style. She's a diva Asian sensation.	Nathan He's anal.	None Nobody cooked.	Janet She was taught well.	
LINDSAY	WORST ▶	None We all had a bit of style.	David He's disgusting.	Janet She's not very domestic.	Me I was taught well...but never went by what I was taught.	
NATHAN	BEST ▶	Me I have a diverse array of clothes.	All Next to David, we all look anal.	David He cooks some mean salmon. And he can fillet a fish.	Rebecca She's just a little innocent queen.	
NATHAN	WORST ▶	Irene She wore the same nasty-a** sweatpants every day.	David He doesn't give a s**t what he smells like.	Rebecca Her pancakes drowned in olive oil.	David I want to take a f**king baseball bat to his head, he eats so loudly.	
REBECCA	BEST ▶	Janet/Stephen Janet: best put together; Stephen: most fashion conscious	Nathan He was always cleaning everything, including himself.	Stephen He's pretty comfortable in the kitchen.	Janet She's well-mannered.	
REBECCA	WORST ▶	David He didn't care.	David He never bothered.	Irene She only uses the microwave.	David Etiquette is not his strong suit.	
STEPHEN	BEST ▶	Me I've got a great fashion sense.	Me I worry about my personal hygiene.	David and Me We're the only ones in the house that knew how to cook.	Rebecca She's a proper little girl.	
STEPHEN	WORST ▶	Irene She doesn't know how to dress.	David He's a pig. He's gross.	Janet Her pancakes had more oil than pancake.	David He farts at the table.	

W O R S T

MUSIC	SINGER	DANCER	PICKUP ARTIST	
Rebecca She has great taste in music, from moody rock to acid jazz.	**Rebecca** She's got a sweet voice.	**Stephen** He knows how to move.	**Rebecca** When she plays the stranded princess, she can pick up anyone.	
Stephen He always listened to Janet Jackson remixes and Celine Dion.	**Me** I sound like a frog when I sing.	**Rebecca** She has the rhythm of a wounded slug.	**Stephen** He'll ask a girl to give him some a** in the first sentence.	
Nathan 'Cause he likes Ben Harper, like me.	**Rebecca** She doesn't have the best voice, she just sang the most.	**David** He's got that good hip thing going on.	**David** He's a player.	
Irene She had no music.	**Lindsay** When she sang, she sounded awful.	**Rebecca** She doesn't have a beat.	**Irene** She's afraid of guys.	
Me My music rocks!	**Irene** She has this great Mae West voice.	**Janet** She just knows how to move.	**David** He's a schmoozer.	
Me, too But it's not everyone's cup of tea.	**Me** I can't hold a note.	**David** He's too sexual with his pelvis.	**Me** I don't give a s**t.	
Me I love my music. And no one can tell me otherwise.	**Rebecca** She has a beautiful voice.	**David and Me** David's got that Elvis thrust, and I can hip-hop the best.	**David** He's got the rap down.	
Irene Neil Diamond's cool. But her other music sucked.	**Me** I can't sing for s**t.	**Irene** She just can't dance.	**None** We all could hold our own.	
Me I like my musical tastes	**Me** At least, I hope so.	**Stephen** He knows how to move.	**David** He has a way with the ladies.	
Irene She digs Air Supply.	**Lindsay** She won't sing.	**Me** I've mastered the art of bad dancing.	**Irene** She refuses to pick up people.	
All but Irene We all brought good music, except Irene.	**Rebecca** Her voice is really gentle and soothing.	**Me** I've got style and rhythm.	**David** He could pull a chick right out from under your nose.	
Irene She doesn't listen to music.	**Lindsay** She can't sing at all.	**Nathan** He's always off the beat.	**Irene** She has no personality to pick up people.	

Real World HONOR

	David 	Janet 	Lindsay 
Most likely to become President	No one Who would vote for us?	Irene She was the most politically astute person in the house.	No one We are all such perfectionists, I don't think any of us could stomach being President.
Most likely to go to prison	Me I'm most prone to that kind of stuff.	David He's "Double-Life David." I don't know what he does in his second life... but I bet it's pretty sketchy.	Janet She'll finally be arrested for wearing that leopard-skin underwear.
Most likely to appear in a tabloid	Me Drama follows me.	Nathan He's the most scandalous.	David He screams tabloid. I see him having 15 wives.
Most likely to join the clergy	Irene She'd look great in a nun's uniform.	Irene She's the most religiously inclined.	Rebecca She's more innocent than anyone else.
Most likely to win the Nobel Peace Prize	Rebecca She's a kindred spirit and has a beautiful heart.	Stephen His anger management is teaching him how to be peaceful.	David He always yelled, 'Shut it and stop fighting.'
Most likely to marry a billionaire	Lindsay Because she already is a billionaire.	Lindsay She'll need a rich husband to maintain the lifestyle she's grown accustomed to.	Nathan Because he loves money.

ROLL

 Nathan	 Rebecca	 Stephen
Me Because I'm a take-charge kind of guy.	**Irene** She's pretty funny and pretty good with people.	**Me or Nathan** Me, the honest way. Or Nathan, the dishonest way. I'd get there through leadership; Nathan, through dirt.
Stephen He's bound to do something really stupid one of these days.	**David** Funny things always happen to David.	**David** He gets himself into some bad situations.
David He's goofy as s**t. He's asking for it.	**Nathan** I see young girls being drawn to him.	**David** He does tabloid-type things, like stripping in public. Nothing wrong with that, but it'll get you into the *Enquirer*.
No one We aren't that holy.	**Stephen** I could see him becoming a rabbi.	**No one** Other than me, no one's religious except Irene... and she's too far gone.
Rebecca She'd love to have that label.	**Me** I don't like confrontation.	**Janet** She's so good at solving things and keeping things peaceful.
Janet That's just something she'd do.	**David** He can talk his way into anything.	**Rebecca** She's got this suave way of appealing to all the rock stars.

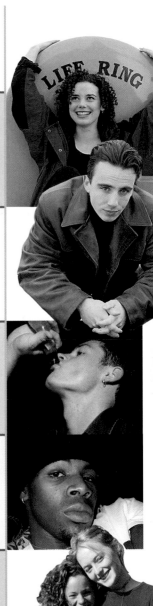

The Creators on Casting: Round by Round

Round 1

Number of applications: 11,535

BLOW-BY-BLOW: *The Real World–Seattle* applicants began the casting process in two ways. Either they put together a 10-minute homemade video telling the casting directors why they ought to be cast on the show. Or, they attended an open casting call, which were held in several major cities. The open call audition usually consisted of a brief interview.

Round 1A

The Home Videotape

MARY-ELLIS: With the videotape audition, we look for genuineness. We look for a sense of humor. We look for a relatability. And we look for an appealing face. They don't have to be stunningly beautiful or handsome, they just have to be appealing.

We don't care if the tape is technically brilliant, or even edited at all. A number of people we've cast have just talked straight into the camera for five minutes and then turned it off. After all, we're casting for people—not filmmakers. Just make sure you're not back-lit so strongly that you appear in silhouette.

JON: ...And the tape must somehow give us the essence of who you are. Of course, that essence has to be interesting to us. Yes, humor is great. But singing naked on camera is not necessarily going to get you cast on the show. It might demonstrate your musical prowess, and even land you on the casting special, but it doesn't say enough about you to tell us who you are.

A lot of kids begin their tape with, 'I want to escape my parents' house.' Then, they talk all about what they don't like about their parents. But, they don't really tell us who they are...or what they want to do with their life. They just talk negatively. We look for people who are trying to turn their life in a positive direction.

Round 1B

The Open Call

MARY-ELLIS: Each candidate only gets about two minutes during an open call, so you really have to get right to it. It's much easier for the casting directors to tell who the real possibilities are in an open call because they're seeing the applicants in person. The people with the most charisma just tend to stand out.

JON: Basically, we're looking for people with enough strength of character to be immediately drawn to that person. Yet, there has to be enough underneath the person, so that we feel like there are still many more layers to explore.

Round 2

The Written Application
Number left: 420, percent remaining: 3.6

BLOW-BY-BLOW: A fraction of the Seattle applicants were sent an in-depth written application to fill out.

JON: The written application is a real chance for people to show some depth. I mean, there are so many good questions on that application, so we're looking for people to really take the questions seriously. We want people to use it as an opportunity to explore their personal histories as well as their likes and dislikes.

MARY-ELLIS: There's a big difference between someone who tries to sketch out the answers in an hour, versus someone who really thinks about each question and gives thoughtful, incisive responses. There are times when a person might be iffy on his or her tape, but the written application is so good it carries him or her into the next round.

Round 3

The Video Telephone Interview
Number left: 105, percent remaining: .9

BLOW-BY-BLOW: The remaining applicants were interviewed by a casting director over the telephone. The applicants recorded their side of the conversation on videotape, so the producers could watch them respond to the questions.

MARY-ELLIS: The questions asked over the phone are usually based on things the applicants said in their home videotape and their written application. We look for variety and more depth.

JON: I want to see if they have an unusual take on things. Or, if they're just giving me the same old drivel that everyone gives you. I want to know if they have something unique to say about their situation, as opposed to just saying what ninety-eight percent of kids would say about it.

Round 4

The Semifinals
Number left: 37, percent remaining: .3

BLOW-BY-BLOW: The casting directors and producers flew to several regional sites to conduct a series of in-person interviews.

MARY-ELLIS: The semifinals is usually our first opportunity to meet the applicant face-to-face. It gives us a chance to sit and talk with them about a variety of issues.

By the semifinals, we're seeking out a kind of staying power. Some people tend to tell the same stories over and over again, so by the fourth round we're beginning to lose interest.

JON: From the moment the candidate walks in the room, you immediately get a sense of them. Sometimes, it can be terribly deflating when you've had such great hopes for someone – and you can just tell it's not going to happen with them. Your gut usually tells you if a person is right for the show.

Round 5

The Reference Check

BLOW-BY-BLOW: Personal references were called if the applicant was seriously being considered for the final round.

JON: Just before finals, we call the applicant's references because we want to know what their friends, and even what their enemies, might say about them. Sometimes, we bring those things up during the interviews to see how they respond.

MARY-ELLIS: We also find out really strange things about people from the reference check. For instance, we recently found out that a guy was lying about his age. He wasn't in his early 20s as he told us, but was actually 28 years old. It concerns us a great deal when we find out people haven't been truthful with us. It makes us question everything they've told us.

Round 6

The Finals
Number left: 14, percent remaining: .1

BLOW-BY-BLOW: The finalists were brought to the producers' offices in Van Nuys, California, for a half day of in-depth interviews. Each of the finalists was prevented from seeing each other, so their first meetings at the beginning of the show would be actual first encounters.

MARY-ELLIS: By the time we've reached the finals, every one of the people involved in casting might have their own favorites, but we still haven't pinned down exactly whom we're going to cast.

We often send out the finalist with one of our younger staff members to a dinner or miniature golf, so we can get them out of the regular interview situation. All of this is done on-camera, as though it were a day on *The Real World*.

JON: That excursion will often tell us a lot about the applicant, like whether they ask questions, too...or just sit there and wait for everyone to react to them. Ultimately, for me, the final decision comes down to: whom do I continue to enjoy and be fascinated by? Whom do I actually want to watch the whole interview of? Or, whom do I get bored with? If I get bored with them, I figure the audience is going to get bored with them, too.

Round 7

The Security Check
Number cleared: 7, percent remaining: .06

BLOW-BY-BLOW: After selecting the "Chosen 7," the producers hired a private firm to run a security check on each cast member before they were officially cast.

MARY-ELLIS: We do the security check just to make sure the people we've picked have no, you know, major felonies—things like aggravated assault convictions. Basically, anything that would make us believe they're too dangerous to put in the house.

JON: We've never disqualified a finalist from one of these security checks. Generally, most people tell you early on if there's something major in their past. And the ones that wish to hide something likely to appear on a security check usually don't apply to a show like this.

Round 8

The Notification
Number left: 7, percent remaining: .06

Blow-by-Blow: The 'Chosen 7' were hand-delivered invitations to join the cast of *The Real World-Seattle*.

MARY-ELLIS: By the time we've cast someone, we're almost as excited for them as they are. After all, we've been through thousands of people just to reach the final seven. We usually notify our new cast in innovative ways. But it's hard to stop ourselves from just picking up the phone and calling them ourselves. We're just so excited to share the news.

JON: The casting process isn't foolproof, not by any means. After all, it comes down to human judgment. And naturally, we all make mistakes. Nevertheless, it's such a rigorous process that we feel confident we've picked a pretty special group. You know, we're not selecting the best and brightest seven, but rather a group made up of seven dynamic and charismatic individuals.

The Creators on Casting

What do you look for when you cast for *The Real World*?

MARY-ELLIS: Well, first of all, we strive for diversity. Then, the individual person, no matter what ethnicity, or socioeconomic background, has to be willing to share their lives with us, and has to be able to communicate their feelings and opinions to us. We really respond to people who express themselves in surprising ways—and are willing to share their deepest thoughts.

The Real World chronicles a rite of passage that just about all 18- to 25-year olds go through. It's about that first experience with independence from your parents. It's about making choices in your life for the first time...without your parents telling you what to do. The most interesting people to cast are those who are going to make bold choices...and then stand behind them. And, of course make mistakes, too. So we can see them learning from them. That's what makes the show resonate with the viewer.

JON: That means we need to find people who aren't afraid to see their mistakes...and have other people see their mistakes, too. That requires a certain degree of self-confidence. Yet, as Mary-Ellis says, they can't be so comfortable with themselves that they're beyond making mistakes. So it's a fine line.

No, we don't designate casting slots, as though we want one from this pile and one from another. But we do believe the show works best when each cast member is unlike the other. We try to reflect all of America.

What aren't you looking for?

MARY-ELLIS: We're not looking for people who think *The Real World* is going to spin them off into their own series...because it doesn't happen.

We're looking for people who genuinely want this experience to help them grow as an individual. And people who are really curious about others —not solely focused on themselves.

JON: The first thing that gets an applicant disqualified is if we sense they're holding back too much, or that they're too afraid of something being revealed. Like someone who constantly says, 'I don't want my mom or dad to know.' It doesn't make sense to put that kind of person on the show.

We're also not looking for actors, who want to come on the show and portray something they think we want. We want people to be themselves. Also, if you're dishonest with us that's an instant out. When you begin to hear inconsistencies from round to round, you know that person isn't being truthful. We don't want to deal with those people, either.

Do you look for people who will fight?

JON: We look for people, who aren't afraid of conflict...who don't back up from it. But we don't look for people who are going to provoke conflict, or go out of their way to make their roommates' lives more difficult. Though that has happened—like with Puck.

MARY-ELLIS: The conflict comes from the diversity we've deliberately cast. We put seven very different personalities together. There's bound to be an adjustment that happens during the course of their bonding—or conflicting.

Casting Seattle: David

OPEN CALL

PLACE: The Cobblestone, Richmond, VA
DATE: October 10, 1997

DAVID on the OPEN CALL

One night, I went to this bar called the Cobblestone, and saw a notice about a *Road Rules/Real World* open call the next morning. Well, I showed up and it was just a bunch of silly college kids trying out. They were all standing around with their *Melrose Place/Wallflowers* gear on, trying to ham it up....Then I strolled in out of nowhere and was called back for an interview two days later. To be honest I never thought I was going to be picked. I'm a skeptic by nature. You know, people are gonna blow smoke up your a**. I figured they were being encouraging 'cause that's the way they are. I assumed it would all end at some point.

SEMIFINALS

PLACE: Embassy Suites Hotel, Arlington, VA
DATE: November 13, 1997

(excerpts)

DAVID: Your first year at the Virginia Military Institute, they put you through a sort of torture for six months.
RW: Define torture.
DAVID: In two words: 'monotonous aggravation.' That's what it is and it goes on forever. At first, it's really intense. The upperclassmen are always in your face. You're doing push-ups, one thousand a day. They're shaving your head. Screaming at ya'. On top of that, you're taking twenty credit hours per semester. You're getting three hours of sleep a day. And you're like, 'They call this a school? It's a boot camp for delinquents.'
RW: How do you feel about that type of discipline?
DAVID: What it does is teach you how to react levelheaded in really tense situations... like *The Real World*.

* * *

RW: Why do you want to do this show?
DAVID: I have yet to see people on it talk about things that really matter. I've just seen them get caught up in petty things that go on in the house.
RW: What are some topics you think should be discussed?
DAVID: Spirituality. How do you feel about your existence? Like, honestly, what do they believe? I think that would help all the different personalities get along much better and achieve a higher state of consciousness.

DAVID'S WRITTEN APPLICATION

(excerpts)

Is there any issue, social or political, that you are passionate about?
Drug abuse among the young. I know that this issue is very broad, but heroin has been destroying the younger generation in my neighborhood. My mother and I started a neighborhood task force to fight the problem.

What are your best and worst traits?
My best traits...umm...well, I'm a vibrant guy, who just loves life and it tends to rub off on people. Well my worst trait–I'm very blunt!

What ways have you treated someone important to you that you're proud of?
I had the privilege of helping my mother get sober, even though I was ten years old. I stood by her side and went to AA meetings with her five times a week. I'm proud because that helped me get her back and taught me how to be a friend.

If you had Aladdin's lamp and three wishes, what would they be?
1. Knowledge–I'm talking boundless knowledge.
2. Peace–Although that doesn't usually come with knowledge. But hey, I've got the lamp.
3. The cure for AIDS and other terminal diseases, if the lamp agrees.

Getting Cast

DAVID on GETTING CAST:

All the cadets at VMI were called into the old courtyard at school. Well, MTV was filming me for the casting special, so I knew something was going down. But the crew had been pulling my string, so I didn't know what to expect. And then our Colonel announced to us that Nate and me had been picked...and I was really, really happy. Everyone crowded around us. All the cadets were getting into it. Like two of their own had made it.

I was skeptical throughout the whole process about getting picked. And the more it went on, the more I wanted to be a part of it. I'd started picturing what it would be like to be filmed for six months and have millions watch it...and I couldn't believe it when Nate and I made it together. We've been through so much together. I'd never have fathomed that he and I would be cast on the same show. I thought maybe we'd both be cast, but on different shows. Me on *Road Rules*. And Nate on *Real World*. Or vice versa. Not in a million years did I think we'd both end up on *Real World*. I thought the show was about seven strangers. I never thought they'd change that for us. But it's so great they did.

DAVID on the FINALS:

Did I think this was an easy process? Yeah and no. No, 'cause I did a lot of interviews. But yeah, because the people I did them with were really heartfelt. Initially, I figured they were just blowing smoke up my *ss. I thought they just wanted to see if I'm the poor city kid. Or a crazy country man. But instead, they had me talking about some things I haven't talked about in ages. I got a chance to look within, to delve within my soul.

I understand that the show takes a big chance on the people it casts. A person can seem one way off-camera...then another on-camera. The casting people have to look deep within each applicant. I tried to tell them, 'This is me. And this is the only me you're going to get.'

FINALS

PLACE: Bunim/Murray Offices, Van Nuys, CA
DATE: December 4, 1997

(excerpts)

RW: Are you a player?
DAVID: No.
RW: Bulls**t, come on.
DAVID: Why the f**k are you trying to play this out of me?
RW: Because you're a player. How many bags of peanuts did you scam out of the flight attendant on your flight out here?
DAVID: None. But I was stoking on the cereal and yogurt...And that makes me a player?
RW: A 'player' doesn't have to be sexual.
DAVID: I thought it had sexual connotations. I thought you were saying that I'm banging all these chicks.
RW: You know how to size up situations. You know how to get what you want from people.
DAVID: Yeah, but no. It's just something you get growing up in Charlestown, Massachusetts.
RW: I could plunk you down in Nairobi and you'd get by.
DAVID: Yeah, that's me. Plant me anywhere and I'll adjust. You got to kick and scrape.

*　　　*　　　*

RW: Do you know there is another person from the Virginia Military Institute being considered?
DAVID: Nate is my bro', man. We lived together in Europe. We did things together on that trip that I only see in the movies. I'm so happy for him that he's being seriously considered.
RW: Have you guys talked about it at school?
DAVID: I want to talk about it with Nate, but we're getting choked at VMI. Everyone has been coming up to us and asking us questions about it. I'm glad his girl, Stephanie, is in the finals with him. Now, you guys are getting original. You guys are starting to think.
RW: Do you think you and Nate will both end up on the same show?"
DAVID: That's bulls**t. I know that ain't going to happen. But I hope him and his girl show up. Man, he loves that girl and she loves him with all her heart.

The Creators on
Casting David

MARY-ELLIS: David's back-story is just amazing and inspiring. The way he was able to extricate himself out of a very dangerous environment in the projects and into the world of VMI is extraordinary. It seems to have surprised him as much as anyone else. Like what's a Boston street kid doing in a Southern military college? We just thought he had an incredible story to tell.

We just wish we'd known about his love affair with Kira before we cast him. We would never have cast him knowing that he'd been involved with someone on our staff during casting...and then planned to continue his involvement with her during the show. Casting a person on this show is based on our feeling that we know them very well and the belief that what they've represented to us is honest. What David and Kira represented to us was completely dishonest. It shook my confidence in him the moment I found out.

JON: ...And we didn't know how much Kira had shared with David about our other casting choices. It would be unfair for David to know why his roommates were cast, if they didn't know the same information. So, it was a very unfortunate situation, too.

DAVID'S TIP:

Don't come with your sob stories. People think that to get on the show, you've got to present some deep-rooted personal problem the masses will identify with. If you're an every-day Joe, who likes beef jerky and drives pick-up trucks, then say so. Don't try presenting yourself as someone you're not.

David's Confessional:

There are times I can communicate a lot more with silence than words. I've been talking way too much. I know I have to talk to get you to know me, but I've been f**king shooting my mouth off all morning. I just want to be quiet now...read my face...see what's going on. I look tired. To tell you the truth, right now I want to cuddle in the fetal position. I am *so* done with this confessional.

Casting Seattle: Irene

IRENE'S WRITTEN APPLICATION

(excerpts)

What is your ethnic background?
White trash.

Describe your most embarrassing moment in life.
I usually don't get embarrassed. But I always trip or spill or walk into glass doors.

Do you have a boyfriend or girlfriend?
I'm too much for most guys to handle. I want a Chia Pet, though. Cha-cha-cha-Chia!!!!

What do you do for fun?
Everything I do in life is for fun.

What bothers you most about other people?
People usually don't bother me. I usually just feel sorry for them because they're not honest with themselves.

SEMIFINALS

PLACE: Embassy Suites Hotel, Arlington, VA
DATE: November 13, 1997

(excerpts)

RW: Have you ever been in love before?

IRENE: No. God, no. But I think I've had much more mental intimacy with guys than I think most girls have…. Like, I get to know people very well. And I think guys will like me more than I will like them.

RW: What is it about you that allows you to have this special mental bond with men?

IRENE: Well, I can just hang out with people. I mean, I don't think it's just men. I think it's with females, too. First of all, I don't categorize somebody for how they look. I just wait 'til I'm hanging out with them. I usually make people feel comfortable. And like, I make people laugh.

RW: What do you think it would be like to be on *The Real World?*

IRENE: Being on *The Real World* would just be fun. I'd get to live with new people for several months… but you've got to give me fun people to be with. I mean, I'll be fun, too. I love people, so it should work out great. Just think of how much fun it'll be living in Seattle. The only problem is that I could potentially have a bad hair day every day because it rains there a lot. I admit I'm a little upset about the location choice. Obviously, nobody was thinking about curly haired people when they made that decision.

FINALS

PLACE: Bunim/Murray Offices, Van Nuys, CA
DATE: December 2, 1997

(excerpts)

RW: Do you have a hard time playing by the rules?

IRENE: No, I'll be able to play by the rules.

RW: That's not answering the question. In the past, have you had a hard time playing by the rules?

IRENE: Well, what kind of rules are you talking about? Like, 'Don't do crack on a regular basis'? I manage to stay away from crack. Like, what type of rules?

RW: Do you chew gum in class?

IRENE: Of course. I eat in class.

RW: Do you run on the pool deck?

IRENE: No, I don't. See, that's a risk I wouldn't take. Chewing gum, I don't have a problem with. But running on a pool deck, well I could fall and get hurt.

The Creators on
Casting Irene

MARY-ELLIS: We cast Irene because her responses and opinions were always surprising. She has this knack of distilling moments into the pithiest statements. And she had a different energy from everyone else. A slower speech. A nasal voice. She was seldom concerned about her hair and makeup, which is rarely the case during the casting process. She was just very relatable and real. And we thought she'd be a challenge to her fellow cast because she's so smart.

JON: We cast Irene because she's delightful. She's so entertaining. She's so smart. She just has a way of observing life, and doing it in a way that's fascinating. She's a total original!

Irene's Confessional:

I hope I make the show. I'd have a very hard time if I made it this far but didn't make the show. If I find out you used me as one of the losers for some casting special, I'm going to show up here with a butter knife. I don't want to become the poster child of rejection for Generation X. That would mortify me. I mean, if you do that, don't drag it out and make me watch myself get rejected every time...and don't leave me nameless, either. I don't want people coming up to me and asking, 'Was that you I saw on MTV?'

Casting Seattle: Janet

PLACE: Viacom Store, Chicago, Il
DATE: November 5, 1997

JANET on the OPEN CALL

A friend of mine told me about the open call for the show at the Viacom store in Chicago. They were running this promotion, where you'd show up at the store and make an audition tape. When I got there, I had to wait three hours in line, and I pretty much sat there the whole time thinking, 'What am I doing here?'

A lot of people had these platforms prepared. You know, like how they were gay, how they were bisexual, how they were beaten by their father. So, I thought I wasn't being creative enough and would need to make something up. But then I thought, if I created a facade, I couldn't keep it up for the entire six months.

My audition lasted about five minutes. I had to talk into a mirror with a camera behind it. I just thought the whole thing was a waste of time. After the audition, I didn't give it much thought. I felt really stupid and didn't tell any of my friends about it. I just forgot about it. Until they called me back.

JANET'S WRITTEN APPLICATION

(excerpts)

What are your personal goals in life?
To have as much power as the President of the U.S. To be content with love, finance and career.

How would someone who really knows you describe your best traits?
Passionate, extroverted, compassionate, ambitious, great with people.

How would someone who really knows you describe your worst traits?
Self-involved, argumentative, a bit flighty, not very committed to anyone, irresponsible, gets bored easily.

Describe your fantasy date.
Downtown Chicago for dinner and drinks. New York City for an opera. Jet to Vegas for Club Rio. Jet to Red Rock in Colorado for sunrise.

If you could change any one thing about the way you look, what would that be?
I'd want longer legs and green eyes.

If you could change any one thing about your personality, what would that be?
I'd want to know how to love more. I'd be closer to my Korean culture.

If you had Aladdin's lamp and three wishes, what would they be?
1. My grandmother would live forever.
2. My parents could stop working.
3. I would be a dancer.

PLACE: Harley Hotel, Columbus, OH
DATE: November 12, 1997

(excerpts)

RW: Do you ever feel really alone?

JANET: Oh, completely. All the time. I used to really rely upon guys for my sense of security and self-esteem. But since I've been in college, I've changed. I've almost taken a complete reverse turn. Now, I'm almost too cold-hearted and really indifferent toward things like that.

RW: Tell us about the time you slapped the pom-pom girl.

JANET: It happened my senior year in high school. My boyfriend was a football player and I was a pom-pom. We were like the stereo typical high school couple. One weekend, I went away and he cheated on me with one of the girls on my squad. I just couldn't believe it.
When I heard, I confronted him. And he was like, 'Yeah, it happened.' I've never been so ballistic, to this day. It was the first time that anyone had ever cheated on me. So, I started showing up at every party this girl went to. I started talking behind her back to everyone. Just stupid s**t. Getting people to hate her. And finally, she came up to me at practice and said, 'Janet, I can't deal with this. Like, if you wanna get it over with, just hit me. But you've gotta stop this.' I'd never hit anyone before. But all I needed was an invitation.

RW: So, what did you do?"

JANET: Oh, I slapped her. She had a big palm print. She didn't show up at practice for a day or two. After that, we just kinda never talked again.

PLACE: Bunim/Murray Offices
Van Nuys, CA
DATE: December 4, 1997

JANET on the FINALS:

I never talked about myself so much in my entire life. It was a little odd. But it was really interesting, too. I'm extremely extroverted and just tell the whole world my problems anyway. So, it wasn't really a big deal. Most importantly, I'm glad I didn't lie during the casting process. They asked the same questions over and over again. I would've ended up getting caught in a lie.

JANET'S TIP:

Never depend on getting cast. If the call comes, great. If not, no big deal. During the casting process, I never told my friends about it. I didn't want to get hyped up over something that was such a long-shot. So, remain even keel. And also, remember to tell the truth. They ask you the same questions so many times, your lies will be exposed.

Getting Cast

JANET on GETTING CAST:

When I found out I was going to Seattle, I didn't know how I was supposed to feel. It was all so unreal. I got the call while eating dinner in my dad's restaurant. One of the casting people from *The Real World* said to me, 'What are you doing in January?' And I said, 'Not a whole lot.' And he replied, 'Well, you're going to Seattle!' So, that's how I heard.

I have no idea why MTV chose me. Honestly, the only thing I can think of is I'm an Asian female that's not pre-med.

JANET on her FAMILY'S REACTION

My family had absolutely no clue about what *The Real World* was. They're very traditional. My uncle was watching one of *The Real World-Miami* episodes and he's like, 'Oh, the boys and girls live together?' So, he started putting all these ideas into my dad's head and my father freaked out a bit. He wanted to know if we all slept in the same bed. My mother asked me, 'This isn't a form of pornography, is it?' I almost died.

The Creators on
Casting Janet

MARY-ELLIS: We cast Janet because she's an extraordinarily bright, beautiful and well-spoken young woman. She's also from Chicago-an area of the country that's been underrepresented on the show. And we thought she might really get into the radio station job because she wants to be a journalist.

JON: We also felt her cultural background was so interesting. Her parents came to America with virtually nothing and worked incredibly hard at their restaurant. So hard, in fact, that Janet felt like they'd rarely had enough emotional time for her. So she'd developed a close bond with her grandmother, with whom she only speaks Korean. The only Asian-American we'd ever cast on the show was Pam from *The Real World-San Francisco*. But Pam wasn't really immersed in her Asian culture. We thought Janet would provide an insight we'd never had before.

Janet's Confessional:

I'm a little nervous that you guys are hiding the other Seattle candidates from me. I'm really interested in knowing what they're like. It weirds me out that I haven't seen any of them...I haven't exactly told my parents what this is all about, yet. And that's making me nervous. I don't think they'll have a problem with it, but I think it'll take me hours and hours and hours to convince them. So, I don't plan on doing that until I absolutely have to....It's been a good time doing this whole casting process. I haven't had this type of sheer adrenaline excitement in a long time. Outside of boys.

Casting Seattle: Lindsay

OPEN CALL

PLACE: Touchdown Café, Ann Arbor, MN
DATE: October 29, 1997

LINDSAY on the OPEN CALL

One of my closest friends, Maggie, told me about the open call in Ann Arbor. She thought *The Real World* would fit my personality, so I went and waited in line for an hour. There were so many people there, it was ridiculous. It seemed like 500, at least...

It was weird because everyone on line around me was talking about how they had an uncle or cousin in the 'business' and that if they really wanted to be on the show, their relative could say a few words on their behalf and they'd get on. Honestly, I heard this five or six times.

The actual first interview was around a bar with five other people. We just kind of shot the s**t—random people talking about random things. As I was leaving, I gave one of the assistants a videotape application I'd put together. It's ironic 'cause I thought about not bringing it. Well, I gave it to this assistant on the way out. And she gave me her number and told me to call her to set up an interview. That's how it all started.

LINDSAY'S WRITTEN APPLICATION

(excerpts)

What habits do you have that we should know about?

I sleepwalk and eat. I guess I've got low blood sugar, and if I don't eat before bed, I'll get up and make something while I'm asleep. I've held conversations in my sleep, and walked into rooms filled with people when I was wearing inappropriate attire.

How important is sex to you?

Sex is a great thing, and I have experienced it with only two people. My boyfriend Alex and a 6'7" basketball player named Ben. I'll be very honest—with Alex, since I see him so little, the sex is on and off. But when I dated Ben, it was *all* the time. One rainy day, he and I drove up to Independence Pass in Colorado and "made it" on a rock next to Roaring Forks Rapids. We were almost *on* the rapids *and* in plain sight of anybody driving by.

What are your thoughts on other sexual orientations?

Like positions? Kidding!!! Whatever one's sexual preference is, it's fine with me. I often find homosexuality much more interesting than heterosexuality—I guess that's why a lot of my friends are gay.

Other than your boyfriend or girlfriend, who is the most important person in your life?

My mother and my brother are the most important people in my life. After my father died, we weren't really a family. No one knew what to do or how to act because we were all dealing with my dad's death individually. In the last few years, we've all come to terms with what we never thought we could. I guess you could say we are a family again. We are as close as we can be, and as "normal" a family as we can be considering our situation.

Name three people you would like to meet and why.

1. Kitty Dukakis—I'd ask her how she got into rubbing alcohol.
2. Elvis—Because I know he's still alive. 'Where have you been hiding yourself? You rascal.'
3. Bill Gates—I'd like to ask him how it feels to lose the pocket change of $1.76 billion in one of the stock market's recent falls.

SEMIFINALS

PLACE: Harley Hotel, Columbus, OH
DATE: November 11, 1997

(excerpts)

RW: If the right guy came along, could you be swept off your feet ?

LINDSAY: Yeah, I think most people could. I know I could. But it would take me a lot of time to really trust the person.

RW: What would he be like mentally and physically?

LINDSAY: You guys are going to laugh, but in the physical sense it would probably be like my boyfriend, Alex.

RW: Which is?

LINDSAY: Greek, very Greek.

RW: By Greek, do you mean Mediterranean?

LINDSAY: Latin would also work.

RW: But super-pale wouldn't work?

LINDSAY: I guess I don't think it would make a difference, but I'm physically more attracted to the darker lot. Greek. Latino. It's the real blond that I'm not that attracted to. And I don't really care if he's that muscular or anything like that. Just athletic.

RW: How tall?

LINDSAY: Not 6'7", like the basketball player I dated. It makes things kind of difficult sometimes. After all, I'm only 5'1".

RW: What about the personality?

LINDSAY: Reserved, but able to deal with my hyperness...and intelligent. Extremely intelligent.

PLACE: Bunim/Murray Offices, Van Nuys, CA
DATE: December 1, 1997

LINDSAY on the FINALS:

Making it to the finals and meeting everybody at MTV was a real nice feeling. It put me on a euphoric high. It was unbelievable. But when I went back to my hotel, I hit this rock-bottom low because I didn't know if I'd ever be called back again. Or if they really liked me. Perhaps they were just putting on a smile to make me feel good.

After my interview, I called my best friend and told her there was no way they wanted me. They'd interviewed so many people, so, why would they want me? I just figured they'd been so polite 'cause they'd decided against me.

Getting Cast

LINDSAY on GETTING CAST:

I was sitting in the library at the University of Michigan, when I got the phone call from MTV. The library had been dead silent, and suddenly a phone rang. I said to my friend Maggie, 'That's so obnoxious. I can't believe someone would call here.' Next thing I knew, someone came up to me and said, 'Are you Lindsay?...the phone's for you.'

I'll tell you I was just sure they hadn't cast me. When they told me I'd been picked, I didn't know what to say. I just went outside...and then I screamed. I called my mom...and she screamed, too. You know it was one of those moments in life I'll never forget.

Lindsay's Confessional:

This whole thing has made me think about my dad a lot more than I expected. There are still a lot of issues with my dad that are hard for me to deal with....I think this casting process has made me appreciate my family even more. My mom has been so supportive. And my brother has been so excited for me, he's called me a million times. He told me he was so proud of me. I haven't had a male tell me that in a long time. I'm going to start to cry, um...whenever I had soccer tournaments or anything like that, my dad would always say that he was proud of me. I never wanted to disappoint my father. So, it's been nice hearing it from my brother.

The Creators on
Casting Lindsay

MARY-ELLIS: Lindsay is just a ball of fire! She had the most energy we'd ever seen in a little package. This girl was irrepressible during casting, just all hair and energy.

JON: And we had a feeling that perhaps all this energy was masking something—like her father's death, which she hadn't fully dealt with. Or her relationship with her boyfriend, Alex, who seemed more like a friend than a real boyfriend. We thought Lindsay had a number of issues that might prove interesting for the show. Also, Lindsay had prior experience working at a radio station, which we thought would be useful for her fellow cast members.

LINDSAY'S TIP:

Be yourself. If you try to be someone or something else, you're going to shoot yourself in the foot. Eventually it'll catch up to you.

Casting Seattle: Nathan

OPEN CALL

PLACE: The Cobblestone, Richmond, VA
DATE: October 14, 1997

NATHAN on the OPEN CALL:

I received a flyer at school saying MTV was having an open call for *Road Rules* and *The Real World*, so, I decided to give it a shot. I think seven or eight of us applied from the Virginia Military Institute, including David. We all filled out a one-page application and had an interview right on the spot. They told me to come back the next day for a taped interview. I did...and I was on my way.

NATHAN'S WRITTEN APPLICATION

(excerpts)

Describe your most embarrassing moment.
My friends were taking me to a party being thrown for me. I got out of the car and thought I just had gas. Well, everything but gas came out. And I couldn't say anything. I had to stand around at the party for at least 20 minutes being social to my friends before I could go to the bathroom and clean up.

What habits do you have that should we know about?
I tend to be a "smarta**," if you consider that a habit.

Describe a major event or issue that has affected your life.
The death of my father changed my life forever. I was 15 and I had to mature to a much higher level. I had to be responsible for myself. My father's death taught me responsibility and courage.

What is the most important issue or problem facing you today?
Money!!! Since the death of my father, I have basically had to support myself. Financing three years of college without outside help has been difficult. This has given me tremendous incentive to work hard, so that I, nor my future family, will ever have to worry themselves with financial problems.

If you had Aladdin's lamp and three wishes, what would they be?
1. I would love to see my father one more time to tell him I love him.
2. For my family and friends to have happy, stress-free lives.
3. To get rid of poverty and taxes.

SEMIFINALS

PLACE: Embassy Suites Hotel, Arlington, VA
DATE: November 13, 1997

(excerpts)

RW: What would happen if we asked your girlfriend, Stephanie, to come on the show?

NATHAN: Together? I would love that! It would kick a**. We'd be together all the time. I mean, I'm sure we'd get into arguments. But it would be a hell of a lot better than what we have now. Because we're both at school and we only see each other on weekends.

RW: So, what do you love about this guy?

STEPHANIE: Not his feet. Um...

NATHAN: What?

STEPHANIE: I'm just kidding. I don't know, he's...

NATHAN: It's time to get cheesy.

STEPHANIE: Just the way he's turned out is absolutely amazing. Just the crap that he's had to put up with. I just have so much respect for the bonehead.

NATHAN: Thanks, little bonehead.

RW: Now, your turn.

NATHAN: What do I? What do I? What don't I like about her...

RW: How would you feel, if he went away?

STEPHANIE: It would just suck....you know just (starts to cry). Hold on. I don't want to talk about it. Next question.

RW: Could you honestly say you wouldn't feel resentment toward him?

STEPHANIE: No, not resentment. I mean, if I was in his position, I'd go.

NATHAN: Yeah, there'd be no question [kissing Stephanie].

Getting Cast

NATHAN on GETTING CAST:

When I found out I'd be on *The Real World*, I had mixed emotions. On the one hand, I was very, very happy and excited, but on the other, I was disappointed for Stephanie. After the final round of interviews, I was sure we were both going to be cast. I was just sure. Of course, I was a bit worried about how we were going to get through those 18 weeks being separated.

But it was real nice that David was cast with me as well. We've been through a lot together and have grown really close. He knows just about everything about me. So that's a great consolation.

MTV called me at my mother's house to tell me I'd reached the finals. And it was like, 'Wow! I might really be on the show.' But then I looked over at Stephanie and she was noticeably upset, and not because she didn't make the finals. But because it was just another step closer to us being apart from one another. So, we went off and talked about it. I reassured her that nothing bad was gonna happen to us.

The next day MTV called again, and this time they wanted to talk to Stephanie. They told her she had made the finals, too. She was just jumping up and down. Totally excited.

FINALS

PLACE: Bunim/Murray Offices, Van Nuys, CA
DATE: December 8, 1997

(excerpts)

RW: Are you a jealous person?

NATHAN: My downfall is that I'm very jealous, but I'm getting so much better about it, especially since I first started going out with Stephanie. Still, I get jealous. It's not that I don't trust her. I just don't trust other people. You know, I finally have something good, and I don't want to lose it.

RW: Is she jealous, too?

NATHAN: Yeah, but she really doesn't have the opportunity to be jealous. I go to practically an all-male school, she goes to Virginia Tech with 28,000 people ready to party and hook up.

REUNION

PLACE: Kansas City, KS
DATE: November 22, 1997

NATHAN on meeting his MOTHER and LITTLE BROTHER

With Stephanie and MTV by my side, I met my mother for the first time since I was in fourth grade—more than 15 years ago. And I met my little brother, Skylar, whom I'd never seen before, and my mother's husband, Sean.

It was a trip planned before I'd auditioned for the show. But the producers wanted to film it for their casting special, so I let them. Anyway, I was so scared at first. Stephanie flew with me to Kansas City. She practically talked me into it. I made Stephanie get off the plane first because I was so nervous. But once I saw my mother, I recognized her right away. Looking at her, I felt like I was looking into a mirror. Once we started talking, it was like I hadn't been away from her. It definitely felt like a mother-son relationship, which is not what I expected it to be.

It was an experience I really can't even put into words–like a part of my life was complete now.

MARY-ELLIS: In addition to Nathan's charming sex appeal, we thought his life story was just fascinating. His mother left him to tour with a country singer. She deposited him with his father, who didn't tell Nathan he was dying. When his father died, Nathan's grandmother thought Nathan was the devil incarnate 'cause he wasn't a born-again Christian. Nathan was so alone that he was virtually adopted by his girlfriend's parents. And on top of that, he and Stephanie have an incredibly tumultuous relationship. So, we thought he'd be great for the show.

JON: We also thought Nathan was a real Southern boy with a warm heart...and with a little bit of redneck tossed in. As for considering Stephanie, too, we had a hunch their relationship might prove interesting to watch. In fact, she didn't even apply for the show. We asked her to do so, and at the casting finals, we were choosing between her and David. Had we known David was involved with Kira, we'd have chosen Stephanie instead.

Nathan's Confessional:

This has been a crazy experience. As I look back on it, it was something like a dream, like, 'Let's give it a shot and hope it works out.' And I never knew I'd be sitting in this chair today. I hoped I would be. But it's really cool to have made it all the way to the finals.

The whole casting process has been a life-building experience. I've really liked the attention. I like to make people laugh. I like to be in the middle of a crowd. I'm just so stoked and excited I've gotten this far....During this time, I've gotten to see my mom for the first time in, like, 15 years. And I've gotten to see my little brother for the first time ever. That was just unbelievable.

That was one of the best experiences in my entire life.

And Stephanie has been just wonderful throughout. I love her more today than I did yesterday. When I look to the future, I see me and Stephanie. I know a lot of people think I'm just young, dumb, and in love. Well, I just want to throw them into my body for a day and let them feel this way.

I pray that we make it through this show, that if we both get chosen, we'll survive. And if one of us gets chosen...but not the other...we'll also make it, because I don't know what I'd do without Stephanie in my life.

NATHAN'S TIP:

Don't try to be somebody you're not. Just be yourself. If you have a good personal story, a good personality and you're a good person... then you have a good chance of making it on the show.

Casting Seattle: Rebecca

PLACE: The Cobblestone Brewery, Richmond, VA
DATE: October 14, 1997

REBECCA on the OPEN CALL:

Ah, the open call was extremely interesting. I hadn't planned on going. My best friend Becky and I were driving along the road and passed by the Cobblestone Brewery. We saw all these people standing outside with their head-shots and pets, or some other kind of selling point. It was like looking at the cast of *Friends*. Everyone had their hair gelled and stuff.

We were like, 'Let's check these people out.' We really went in just to laugh at them. We filled out an application, but decided not to wait around for the interview. Well, just as we were about to leave, my name was called.

After my interview, I remember thinking, 'How weird would it be if I ended up on MTV?' because I don't even watch the channel. I thought the whole situation was complete humor.

REBECCA'S WRITTEN APPLICATION

(excerpts)

How important is sex to you?
It's not important. I haven't had sex before, but it's not a moral choice. I just haven't met the right person. When I do, I'll have no qualms about giving it up.

Name three people you would like to meet and tell us why.
I'd easily like to meet Sinéad O'Connor. That's a woman with clout. She's got a lot to say and she has no qualms about saying it. Al Pacino. He's absolutely brilliant. I'm into theatre and he perfected the Stanislavsky method. Sam Shepard. His plays are amazing. He was from Charlottesville and I've always had quite a fancy for him.

Is there any issue, political or social, that you're passionate about?
Oh, yes. I used to be a rampant animal-rights activist. I protested the circus and almost got arrested.

Describe your most embarrassing moment.
My friends and I were avid Dave Matthews fans a few years ago. I tried to sneak backstage at one of his concerts and he totally nailed me. It was definitely the lowest point of my life.

PLACE: Embassy Suites Hotel, Arlington, VA
DATE: November 12, 1997

(excerpts)

RW: So, are you high-maintenance?

REBECCA: No, I'm not. Like, well, in a way I am. I'm really low-maintenance to begin with. But, then, my guy friends are like, 'Yeah. You're low-maintenance. But that's the highest maintenance of all because you think you're low-maintenance...and you're actually the highest.' I don't need to be catered to, but I like to be the focus of attention.

RW: If you go on a date with a guy, when is he supposed to call back?

REBECCA: Well, I don't have those *Swingers*-like rules.

RW: Should he call the next day?

REBECCA: He doesn't have to call. It's not like, 'You have to do this and that.' It's more like...

RW: Like you have a set of rules in your head?

REBECCA: Yeah, in the back of my head. I'm completely over-analytical and 'glass half empty.' So, like, if a guy bought me a car, I might say to myself, 'Whoa, this guy just bought me a car. He must really like me...but maybe it's a good-bye present!'

*　　　　*　　　　*

RW: So, what religion were you raised in?

REBECCA: Christian Science. But I'm not really that devout. My family wasn't that ardent with it. I think there are a lot of things that are interesting about it, like taking medicine. They rely on God to guide them. The media has taken that to mean, 'Oh, they kill their babies by not giving them medicine,' but it's nothing like that. It's more of a spiritual connection with God. It's like each of us represents God's perfect image. And you don't need medicine 'cause God doesn't take medicine.

RW: Do you take medicine?

REBECCA: No, I don't. Well, a few months ago I had poison ivy and I took stuff. I mean I'm not really... well, I'd feel like such a poser to say that I'm a really good Christian Scientist. But I think the tenents of Christian Science are really deep and noble. I just don't have...I don't know...the willpower to be completely observant.

REBECCA on the SEMIFINALS:
When I arrived for the semifinals, I was really nervous. I guess it was from the impact of making it that far. But after I started talking with the casting people, all the blocks came down and I felt more comfortable. It was just weird, man. Like sometimes I'd think, 'My life is so lame. I don't know if I want to share it with everyone in the world.' Besides, who'd actually want to watch my life?

PLACE: Bunim/Murray Offices, Van Nuys, CA
DATE: December 4, 1997

(excerpts)

RW: You like bad boys and tattoos?

REBECCA: No, I don't like tattoos. But, yeah, I like bad boys. I like people who go against the norm. I like that bad boy to be the good boy that everyone is misinterpreting. And I don't like guys that like me a lot, either.

RW: So, you want them to treat you badly?

REBECCA: No, I don't want that. I want them to play games with me at first. Like, it's got to be my conquest, or a trophy, of sorts. I have to be like, 'That's my man!' I've got to feel proud of him.

REBECCA on the FINALS:

My whole trip to Los Angeles was kind of fun. A friend of mine works for Paramount Studios and invited me to check it out. So, I went to visit him and we checked out all the buildings, and we came upon this parking lot that was filled with limousines. Well, I just figured it was a normal occurrence. But then, we saw all these tents filled with people in black ties and dresses. So, we were like, 'Lets go in.' Well, I'm in my khakis with a tank top and boots. The moment we entered, we ran right into the entire cast of *Friends* and *NYPD Blue*. Cindy Crawford was there and so was Dustin Hoffman. It was wild.

REBECCA'S TIP:

Really think about whether or not you want to do this. Make sure you are completely comfortable with yourself. That you're not carrying around some thing that could be burdensome to you. And make sure everyone in your life understands why and what you're doing, and that they're comfortable with it, too. If they're not, respect their privacy. But I could give you any casting tips and it wouldn't matter. 'Cause regardless of the warnings I give, no one's going to adhere to any of them. I know I didn't!

Rebecca's Confessional:

As far as a boyfriend, or future husband is concerned, I need my needs to be met. And if my needs aren't met, then it will not work out. So, either I find someone who meets my needs, or, I'll be alone. I won't be settling. And I'll be happy that way, because I won't feel like I'm compromising. I'll be true to myself... but then again, I have a really big need to feel loved."

Rebecca on her Confessional:

The confessional was interesting. I felt kind of silly talking to myself. But then it wore off and I just kind of rambled.

The Creators on
Casting Rebecca

MARY-ELLIS: Rebecca is a romantic, she's also ethereal, and a patrician, beautiful woman. During casting, we sensed that one of her biggest struggles was not being able to stand up to conflict and not being confident enough to express her own opinions. That's a very relatable struggle for many young girls. So we thought it would be interesting to see how it played out on the show.

JON: We also liked her strong interest in music. Given how important music is to the city of Seattle, we thought its music scene might draw Rebecca in.

Getting Cast

REBECCA on GETTING CAST:

When I was told I'd be on, my first reaction was total shock. I was just blown away. Like, 'I'm going to be on TV, living in some place so different from what I'm living in now.' It was all so completely unexpected. The casting process is very mysterious and secretive. I just had no idea what the hell was going on. And no expectation I'd be picked for the show.

Casting Seattle: Stephen

STEPHEN on the VIDEO APPLICATION:

I kind of applied on a whim. My friend, Jerry, saw an ad for the show on MTV. He yelled out at me, 'Dude, ya got to give it a shot. You should be on *The Real World!*' And a number of my friends agreed, so, I was like, 'I'm gonna do it for you guys.' It was just two days before the video applications were due and I still needed to find a camera. Luckily someone had one I could borrow and the next day a friend filmed me doing whatever I normally do. I mailed it off the next day and got the whole thing rolling.

STEPHEN'S WRITTEN APPLICATION
(excerpts)

Do you have any habits we should know about?
I have the habit of walking around in my underwear on occasion.

Describe your fantasy date.
My fantasy date would be with a beautiful young or older woman (up to 25) out at San Francisco's Vertigo Restaurant, atop the TransAmerica Building. A nice walk in the Berkeley Hills. Ideally, it would end with passion and not necessarily sex.

If you had three wishes, what would they be?
My first wish would be to have the happy "Huxtable" family that I always wanted but could never seem to have. My second wish would be for personal success in life through love, career, family and a healthy social life. My last wish, most important for the world, is that I would like to convince people that we are all people and that's all that should matter.

Describe how conflicts were handled at home as you were growing up.
When I was growing up, conflicts were handled fast and painful. My mom gave all my stepdads permission to spank me, but most of them went past that to hitting me with extension cords, leaving me outside overnight, making me feel like s**t. I guess I'm so outspoken now because I didn't feel safe saying anything when I was young.

STEPHEN on the WRITTEN APPLICATION:

I knew I was applying for *The Real World* as soon as I read the application. I've never been asked such straightforward questions in my life. Before I filled it out, I asked myself, 'Are you going to be open with everything? If not, I shouldn't do it.' And so I decided to go ahead and be real.

PLACE: Bunim/Murray Production Offices, Van Nuys, CA
DATE: November 13, 1997

(excerpts)

RW: Have you had a lot of conflicts in your life because of your color?
STEPHEN: Yeah, I have. The darker you are, the less accepted you are.
RW: You mean in society or in the black community?
STEPHEN: In society and in the black community, the light and dark issue is a huge deal. But I think, the darker the berry the sweeter the juice. Some people think that since I'm dark black, I make up for being black by talking white. People think, 'Oh, you're not kicking it with the black people, or you didn't pledge Alpha Phi Alpha like your father, you must not be a black man.' Well, obviously I am.
RW: Do you have a racial preference in whom you date?
STEPHEN: Well, I usually only date black women. That's just a personal preference. It's not that I don't find other women beautiful, 'cause I totally do. It's just that I date black women because of their unique personality. They have to...and my mom's this way, too...they have to be stubborn, yet movable, punishing, yet rewarding. I've dated one or two white girls, and five or six Latin girls. But black women are very special to me.

STEPHEN on the SEMIFINALS

My mom would like certain things that I've shared with her not to be publicized—like the former jobs I've had, whether that be exotic dancing or working at my neighborhood KFC. She's very proud of who I am, but some of the decisions I've made she's not too proud of. And she's a very, very private person. So, I didn't tell my mom about my applying for *The Real World* 'cause I knew she wouldn't approve of it. I get a lot of encouragement from her. But when she doesn't want something to happen for me, she goes the extra mile to try and make it not happen. You know, by discouraging me. But I wanted this to be my decision. I didn't want to be persuaded by her. And this is my life we're talking about. Since I've lived it, I have a right to talk about it.

The Creators on
Casting Stephen

MARY-ELLIS: Stephen was one of the most articulate people we've ever met during casting. It was clear right from the start that he's still searching for his true self. And we figured his search would bring a lot to the show.

JON: As soon as we met Stephen, it was evident he's a mass of contradictions. He grew up with all these different stepfathers. Yet, somehow he made it through a very tough childhood into Berkeley. He rejected his mother's religion and embraced Judaism. So, he'd obviously been through many interesting stages. And we figured these contradictions might be further illuminated on the show.

STEPHEN on the FINALS:

I had mixed emotions about getting this far. On the one hand, it was a really big deal. On the other, it meant the possibility that I'd be sacrificing whatever privacy I had. I began to think, 'Bye-bye privacy. Bye-bye lonely walks down the street.' 'Cause if I'm cast, everybody will know me after this. Overall, though, I thought it was going to be a great thing for me to do. And I've always been one to accept any challenge at hand...whatever it might be.

Stephen on the Confessional:

After I went into the confessional room, I really don't know what happened. All I know is something really, really personal came out. In a gross way, it was like I'd picked the scab off these personal scars of mine. It felt like the moment of truth for me. It was the final time for me to be in the presence of the *Real World* people and tell them how I really felt.

STEPHEN'S TIP: Ask the directors questions about the process. Ask as many questions as you want–like, 'How do the cameras affect things?' or, 'What's been the experience of past cast members?' I recommend that each applicant knows their insecurities beforehand, because they'll be thrown in your face like baseballs. You've got to know them. You've got to accept them. And you've got to be able to defend them.

As for the people doing the casting, I wish you wouldn't make it seem like we're winning the California State lottery. You made it seem like we were really, really, really lucky to be selected. Yeah, we were in a way. But you didn't really tell us how stressful it was going to be. The only one who did was Craig, one of the directors. He said to me, 'It's hard. Are you really sure you want to do this?' I should've answered, 'No.'

Stephen's Confessional:

Um, confessional...my hands are shaking. I'm still overwhelmed to be here. It's taken a while for this to sink in. But I'm actually content about being here. I actually believe that Stephen's story is something that America needs to see. It's about time that black men, like myself, who are trying their damnedest to do something with their life...that have run into so many obstacles...have their story shown....

I tried to commit suicide over what people thought of the way I looked and acted. All the black kids thought I was white 'cause I didn't talk street slang, and I didn't do street things. But all the white kids thought I was black because I couldn't play soccer or baseball like them. This whole *Real World* process has helped me to finally know that it's cool to be exactly who the hell I am....

And I'm gonna do what the hell I want and feel good about it. Because at the heart of me, I'd like to be the most confident person in the world. Oh, crap [wiping eyes]. I'm sorry. Hold on. At the heart of me, I'd like to be the most confident person in the world. I can act it sometimes, but sometimes, I'm not very confident.

If I make the show I will be very excited to watch myself grow. I hope this show gives this young African-American male the chance to really find out what it means to be someone, who's learning and growing from other people. And I hope that you guys see that I'm someone not like anyone else. I trust that I'd be a really cool addition on *The Real World 7.* And I hope that's how it turns out.

BOSTON

WHERE ARE THEY NOW?

SYRUS

Now Living:
Santa Monica, California

Now Doing:
Promoting nightclubs, sports apparel, and GODDOG.

Now Planning:
To pursue a career in the entertainment field.

Now Seeing:
No one. No longer going out with Jennifer.

KAMEELAH

Now Living:
Palo Alto, California

Now Doing:
Junior year at Stanford University. Majoring in human biology and pre-med.

Now Planning:
To become a gynecologist specializing in public health.

Now Seeing:
No one at the moment. Working too hard.

JASON

Now Living:
Los Angeles, California

Now Doing:
Associate Casting Director–Bunim/Murray Productions. Appeared on *The Real World/Road Rules Challenge.*

Now Planning:
To go to film school.

Now Seeing:
Off-and-on with Timber.

ELKA

Now Living:
Las Vegas, Nevada

Now Doing:
Sophomore at the University of Nevada-Las Vegas. Considering majoring in broadcast journalism.

Now Planning:
To be the next Diane Sawyer.

Still Seeing:
Walter.

SEAN

Now Living:
St. Paul, Minnesota

Now Doing:
Third year at William Mitchell College of Law.

Now Planning:
To take the Wisconsin bar after law school. Then, move back to Hayward, Wisconsin, or out to Los Angeles, California.

Now Seeing:
Rachel from *The Real World-San Francisco* and *Road Rules All-Stars*.

GENESIS

Now Living:
Orlando, Florida

Now Doing:
Working as a restaurant hostess until she goes back to college.

Now Planning:
To return to college, possibly to major in meteorology.

Now Seeing:
Just casually dating–both women and drag queens. But nothing serious at the moment.

MONTANA

Now Living:
Hoboken, New Jersey

Now Doing:
Senior year at Hunter College. Majoring in archaeology. Also temping at MTV Networks. Appeared on *The Real World/Road Rules Challenge.*

Now Planning:
To go to graduate school for museum education.

Now Seeing:
No longer with Vaj. Single, at present.

THE FIREHOUSE

Now Living:
Boston, Massachusetts

Now Doing:
Laying empty.

Now Planning:
To become a neighborhood community center.

Now Seeing:
A lot of dust and many memories.

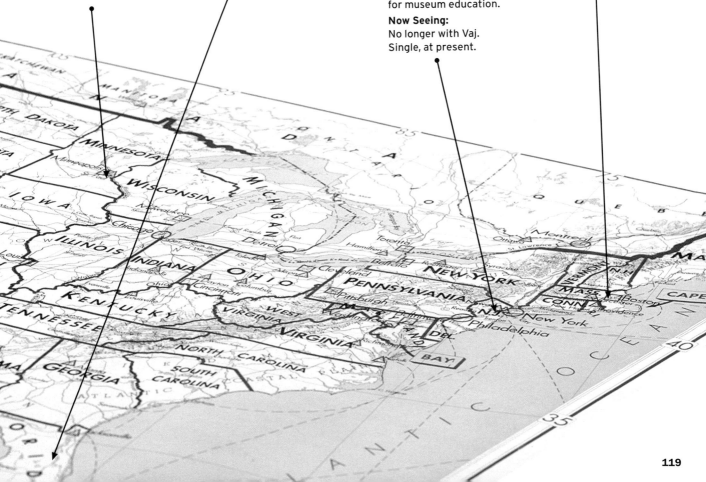

Elka

MOST FAVORITE: I thought they did a great job portraying my trip back to Brownsville. Every time I watch that show it makes me cry. Of course, I would have preferred to visit my mother's gravesite alone. But I understood why they needed to be there for the show. After all, I'd signed up to have my entire life filmed and a lot of viewers have told me it helped them cope with their mother's or father's deaths. So, that makes it even more worthwhile.

LEAST FAVORITE: The sequence where I fought with Kameelah at the After School Program. Not because I got in a fight with her, but because they didn't air the whole conversation. They showed her saying, 'I'm going to knock you out,' and then showed me responding, 'No, you're not,' in this little meek voice. Well, they should have turned up the volume on that, man [laughing] or they should have run it the way it actually happened. 'Cause I stood up for myself a lot better than that.

> "Listen, if I'm going to be famous for something, **I might as well be famous for who I am.** And *The Real World* was a true and fair representation of who I am."

I think I kept myself up pretty well. My hair was in place — most of the time. My taste in clothes was all right. Yeah, I could've worn a little more makeup in the morning. OK, I admit I made myself up a bit more than usual for the cameras. On a scale of 1 to 10, I was in '8' mode in terms of preparation, when I'm usually at '5' or '6.' Towards the end, I slacked off a bit as I got more comfortable...and more like myself.

But my true qualities did show. Like the morning the After School kids appeared at the Firehouse to sing to us, and I was such a grouch about getting up. That's me in the morning. If I don't get my sleep, then you'd better get out of my way [laughing].

My 7-Eleven call to Walter was the only time I was real embarrassed about something on the show. You remember the one...where I mentioned sending my panties to him. Of course, my phone rang immediately after that aired. It was Kameelah, who was breathing hard into the phone, saying, 'I've got these black lace panties I'd like to send to you!' Goodness, I thought I'd completely covered my mics that time. Those mics must be incredibly high-tech and expensive.

"But I'll tell you, as I watched *The Real World* episodes on TV... I was real proud of the way I handled that entire experience. I thought I did my best to reach out to every single person in the house. Like the way I was accepting of Genesis from the start. She said, 'I'm a lesbian.' And I responded, 'That's cool!' Given the fact I'd never known a lesbian before, I look back on that moment with pride.

I was the Julie, the Sharon, the Jay, or the Rachel of the Boston *Real World*. The person from a small town who has been very sheltered. I'd never had gay friends. Nor any friends, for that matter, like the others in the house. Everyone was either older than me or had lived in bigger towns—with the exception of Genesis. They'd all had more exposure to a variety of topics—from sex to drinking. On top of that, I was arriving soon after my mother's death. So I was this great story, if you can call me that.

Well, I felt like I accepted them all just the way they were. Like the way I was with Genesis. But I think some of them weren't always as accepting of me.

For example, I still can't understand why some people were so appalled that first day about my being Catholic. When I saw that episode of the night we arrived, I couldn't believe all those conversations that went on behind my back. Why were my roommates so hell-bent on corrupting me right from the start? Why couldn't they just accept that's the way I am?

If seven people are going to live peacefully together, then you have to compromise your own ways. I did. Some did not. Of course, I didn't prefer to be around that constant crude language. But I lived with it. Because if I *really* said what I thought or felt...it would have ruined me. It would have made me a complete outcast and exile. I just kept in mind that this is the way they were. And if I wanted to be accepted, I had to accept them, too.

Close Encounters

I speak with MONTANA the most, just about every week. And I talk to SEAN once a month. My father and I invited GENESIS to come down to Brownsville for Christmas, but we never heard back from her. So, I'm kind of mad at her and haven't spoken with her since. KAMEELAH and I have talked a few times, but not too regularly. And SYRUS and JASON are nearly impossible to get in touch with.

Impressions

Impression Given:

I think I came across to some people as a goody-goody. I don't believe I am, unless you compare me to the other six. I think some people thought I was really prissy the way I confronted Sean over his 'crusty underwear' comment. But where I come from, it's extremely inappropriate to talk to a girl that way. I think some people thought I was strange to still be a virgin, but those are the values I grew up with. Perhaps, around the country, people are just not used to seeing someone raised like I was.

Impression Desired:

I think from watching the show, people think I'm really quiet and meek. But I'm a much more outgoing person than the Elka they showed. I love having a good time. I'm not exactly 'Crazy Girl,' but I'm certainly a lot louder and more of an extrovert than the viewers would think. Look at my boyfriend, for goodness' sakes. He's no accountant. He's a rock star.

"And that's not to say that I didn't enjoy my *Real World* experience. It's one of the greatest things that's ever happened to me. Where else am I going to find people like Jason, Montana, Genesis, Syrus, Sean, and Kameelah...under one roof? You just don't run into people like that every day. At least, I don't. Not a group with such strong and conflicting personalities.

So much of me wanted to stay in Boston and have *The Real World* go on longer. I was also apprehensive about going home and not having my mom there. But I think those few days I'd spent in Brownsville during the show really eased the transition. It sort of broke my fall.

When I left Boston, my dad met me at the airport in Brownsville with a huge entourage and a big sign that read, 'Welcome Home Elka from *The Real World–Boston*.' It was such a wonderful welcome, it made me feel a lot less sad. Though I still felt kind of naked without the microphones and the cameras following me wherever I went. And frankly, I probably missed the attention a little bit too.

But my life's been good back here in the real world, especially now that I'm nearer to Walter. I'm enjoying my classes at UNLV and bit by bit getting over my mother's death. I've received so many wonderful cards from people who watched the episode about her. The cards and comments have really touched my heart. So, thank you all for sending them...thank you very much!

The Creators on Elka

Mary-Ellis:
Elka had each foot in a different culture—Mexican and American. She felt a responsibility to live up to both—and even more so, to live up to her family's expectations, particularly her father's. Having just gone through the tragedy of losing her mother, she was extremely vulnerable when she arrived in Boston. But Elka remained true to her ideals. Yet at the same time, she was still open-minded enough to embrace other points of view.

Jon:
I compare Elka a little bit to Jon from *Real World-L.A.* Like Jon, she was someone you'd have expected to be more narrow-minded. But she was usually one of the first to see another point of view. Like Jon, Elka was also the youngest in her cast. But she and Jon were in some ways the most mature of their respective groups. To her credit, Elka refused to side with either faction in the Boston house.

ELKA & WALTER

Elka: I really wanted to move to Las Vegas, so I could be nearer to Walter. But I was scared to ask my dad if I could go. I was just sure he was going to say no.

Last fall, I finally got around to it. I said, 'Dad, this is what I want to do. Hear me out before you say anything.' Well, instead of saying 'No,' he said I could go as long as I continued my education. I was stunned. I know he'd have preferred me to stay in Texas, but he understood how important Walter is to me. I think my being on *The Real World* also had a lot to do with it. He saw how I stood up to that challenge without compromising my —and his—values.

So, now I'm livin' in Las Vegas, and seeing a whole lot of Walter. We're really happy together now, and everything seems to be working out for the best.

Now, I know some of you are interested in only one thing. Like whether or not Walter and I have had sex. All I will say is that I still have the same view regarding premarital sex... that I plan to wait until I'm married. So, yes, I'm still a virgin.

Walter: A lot of people come up to me and ask, past-tense, 'Were you Walter? And were you going out with Elka on *The Real World?*' And I reply, 'I *am* Walter. And I *am* still going out with Elka in the real world.'

Elka and I are still very much in love. The magic is exactly the way it was when I got off the plane in Boston and hadn't seen her for ten months. I've never felt this way about anyone in my entire life.

So, sometime in the future... we'll *definitely* be heading down the aisle.

Celebrityhood

Best Part:
I am so glad I did the show, so it never bothers me when people recognize me. And I definitely feel good about the way I handled myself in Boston, so I'm not afraid of what they are going to say. Just about everyone I met has said something nice to me. Either, 'You helped me deal with my own loss.' Or, 'You represented Catholic girls in such a good way.' So, it's all been a very positive experience.

Worst Part:
No negative vibes, yet. No one's said, 'You were such a bitch.' Or, 'You really sucked.' And they've never been rude. No one hangs on to my sleeve for the entire evening. They just ask a few questions or get an autograph.

Besides, it would be real arrogant and selfish of me to say to some fan of the show, 'Get away from me.' After all, I remember how important it's been to me in the past whenever I've asked someone for an autograph. Although I must say, it's really, really strange to be the one signing autographs now. All I've done is appear on TV. But I didn't show any unique talent. I can't sing or act. I was just being me on TV.

The only major downside of my so-called fame is how hard it's been to make real friends since the show. People are affected by it one way or the other. Either they feel, for some reason, that they're not good enough and have to impress you. Or, they look down upon you for some other reason. It's been one extreme or the other. So, it's always refreshing to find a person who's never seen the show. Whenever I do, I'm like, 'Hey, want to be my friend?'

Coolest Celebrity Encounter:
I got to meet Neil from *The Real World - London.* I'd always had such a crush on him.

Above left: At eight months with her mom. *Above right:* With her dad after returning home from *The Real World-Boston.*

The Contract with Elka

ELKA'S DAD: When Elka was picked for *The Real World*, the producers sent her a 25-page contract to sign. I figured if she was willing to sign something like that for complete strangers, she ought to sign a one-page contract of my own.

So I put together a contract between us regarding her conduct in Boston. It said, 'I will not engage in any smoking, drinking, drugs or sexual activity....'

During the show, Elka wrote me saying that she'd broken one of our rules. I was so worried about which one. When I found out it was the one rule about smoking, I was so relieved that I felt like sending her a carton of cigarettes myself [laughing].

ELKA: The whole contract thing is kind of embarrassing, don't you think? Well, that's my dad for you. He likes to embarrass me [laughing]. You know there was nothing I could do. My dad required I sign it before he'd let me leave. I wasn't real worried about breaking any of the rules, except for the one about smoking.

I started smoking at the end of sophomore year in high school. I'd tried to quit many times before. When I got to Boston, everyone else was smoking so it was really hard to stop. But I didn't drink, do drugs, or have sex while I was in Boston. So I guess I lived up to three out of the four rules...and that's not too bad. And, I'm pleased to report, I stopped smoking New Year's Day, 1998...and haven't lit one up since!

Inquiring Minds

Most frequently asked question
Did I have a good time doing the show?
Elka's answer
Of course! Or else I would have left the house.
Strangest question
Can I get Syrus' phone number?
Elka's response
Who the hell are you [laughing]?
Most obvious question
Has anyone ever told you that you look just like that girl on *The Real World?*
Elka's answer
Oh, my God. Really?

Strictly platonic: Meeting Neil from *The Real World-London* at the wrap party for the Boston season, where Neil's band played.

the real world

A lot of people ask me if it was difficult doing *The Real World* so soon after my mother's death. It was very difficult. But I don't think *The Real World* could have come at a better time. I think if I'd stayed in Brownsville, I would have self-destructed. When I was in Boston, I thought about her every day. I mourned, but I didn't damage myself. Instead, I was being productive and expanding myself, which is something she would have wanted.

The first month back home was hard. The food smelled the same. The sounds were the same, but I was constantly aware of this big void. I'd be walking down the stairs in my house and I'd sound just like my mom used to.

I miss her a lot, but gradually it gets easier.

Kiss and Tell

MONTANA:

Elka's got sticky fingers. She's not real big on whatever commandment deals with stealing. She likes taking little knick-knacks and souvenirs wherever she goes. I was shocked the first time we walked out of a store together and she was giggling with a stolen 'I Love NY' key chain tucked in her pocket.

ELKA'S RESPONSE:

Yeah, it's true. Well, about the key chain, it's true. I took it. The line was incredibly long. And they were charging $5 for that little thing. It was such a rip off. But I'm not a 'klepto,' or anything. It was only that one time. Montana just assumed I did it all the time. Well, occasionally I'll take a small souvenir. But not big things. Jason is the one that takes big things. Like furniture. He's even stolen a car.

JASON'S RESPONSE:

Yeah, it's true. When I was 15, I stole a four-wheel drive off a car lot in Arkansas. I took it for a joy ride through the woods with a few friends of mine. We trashed it, then parked it back on the lot with a note that said, 'Thanks a lot for the ride.'

As for Elka, she's got a pretty clean record, I think—except for the fact that she chain—smoked the entire time. But we all did that.

Genesis

MOST FAVORITE: I had so many great moments, but I'd have to say my most gratifying moment was Mother's Day night. The house was empty, except for Elka and me. And we both stayed up 'til 7 o'clock that morning really opening up to each other. She talked about her mother and her childhood. And I told her all about mine. That night was special... and really therapeutic, too.

LEAST FAVORITE: The fight I had with Sean, definitely. Life's too short to waste time fighting. After that fight, we avoided each other for the next few months. What a waste! Instead of avoiding each other, we should have been getting to know each other better. We were both such idiots! I regret that fight ever happened.

"Frankly, I'm surprised any viewers can even remember my name. I figured no one would know who I am, 'cause I thought I was barely on the show. But It's turned out to be quite the opposite. In fact, I've gotten a ton of fan mail since the show. And people approach me all the time and tell me I changed their lives."

I've been told I made it easier for some gay women to come out of the closet. And some lesbians, who are attracted to drag queens, say they're no longer afraid to admit it, on account of me. That I've made some people feel more comfortable about themselves makes me feel good. Especially since I felt like I'd accomplished so little at the end of my stay in Boston.

You know, I was so intimidated inside that house. I just don't think my true colors ever showed. I'm usually an outgoing smart-a** back home. But in Boston, I was real quiet and separated myself from the others. The only time I ever really let go was when I fought with Sean over the Genesis-isms.

"The cameras made everything so intense. After I left Boston, I'd still hide in my bathroom for privacy even when no one else was in my house. To this day, I still feel like people are constantly watching me, or listening in on the other phone line. I guess I'm going through what you might call 'Real World withdrawal.'

I'm certainly far less open now than I was on the show. I feel like I gave away too much of myself, so now I don't disclose nearly as much. I'm also not as trusting of people as I was before. In the past year, I've been befriended by a number of people only to learn they had ulterior motives.

In Gulfport, there were false rumors spread that I'd made a lot of money from the show. Suddenly, all these girls were trying to be my friend or girlfriend...until I heard the rumors a month later and realized what they were doing. And in Orlando, several actresses and singers befriended me, thinking I was their meal ticket to MTV, then dumped me as soon as they learned I had no inside connections.

But I'm still really glad I did the show. It gave me a lot more confidence. It got me out of Gulfport, Mississippi, where I wasn't happy. I'd probably still be there living with Tammy, if I hadn't done the show. I wouldn't be in Orlando trying to keep the growth process going. And my friends were real proud of me for doing the show. Some of them teased me a bit. They told me my hair and makeup looked like s**t which it did. But they were real proud of the way I'd presented myself.

Best of all I never could have predicted the positive effect *The Real World* would have on my family. Since the show aired, we've gotten along so much better than we ever did before. When I first 'came out' to my family, they went upside down–particularly my grandparents, who raised me. For a couple of years after, we barely spoke and I never visited.

Impressions

Impression Given:

I'm not sure if it was intentional or not, but the show portrayed me like I was really confused about my sexuality. So people now come up to me all the time and ask, 'Have you figured out your sexuality yet?' Well, I figured it out years ago. Just 'cause you don't understand me, doesn't mean I'm the one that's confused. I know exactly who and what I am. And what I like.

Impression Desired:

When we were living in the Firehouse, I had lots of discussions with Kameelah and Jason about my sexuality. But for some reason, they never showed any of them. I think those would have explained where I stand. In short, I'm just me. I'm sexual. As far as labeling me, it's in the eye of the beholder. I'm attracted to transsexuals

and drag queens. To me, they're women. Not men. So, that would make me a homosexual. But because a drag queen has a penis ...he's technically a man. So, some people would label me a bisexual. Frankly, I don't care. For the sake of argument, just call me 'sexual!'

Well, last fall, I sent them a couple of tapes of our show. And I don't know what happened exactly, but all of a sudden they accepted my lifestyle like never before. Not just the fact that I like women...but drag queens, too. My grandfather even jokes now that he's going to put on one of my grandmother's dresses, so he can go to a drag club with me.

They've taken the mentality that whatever makes me happy, makes them happy, too. And that makes me feel really great. I go home all the time now. And for the first time in my life, I feel like I can talk to them about anything I want.

My mother is also doing better as well. After the episode aired about her falling off the wagon, she called me up crying and said I was the best daughter in the world. She hadn't raised me, so she'd never actually seen my reaction to one of her relapses. And since that episode aired, she's tried much harder to improve herself. For sure, it's been a struggle for her. But I think she's made progress.

You know, I must admit, I really miss *The Real World*. I even miss the cast members I didn't get along with so well. We may have argued, but we always had an underlying unity that made us a kind of family. I know what we did is now a TV show, but to me, it's a home-video of our time together.

Genesis and Tammy

The summer after I lived in Boston, I moved back to Gulfport. I needed a place to stay and moved back in with Tammy. Well, actually, I moved in with Tammy and her new girlfriend. They were in my old bedroom and I slept in the spare. Yes, it was

bizarre. I knew I didn't want to stay there, but kept prolonging it for some reason. Eventually, I moved out and in with friends. And then I moved to Orlando. But Tammy and I are still very close, and we talk a few times a week. She was all right with most of the stuff that appeared on the show. She got pissed off at me for the episode where I called her a bitch, the one where I was piss-poor and she refused to loan me any money. But after we discussed it, she said to me, 'You were right! I was being a bitch!'

The Creators on Genesis

Mary-Ellis:
I have such a special connection with Genesis. I really like her and worry about her. We've all been encouraging her to go back to school. Our company has an academic scholarship, which we award to one *Road Rule-r* and one *Real World-er* each season. We pick the winner based on who we think deserves a boost. We offered Genesis a scholarship, but she turned it down, and ever since then, she doesn't return our phone calls. I would just like to see Genesis make some positive choices in her life, to go for something that's good for her, not just party.

Jon:
Clearly, Genesis had a tough childhood. And it's been tough for her to overcome some ingrained behavior, which she's been stuck with. It's left her with major self-esteem problems. Every time she seems on the verge of lifting herself up, she falls back into a rut. All sorts of people, including Jason, have tried to help her since the show. But she's refused all of them. Frankly, I don't know if she can make it happen for herself on her own. If she can, wonderful. If not, I would hope she would accept some help.

Celebrityhood

Best Part:
Perhaps the only good thing about being a sort-of celebrity is that I seem to have touched a few people's lives. And that makes me happy.

Worst Part:
It upsets me that people now watch me like a hawk, especially when I'm in clubs. They stare at me for hours and hours. Whenever I go to the rest room, people watch me as if I'm going in there to do drugs. I've even heard rumors in Orlando that I'm a coke addict. Hell, no, I don't do drugs. When I'm at the drag clubs, I feel like I'm back on the show again. My privacy is totally being invaded.

Strangest Part:
I got a letter from a girl in Illinois, who wrote that she'd fallen in love with me and was leaving her boyfriend for me. She included a copy of a plane ticket, which she'd booked to Orlando. I was like, 'Holy s**t!' So, I stayed in my apartment the whole time she was scheduled to be in town. Thankfully, I never saw her, nor heard from her again.

Dating

The biggest impact of the show on my love life has been that I no longer feel guilty about what I'm attracted to... whether it's a woman or a drag queen. Since Boston, I've had only a few short-term relationships with women and drag queens. But now I feel free to date whomever I choose.

I'm not attracted to natural beauty. I'm attracted to people who are heavily made up. I like a lot of hair. I like fake nails. I like fake breasts. I like all that s**t. And I like someone that I can take care of, too. I want somebody who has trouble taking care of themselves, so I feel needed. I find that drag queens are needier than most women I know. Without question, *The Real World* has increased my standing in the drag queen community. It takes a lot of 'balls,' so to speak, just to become a drag queen. You have to put up with a lot. I think drag queens respect me for having been on *The Real World*. They know it took a lot of 'balls' putting myself through that as well.

Close Encounters

At first, I spoke with **JASON** and **KAMEELAH** just about every week. And **ELKA** nearly as often, but as time has gone on, we've either moved or gotten caught up in our regular lives. But I'd still like to keep in regular contact with those three. As for **SYRUS**, **MONTANA** and **SEAN**, I'm perfectly happy seeing or speaking with them whenever, but none of us really makes the effort. Occasionally, I'll run into one of them at a *Real World*-related event. But that's about it.

Kiss and Tell

JASON:
I got to see Genesis' bare breasts in Martha's Vineyard. And they are perfect, little breasts. Small and firm. She wants to get a boob job, but she's got great breasts just the way they are.

ELKA:
One day, I brought this children's Ouija Board back to the Firehouse. And I started secretly moving it around, as if it had powers of its own. Well, Genesis freaked out and started screaming, 'I'm getting really bad vibes,' and she was crying and everything. So, I convinced her the only way to get rid of the demons was to set the Ouija Board on fire. Well, we went outside and burned it in the middle of Beacon Hill.

Afterwards, she was like, 'Thank you, Elka. I feel so much better now. Now I can go to sleep.' And she was serious!

Inquiring Minds

Most frequently asked question
How was the experience?

Genesis' answer
It was the most amazing, eye-opening, horrifying situation you could possibly put yourself through.

Strangest question
Did you and Elka sleep together?

Genesis' response
No. And what could possibly make you think we did?

Kameelah

MOST FAVORITE: I really liked the scene where that guy hissed at me on the train platform. The one where I said to him, 'Don't address me like that!' That moment resonated with a lot of people I know. It sparked some discussion about how men ought to approach and respect females.

I also like the moment where I talked about homosexuals with the little girl at the community center. A teacher told me she uses that segment in one of her university classes. She says it serves as an example of how to talk to children about sexuality without confusing them.

LEAST FAVORITE: When Montana said to Sean that I ought to play Russian roulette by myself. I can accept them talking behind my back, but wishing I'm dead? That's plain evil!

> "Being on *The Real World* was like being a part of history—at least, a part of our generation's history. Someone who grew up in the 1960s might say, 'I went to Woodstock.' Now I can say, 'I was on The Real World.'"

It was the best experience I've ever had. A chance to leave my normal environment. To put myself in a pressure cooker...and see how I could respond.

Overall, I'm proud of the way I handled it. On top of that, I met some wonderful people. Got some free trips. And had a really good time...for the most part.

I learned some important things about myself doing the show. Like I laugh really loud [laughing really loud]. More seriously, though, I learned to be less tolerant of people that don't deserve it. I don't think I should have put up with Montana's and Sean's bulls**t as much as I did. She was constantly lying and always had to be the center of attention. He was always talking about people and being an instigator. So, now I don't feel guilty if I *piece* people out that behave that way. People like that are more trouble than they're worth.

"**M**y friends back home weren't so pleased with the way I was portrayed on the show. They thought it was a very negative and one-sided depiction of me and that one side was ugly and dark. My mom said they made me out to be the Angry Black Woman and I agree with her!

My views on race were definitely portrayed in a skewed fashion. They made me out to be pro-pro black...as well as anti-white. They made it appear like I segregated myself. That I only did black things with black people, and only spoke a black language. That wasn't, and isn't, the case at all.

They also misrepresented my views on interracial dating. Yes, I wanted to know why Syrus *only* went out with blond-haired, blue-eyed women. To me that's strange! Especially considering that Syrus was raised by a black woman. OK, so he says he dates all types of women. But that's not what he brought home...and actions speak louder than words.

As for my opinion of interracial dating, let me set the record straight: If a man is a good man, then I'll date him...regardless of color. However, I'm less likely to date white men, because

About Kameelah & Jason

SYRUS:
I still wonder if Kameelah and Jason fooled around. I'm pretty sure they did.

JASON:
I had the biggest crush on Kameelah, and she for me. But nothings ever happened.

KAMEELAH:
Nothing's ever happened with me and Jason. N-O. No!

my standard of beauty–or what I'm attracted to–tends toward black men. I just prefer their physical features and their essence, but that's not a rule. I'd never categorically say, 'I will not date white men.' Fact is...I already have.

Unfortunately, they cut out that conversation, the one where I told Syrus I dated a white man the year before the show. I sure wish they had not...'cause it would have made me seem less like a hypocrite for showing an interest in Jason.

The Real World is a beneficial experience, but a rough one, for sure. It whacks away at your self-esteem–first in the house, then once it's aired on TV. When you're in the house, these six strangers come down on you at one time. Then, you're forced to relive it again with the entire country, who walk up to you on the street and make comments and ask questions. So I'd say my self-confidence is about half of what it was before the show.

But then again, part of that has to do with my being back at Stanford. It's real hard here. I'm competing against a lot of knuckleheads, who are a lot more academic than I am. But I'm hanging in there and still doing the pre-med thing. Someday, I hope I'll be a gynecologist working with poor women in Africa.

I just don't see *The Real World* as the be-all and end-all of Kameelah. I mean, I was just 19... with at least 40 more years to go. I don't want to be referred to as 'the girl from *The Real World*' the rest of my life. Hopefully, I'll accomplish more than that in life. If not, that would be really sad.

The Creators on
Kameelah

Jon:
To her credit, Kameelah has made it all happen for herself. She got herself into Stanford, she's going pre–med. No doubt, she's extremely smart and motivated. But because she's had to do so much for herself, I think she's a little too intolerant of other people and their weaknesses and that's something she needs to work on.

Mary–Ellis:
Kameelah is really bright. She can be very funny and likable. But she also likes to push the envelope sometimes.

Celebrityhood

Best Part:
It depends on the day.

Worst Part:
It depends on the day.

Coolest Celebrity Encounter:
Not so long ago, I performed for my sorority at a hip-hop diaspora on campus. Chelsea Clinton, who's also a student at Stanford, was sitting right behind us. At one point, I got up and left the room. When I got back, several of my friends said that Chelsea was asking around, 'Is that *the* Kameelah from *The Real World?*, I thought that was kind of funny.

Close Encounters

I talk with **JASON**, **GENESIS** and sometimes **ELKA**. I speak with Jason and Genesis every few weeks. Unfortunately, I've been too busy with schoolwork to talk more often. But when we do hook up, it's usually for an hour and a half. We just get everything out in the air. Then, we hold it in for another two or three weeks 'til we talk again. Elka and I speak less frequently because she's in school, too. I don't talk to any of the others. I have no real interest or desire to. I spoke at a college in Indiana with **MONTANA**. We didn't fight. We were civil. We're not friends, but I still wish her the best.

Impressions

Impression Given:
From the feedback I've gotten, I came across as the angry black woman. I looked like I was always negative. Always giving my opinions. Always bossy. Miserable. Lonely. That I don't like white people. Basically, I don't think I came across as a nice person at all.

Kiss and Tell

JASON:
I saw Kameelah's naked breasts in Martha's Vineyard, the time Gen, Kameelah and I showed each other our private parts. And Kameelahs breasts are huge, and absolutely beautiful. Just big gorgeous breasts.

GENESIS:
Once, I totally trashed Kameelah's bedroom when she was out. I dumped everything of hers upside down. I toilet-papered her bed. I hung my gay pride flag over her pillow and I took this doll she sleeps with and hung it by its neck with a cigarette in its mouth.

Soon as she got home, she knew it was me. She dragged me out of my bed by my shirt and tried to force me to clean it up. So, I told her, 'Shut up, Kameelah! And get your black-ass into my bed.' And she ended up sleeping next to me the entire night.

Impression Desired:
I wish they'd given an impression of me more like I really am. I'm much more upbeat. Much more laid-back. Much more open-minded about race and other things. And much more fun. My mom was like, 'They don't know how many people call this house looking for you!' At first, she thought the portrayal of me was funny. But after a while, she said, 'This is not cool! You're not lonely and desperate. So, why are they portraying you this way?'

Dating

My love life hasn't been affected by the show. It's been affected by my major. Being pre–med takes up a lot of time. Though I will say that being on the show has made me a bit leery of guys. I don't want to be someone's trophy, like 'Hey, I'm with the girl from *The Real World*.' So I'm definitely more cautious when I meet guys. And some of them might've watched the show, so they may be leery of me as well. As for my 'list,' it's still active. And it still serves as a reminder of what I like.

The Firehouse

KAMEELAH: I've gone back to see the Firehouse one time. I never realized how big it was, until I saw it with all the stuff taken out. It was nice seeing it again, but a little sad.

MONTANA: Sean, Jason, Syrus, and I went back to the Firehouse just four months after the show. It was weird seeing it so empty. Everything's been stripped. It brought home the fact that *The Real World* was a one time shot. You can't go back!

SEAN: It was weird seeing it look so small and empty. It's kind of sad. Other people can go back and visit their home, but we can't.

SYRUS: It feels like a haunted house. It's pretty sad. But it didn't make me cry or nothing [laughing].

JIM JOHNSTON (*The Real World* producer): Just about everything is gone from the Firehouse now. The furniture's been removed and auctioned off to raise money for charity. The cameras, lights, and sound equipment are being used on another production. And the construction we did, except for a few walls, has been totally stripped away. The Firehouse is presently empty, but the nonprofit Beacon Hill Civic Association is planning on turning it into a multipurpose community center within the next few years. Still, it's bound to continue to be a local tourist stop, like the Cheers bar and Bunker Hill. In fact, if you take a trolley tour of Boston, they'll point it out as you drive by.

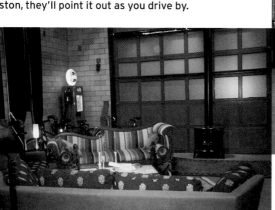

Did You Know?
The Real World–Boston Firehouse appeared as the home of Robert Urich's character in the 1980s hit TV series, *Spenser: For Hire.*

The After School Program

ANTHONY, former director of the After School Program:

A lot has changed at the After School Program since *The Real World–Boston* was last there. There's no more logrolling and no more model airplane-ing, either. And journaling is rarely done. Most of the regular staff is gone, too, included me. I'm now working on a remake of the popular 1970s kid's show, *ZOOM*, being produced in Boston.

But most of the kids are still there at the After School Program, and most are doing really well. I'd say that nearly all of them watched *The Real World* episodes, even the 9- and 10-year-olds. Of course, they were excited to see themselves on TV, though more than a few were upset by what they saw. Especially, seeing the sex, the drinking and arguing that went on in the house. Fact is, the show's not intended for kids that age. So the 9- and 10-year-olds probably shouldn't have been watching the program at all.

But to be honest, the parents were the most upset by what they saw. Of course, many of them were furious that Montana had given alcohol to two of the kids. And they had a right to be. Many parents also complained after the episode aired where Kameelah and Genesis talked about homosexuality with a few of the girls. The parents felt their kids were way too young to be discussing such topics, and they thought Kameelah wasn't qualified professionally to be leading such a discussion. Also, a number of parents were angry to learn that Syrus had dated one of the mothers.

Overall, I'd say that half the parents would have voted against letting the cast inside the ASP, if they'd known then what they saw later on TV. But– and it's a big but–every parent would agree the *Real World* experience–cast, crew and cameras– was a unique learning experience for their kids. A once-in-a-lifetime opportunity that none of their kids will ever forget.

Shelter, Inc.
MARK (Program Director at Shelter, Inc.):

We don't often have MTV on at the shelter, so not many of our residents caught *The Real World.* As for the staff, we were anxious about how we might be portrayed [laughing]. After all, Montana's character was involved in so much conflict throughout the show. But in the end, we were quite pleased the Shelter provided Montana's character with her happy ending.

The Real World was a positive experience for us, too. Especially for the women that come to the drop-in center. It brought excitement and glamour into their lives. I know they appreciated someone from a TV show donating their time. They looked forward to the desserts Montana made and the hairstylist she arranged. And, even more importantly, the women enjoyed the direct contact they had with Montana whenever she was around.

Jason

MOST FAVORITE: When I showed my d**k to Kameelah and Genesis. That entire trip to Martha's Vineyard was such a cool time. Showing my bean. Hitchhiking around the island. They portrayed it just the way it was.

LEAST FAVORITE: The fight I had with Timber outside the bar. It was a nightmare at the time. But having to relive it again on video makes it doubly worse. I'm also not particularly proud about the scene where I kissed that girl. Timber decided not to watch that one.

"I've never had this many women approach me in all my life. **It's fame. It's TV. F**king TV. It surely has little to do with me—the real me.** They see me on television, and they're like, I want to meet that guy. You know, it's about bragging rights. 'Hey, I f**ked the guy on *The Real World*.' Or, 'Hey, I smooched the guy in the Boston house.' A little bit of fame makes you somehow more attractive. Heck, I don't look any different than I did before *The Real World*."

Some of the girls can be really forward, too, especially the 18- and 19-year olds. They seem so much more forward than ones I knew. Now, I don't want this to seem egotistical. Most girls just want to ask me questions. Some want to take photos. But, occasionally a girl will come up to me and say, 'You want to come to my room and make out?' It's happened about ten times. And each time it's blown my mind.

When I was 20, I used to go home with girls and not give a s**t. Now I don't want to get with every girl I possibly can. I guess it has to do with self-respect. In the past, I'd wake up feeling s**tty afterward. But I'd prefer to wake up with a girl and actually want to have a cup of coffee with her...not just want to get the hell out of there. I've had too many one-night stands. It kind of chips away at you after a while.

"I guess it all comes down to self-respect. Which is also the reason why I stopped drinking as much alcohol as I used to. Before, during, and immediately after the show I was getting drunk all the time. Perhaps, it was 'cause I couldn't think of anything better to do with myself. I suspect it was a way of coping with the stress. A bad way, at that!

But seeing the way I looked and acted on some of those episodes woke me up. I hated seeing my body that way. I'd lost so much weight. And most importantly, I wasn't all there mentally. I'd be drinking four-and-five times a week in Boston. So, a lot of those episodes I was a wet-brain. My mind was working real slow, and that pissed me off. I wasn't alert enough to say the things I really wanted to say on the show.

Mary-Ellis, one of the *Real World* creators, talked to me about it after the show. She was real worried about me, kind of like a mother-figure. So I tried being sober for two weeks. And gradually, I could see my brain returning to its proper function. I started eating right. Lifting weights. Getting my s**t together. I feel much better now. I still drink, but much less frequently.

I learned a lot by watching myself on *The Real World*. You can't overlook your character flaws when they're in plain sight for everyone to see. It's a great f**king tool for working on yourself. I'd watch the show and say, 'S**t, I don't like that about myself.' I realized I can be really defensive for no reason. I need to relax and chill more. I'm also never cutting my hair that short again. I looked like a dork [laughing]!

Sometimes, it could be rough watching the episodes. But most of the time it was just good ol' fun. My friends and I would cook up a big fat barbecue and catch the shows each week. They'd just laugh at me. They'd totally give me s**t when I was being a d**k. And during the commercial breaks, I'd either call up Genesis or Kameelah, or they'd call me.

Like, Genesis would ring up. 'Why'd you say this and that about me in your confessional?' Or one time, Genesis criticized me for the way I was talking to Timber. I dialed her straight away and said, 'What the f**k? You're making it look like I talk down to my girlfriend.' She explained what she meant...and all was right with the world.

Listen, *The Real World* opened my eyes to a much bigger world. Man, it got me out of Colorado, which I needed to do. It introduced me to the TV and movie industries, which is where I hope to work. And it made me believe I can accomplish anything I want. Hell, getting picked for the show is an accomplishment in and of itself.

So, someday I hope to be a movie star. And a director, too. Right now, my goals are a little less ambitious. I'm trying to score a gig as a production assistant. Heck, I'd be a coffee-boy as long as I got to learn and meet people. And then, who knows.

JASON & TIMBER

My relationship with Timber continues to be as off-and-on as it was on the show. We moved out to San Francisco together, but then decided to get our own places. We were engaged for a short period in early '98. And now we're not. We got engaged because we thought it was a good idea at the time. Then we got together with some engaged friends, looked at their lives and decided it wasn't such a good idea any more. Our relationship is a weird one, no question about it. We've been together two-plus years and I love her very, very much. But God knows what's going to happen to us in the future.

Above: **Took these at a bar called the 'Elbo Room'.**
Left: **Timber and me getting some sun in Arkansas. We spent half the summer here drinking beer and recovering from Boston.**

Celebrityhood

Best Part:

Free meals and drinks. When I'm broke, it's especially cool.

Worst Part:

So far there haven't been any bad parts. I think if I were really famous, it would really suck, because then I couldn't go anywhere without being mobbed. But that certainly isn't the case now.

Coolest Celebrity Encounter:

I got to meet movie director Ron Howard, the guy that directed *Apollo 13* and also starred on *Happy Days*. He was filming the movie, *ed TV*, in the lobby of the Castro Theater in San Francisco. It's a movie about a guy who gets followed around by a camera 24 hours a day. Pretty ironic, huh? Well, I snuck on the set and introduced myself. I told him that I'd been on *The Real World* and we talked for ten minutes. He was incredibly nice and let me hang around and watch him direct. It looked like the coolest job in the world.

Impressions

Impression Given:

I think the first impression I gave viewers was that I was an a**hole, especially the way I greeted Sean. I looked like some kind of conceited-poet-type-wanna-be-James Dean-hipster-f**khead. At least, that's the impression I've gotten from people who watched the show. They say to me, 'I didn't like you at first. Then, I started liking you. And at the end, you were the only one I liked!' I've heard that about 50 million times.

Impression Desired:

That I'm just like the viewers. Just trying to figure things out like everyone else. And not some wanna-be-cool-hipster-poet guy.

Above: In my hometown of Russellville right before I rode my motorcycle to Graceland.

Close Encounters

It's cool 'cause everyone in the cast is more themselves now. Like they're relaxing back into who they were before the Firehouse. MONTANA seems more centered and happy. She's lost a bunch of weight and looks great. I like Vaj a lot, but I think it's been a good thing for Montana to separate herself from that relationship. ELKA also appears to be doing really well. I visited her and Walter in Las Vegas when I was driving through. I thought it was a big growing step for her moving out there to be with him. It took a lot of courage for her to tell her dad what she wanted to do, and then do it. GENESIS is looking real good 'cause she's happy...and 'cause she spends all her money on clothes. I'm glad she got herself out of Gulfport. I thought I might have to pack

her bags and drive her out of there, 'cause that place was getting her down. Someday, we might live together in Los Angeles, but she likes living in Orlando now.

I haven't spoken that much with SYRUS. But he seems to be happy back on the West Coast. I'm sure I'll see him more, now that I'm in his neck of the woods. SEAN and KAMEELAH have changed the least. Sean is pretty much a constant–happy-go-lucky. He and I hated each other at the end of the show. But he called me up after we left Boston and we talked for a couple of hours. Ever since, we've had a great time partying together.

And KAMEELAH. . . well, Kameelah is always the same. Always strong!

Mary-Ellis:
Jason is enormously likable and smart. He's also in search of something in his life. What he's searching for exactly, I'm not sure. I think he's seeking something solid in his life, which has been missing. In the past, he's tried to fill it with drugs and alcohol. But I understand he's doing less of that now and that's wonderful news! You know, Jason always has interesting plans. Often times, he's gotten in his own way of realizing them. If he can just make some positive choices and impose self-discipline, he's capable of accomplishing a lot of great things with his life.

Jon:
Since the show aired, I think Jason has begun to come to terms with many of his issues. I think the *Real World* experience helped him in that regard. It forced him to take a hard look at himself and see how he was living his life. And it seems he's now moving his life in a positive direction.

Inquiring Minds

Most frequently asked question

Do you still talk to the other cast members?

Jason's answer

Yes, I've either seen or talked with all of them.

Most forward request

A beautiful woman, whom I'd never met before, walked up to me in a bar and asked, 'Will you sleep with me?'

Jason's response

I really wanted to go with her, but I told her, 'No. I'm sorry. I don't know you.' In retrospect, I'm not sure what I was thinking [laughing.]

Most requests

I did a *Real World* appearance at a college in northern New York and 30 girls gave me their phone numbers. I got little notes saying, 'Come over and I'll cook you dinner.' That really freaked me out. The first thing I did was call Sean and say, 'Hey, I just got 30 phone numbers, and I didn't even

ask for any of them.' And Sean replied, 'That's exactly what's happening to me.' But you know, a lot of girls like Sean. And nothing close to that had ever happened to me.

Jason and Kalle of *Road Rules*

JASON: Kalle and I have hung out together a little bit. But nothing sexual has ever happened. Yeah, we lay in bed together one late night. But we were just playing with each other's hair. Yeah, we thought about it. But didn't do it. God, it was tempting, though. She's a gorgeous woman.

Kiss and Tell

SYRUS:
Jason doesn't wear any underwear. One day, he borrowed Sean's corduroys and walked six miles in them. But he put them back in Sean's closet without washing them. My boy, 'Sweaty N*ts', is *nasty*!

Also, remember the girl Jason got caught kissing at that party? Well, a friend of mine had told her beforehand that Jason was a porn star.

MONTANA:
Jason liked to use self-tanner in Boston. He would rub tanning lotion into his face, so it would bronze him.

ELKA:
I've heard that Jason intentionally played up the depressed poet-thing for the cameras.

*   *   *

GENESIS:
Kameelah and I saw Jason's penis in Marthas Vineyard. Now, it was the first penis I'd ever seen, but I thought it was huge myself. I'm serious! It wasn't as scary as I thought it would be. But let me tell you, that Jason's a little boy, but he's not hung like one. I was real impressed. I just figured all little men had little, bitty packages. But not Jason. He's got a pretty penis, I must say.

KAMEELAH:
It was an 'A.'

Real World HONOR

	Elka 	Genesis 	Jason 	Kameelah 
Most likely to become president	Montana and Kameelah It would sure be a bitter campaign between the two of them.	Kameelah She's not a bulls**tter, unlike Sean who'll tell you everything you want to hear. I hope the fact that she's not, wouldn't hurt her chances.	Nobody But President of the Players Club? Syrus. President of Virgins of America? Elka. President of Lesbians for Liberation? Genesis. President of Slackers of America? Me.	Jason He's intelligent. But he's not part of the establishment. I think the country is getting away from bulls**tters, like Sean.
Most likely to go to prison	Montana and Sean They're partners in crime.	Me I've been around a lot of illegal activity the past year. I'm surprised I haven't been arrested yet. A lot of my drag friends do drugs, though I never do any myself.	Me I'm the only one in the house who's ever stolen a car. When I was 15. Thank God I never got caught. And I returned it, too.	Jason Because he's the most likely to be President.
Most likely to appear in a tabloid	Me It would probably read, 'Elka Finally Loses Her Virginity!'	Montana She's a drama queen.	Montana Because she dreams of becoming a professional wrestler. And that would certainly hit the tabloids.	Montana She likes being the center of attention.
Most likely to join the clergy	Montana I think her Virgin Mary night-lite is a sign she's heading for a conversion. Deep down, that girl loves God.	Me Because at one time, I planned on becoming a nun. And besides, I lead a totally celibate life.	Elka She's the only one of us who has any God in her.	Jason I think he has a very intense, spiritual side.
Most likely to win the Nobel Peace Prize	Jason and Me We were the floaters in the house that went back and forth between the two factions.	Kameelah She's extremely intelligent and capable of winning anything.	Me Because I had to negotiate between both sides of the Firehouse.	No one None of us is mature enough to deserve it.
Most likely to marry a billionaire	Sean He needs someone to keep him in the lifestyle he's grown accustomed to.	Elka I can see her becoming the wife of a billionaire rock-and-roll star.	Syrus I could see Syrus meeting a really rich chick and marrying her.	Me 'Cause it's all about the *Benjamins*.

ROLL

 Montana	 Sean	 Syrus
Sean Because he's a straight, white male.	**Syrus** He's such a people-person.	**Montana** Based on the way Clinton is going, she'd fit right in.
Jason He'd be the first to participate in deviant behaviors.	**Jason** Definitely. He's such a shady character.	**Jason** He's kind of wild. Although, I might be the most likely to be arrested... but I didn't do it.
Me For some reason, I can't prevent myself from having a lot of fun in public.	**Montana** She's just so scandalous.	**Montana** Without a doubt, based upon some of the stuff I've read about her on-line.
Genesis Then, she could give up her sexuality altogether and stop trying to figure it out.	**Genesis** One day, she'll come to the realization she can't figure out men and women. So, she'll go to God, instead.	**Elka** She's just about the only one of us who doesn't drink alcohol. Only over-the-counter cold remedies.
Kameelah She wants to go into medicine. That's a noble profession.	**Kameelah** Beause she was always *piecing* people out.	**Me** 'Cause I'm a pretty noble guy.
Elka Her lifestyle doesn't come cheap.	**Elka** She's consumed with money and power.	**Me** There are loads of billionaires out where I live.

Montana

MOST FAVORITE: I liked the scene where Sean, Jason, and me came home slightly tipsy and wrecked Elka's bed. Then, we all messed around on top of the pool table. Elka got so upset. I think her comment was: 'I've never seen drunk people be so crass and vulgar in my entire life. Not even on Spring Break!'

LEAST FAVORITE: My least favorite moment involved my phone conversation with Vaj, where he called me a whore and several other names. There were times I wished the cameras weren't around. That was one of them. It was hard living through that moment—let alone having it shown on TV again and again.

> **"Being on *The Real World* was like being in the middle of a gladiator ring.** There are a million spectators in the bleachers watching you. And then you're put into a pit with six other people to see who comes out alive. I think we all came out alive."

In fact, I'm proud of us for getting through the experience. It's been a very strange and stressful time. High stress, indeed. When things have been good...they've been great! When bad...they've been horrible!

Looking back on Boston, I think I should have let things slide more. But at the time, everything seemed so all-important. When you're living in a *Real World* house, you feel like you've got to represent so many different things—in my case, myself, my family, women, women from New York...on and on.

Without question, the show broke down my confidence a bit. I've been rebuilding it ever since. But I do think I've become a better person as a result of this entire experience. I've seen parts of myself I'm not particularly proud of.

For example, I didn't like the way I handled the situation with Syrus at the After School Program when he dated one of the moms. In retrospect, I should have talked to Syrus first, rather than to the director, Anthony. I would never do that again, and I've apologized to Syrus for that.

"Of course, you can't beat yourself up forever about mistakes like that. I guarantee you that anybody would be embarrassed by their own behavior if a camera followed them around for six months. Listen, I was only 21 when I did the show. I'm still learning things in life. God, I certainly hope so.

It's a pretty scary proposition watching yourself like that. Initially, it was just so strange seeing myself from so many different angles. Like most people, I'm used to seeing myself only in a mirror—straight-on. I never see myself eating, drinking, and sleeping from three-quarters position. So at first, I'd see myself on TV and think, 'Geez, I crinkle my nose in a weird way when I laugh.' But eventually, I was able to sit back and focus on the story lines.

Generally speaking, the episodes were fairly representative of what went on in Boston. But viewers must also keep in mind the show is not total reality. Anyone who takes it for gospel has mental problems. Scenes and dialogue are inserted out of context all the time. One time, they showed me upstairs playing pool with Matt. Then, cut to me downstairs calling Vaj on the phone. Back and forth they went several times, as though I were running back and forth between the guys. But in reality, those two moments occurred two weeks apart. Next time it's repeated on MTV, just take a look! My hair and

Above: The face of victory in the aftermath of the *Road Rules/Real World Challenge.* *Right:* At work in the super-glamourous offices of media behemoth MTV.

clothes are different, but close enough, so you might not notice. The editors thought no one would be able to, so they tried to make me look much more scandalous than I was.

My mom really liked the entire season. She really got into it. After the first episode aired, she called me up and said, 'Well, you looked cute in this one scene. But in the other, your bangs were all messed up.' And I was like, 'Mom, you can't do this for the next 22 weeks. You've got to let it go, 'cause there's nothing I can do about it now.' And she did.

She wasn't upset by any of the things I did—like the stuff with Vaj or getting fired from the After School Program. Her reaction was, 'Hey, I was once 21, too.' My grandma was real cool with it as well. Fact is, I'd rather my family see the stuff I do, than people I don't know.

Now that the show is over, I feel like I deserve my privacy back. I was willing to let people into my life for six months, but not for the rest of my life. I will tell you, however, that I expect to graduate from college in June 1999. And I hope to continue to work for MTV where I've been temping for the past year. It's been great fun working there, especially when *The Real World–Boston* is on the air. I've worked at one of the MTV reception desks, where six television sets are tuned to MTV directly behind me. One time, the 'real me' was receiving a guest at reception, while the 'TV me' was fighting with Vaj. So when I work at reception, I change the channel.

Ultimately, I want to go to grad school for museum education and study art-curriculum development. And, one day, I'll find a nice man...settle down...and squeeze out a few pups! Oh yeah, and one more thing: the other day I was doing body shots of tequila with a couple of 10-year-olds [laughing]. And then I remembered drinking with minors is wrong. Who knew? No one ever told me.

Impressions

Impression Given:

I think viewers got the impression I'm really confrontational, and really wild. In fact, people are always surprised when they meet me now. They say I'm a lot more mellow than they thought I'd be.

Impression Desired:

I don't think I'm as argumentative, opinionated, or confrontational as I appeared to be on *The Real World.* Those scenes just happened to make for good television. Overall, I'm a lot more mellow than they made me out to be.

Montana & Vaj

MONTANA:
A number of people have asked me if Sean and I hooked up. Once and for all, we didn't. And we haven't since the show either!

VAJ AND I BROKE UP last February. Basically, I think the relationship just ran its course. After a year and a half together—including six months following the show—it was time for us to move on. The decision was mutual. Things are amiable between us, and we still speak every so often.

I think questioning my relationship with him was a major reason why I went to Boston in the first place. Clearly, it was the reason why I wanted to see other people. I thought those six months might be a good way to reflect on my feelings for Vaj, and finally decide once and for all if we were truly right for each other.

In retrospect, I should have been more direct with him. I should have said, 'I'm having these doubts. It's better we stop while I'm away, and then see what happens when I return.' Instead of my trying to keep our relationship going.

But I don't think I did anything wrong by dating Matt. Vaj and I agreed we could see other people. He did, so why couldn't I? Yes, I find it uncomfortable to watch that Valentine's Day episode, where I kiss Matt prior to Vaj's arrival. But believe me, a lot of people have done a lot worse.

Vaj didn't watch too many of the episodes, particularly none of the ones involving us. He never liked *The Real World* from the beginning. He finds the whole show distasteful. He always has. And, truthfully, I think that's his prerogative.

Dating

Typically, the kind of guys I tend to date aren't big *Real World* watchers. And that's a good thing, because I prefer dating people who haven't seen the show. When I meet a guy who's really into it, I figure he's only into me 'cause I've been on *The Real World*. It also throws a weird dynamic into a relationship. They know so much more about you than you know about them. And what they've seen, furthermore, is not exactly an accurate picture of who I am. Sometimes, getting recognized can be problematic for dates. Not so long ago, I was on a first date with a guy. And we were eating outside when two girls came up to us. One of them said, 'Where's Vaj?' I told her that me and Vaj had broken up. And they're like, 'Oooh, I liked him.' And I'm like, 'Well, then yoouu date him.' I felt bad for my poor date. Not exactly an ideal way to start a new relationship.

Celebrityhood

Best Part:

We're not very big celebrities, but we do get free stuff from time-to-time. Bartenders will give me free drinks, and occasionally free meals, too. Vaj and I once got bumped up to first class. It was when we were going to visit Sean in Wisconsin. The woman at the ticket counter looked at my ticket and said, 'S**t, I just knew that was you. Glad to see you two are still together.' I guess she'll be disappointed if I run into her again.

Worst Part:

One time, I was really sick and ran to a pharmacy to buy antacid. I was trying to get out of there as quickly as possible without throwing up. Well, just as I was about to leave, these young girls from out of town rushed up to me. 'Oh, can we take a picture with you?' they asked. Of course, I wanted to say 'No,' but I said 'Yes,' instead. And I'm sure when they got home and developed their pictures, they must've thought, 'God, she doesn't look very good in person.'

Coolest Celebrity Encounter:

I got to meet Mike Myers at the Video Music Awards in New York. His wife even recognized me from the show, which was exciting. She said she makes her husband watch the show with her.

Inquiring Minds

Most frequently asked question

What was it like?

Montana's answer

Sometimes, it was really cool. And sometimes, it really sucked!

Strangest question

I walked into a bar and this girl asked me, 'Oh, my God. I've been dying to ask you this question. Are you a Leo?'

Montana's response

'No, I'm an Aries.' She said, 'Thank you.' And walked away.

Most unusual gift recieved

There's one boy who sent me a big box of loose tea. All these different flavors of loose tea. Apparently, he'd seen me drinking tea one time on the show and decided to send me a box of it. I liked the tea. I still drink it. Yeah, I like gifts.

a real world reunion

As you may recall from the show, I grew up not knowing my father. I met him only once when I was an infant, so I have no memory of him at all. When I was eight, I sent him a letter telling him who I was. He sent it back unopened.

Sometime during the airing of *The Real World-Boston*, my paternal uncle was channel-surfing and happened upon MTV. He saw this girl named Montana, who had red hair and looked like some other people he knew. I resembled a half-sister of mine, whom I'd never met, and looked like his brother—my dad—and even acted like him, too.

So, he started watching the show each week. And by the Puerto Rico episode, the one where I spoke about my father, he was sure I was somebody he knew.

After much deliberation, he decided to call up MTV to check on my exact identity. Fortunately, a friend of mine was working reception that day. She knew my personal story and immediately called me at home.

'This man just called,' she said, 'claiming to be your uncle.'

'I don't have an uncle,' I said.

'Your dad's brother,' she replied.

Well, long story short...of course, I was shocked. I rang my uncle back and the rest is history. Since then, my family circle has grown fivefold. I've spoken with my paternal grandparents in Texas and several others from that side. Just hearing their excitement makes me realize that my father's absence was his own trip, and not the result of something I did.

As of now, I still haven't met my father. It's a scary proposition for both of us. But I know it's only a matter of time. I always figured some things I'd never get to have in my life, like being walked down the aisle by my dad. Now I feel like I might get that, too.

Close Encounters

I've seen everyone since Boston. I talk to SEAN several times a week and ELKA nearly as often. The three of us talked all the time when the show was airing. Like Sean would call to ask, 'Did it look like I had a gut in that scene?'

I spent ten days with Sean over Christmas in his hometown of Hayward, Wisconsin. Vaj came, too. In fact, Sean's brother is a dentist and he fixed my tooth for free. Went for the social call... stayed for the free dental work.

After I broke up with Vaj, Elka tried convincing me to come room with her in Las Vegas. But I can't see myself living there, though it would be nice to see her more often.

I speak with SYRUS as frequently as possible. JASON is rarely in one location, but we try to stay in touch.

And KAMEELAH and GENESIS I might see at a speaking engagement from time to time. Whatever animosity existed among us three has dissipated now. I'm glad we're no longer living together. But we're certainly cordial.

The Creators on
Montana

Mary-Ellis:
Montana has really turned her *Real World* experiences into an asset and advantage for herself. She's in tremendous demand as a speaker on college campuses, because she's really a gifted speaker. Funny. Smart. Engaging. She's someone who's going to be real fun to watch as she grows into a full adult. I look forward to seeing what she does with her life.

Jon:
Montana has made the most of her *Real World* experiences just the way she handled herself in the Boston house. She got fired from the After School Program, but ended up succeeding at the shelter. The fact that she doesn't take herself too seriously has something to do with it. Like the time when Sean and Syrus played a practical joke on her. They told her she'd been voted out of the house for getting fired. Well, she was able to laugh at herself the moment she discovered they'd tricked her. Not everyone could have done that.

BEST +

		DRESSED	HYGIENE	COOK	TABLE MANNERS
ELKA	BEST ▶	**Syrus and Me** I've got a good sense of style, and Syrus picks beautiful colors.	**Me** I was the only one who cleaned the fish tanks.	**Kameelah** She could make any number of things.	**Syrus and Sean** Rarely did you ever see their elbows on the table.
	WORST ▶	**Jason** He wore the same clothes every day.	**Jason** Just smell his boots!	**Me** I can't cook, period. All I can do is mac and cheese.	**Jason and Kameelah** Both of them were atrocious.
GENESIS	BEST ▶	**Kameelah** I love her style. Very casual, but very classy.	**Kameelah** She always smells good. The girl can kick it with the perfume.	**Kameelah** That girl knows how to make *good* cornbread.	**Elka** She's very prim and proper about everything.
	WORST ▶	**Me** I had to borrow winter clothes. I was always mixing and matching.	**Montana** It's unhygienic for her not to shave under her arms.	**Me** I made chicken that was raw inside and burnt outside.	**Jason** He'd stick gum on his plate and chew it when he finished eating.
JASON	BEST ▶	**Elka** She has nice clothes. And she looks good in them.	**Syrus** He always smelled good. Like a Player.	**Kameelah** Without a doubt.	**Elka** She was very prim and proper about everything.
	WORST ▶	**Sean** He dresses like a frat boy–jeans and a T-shirt. Every day!	**The cameramen** They had to carry 35-pound cameras. Sometimes they just stunk.	**The rest of us** Without a clue.	**Me** I was the worst, for sure!
KAMEELAH	BEST ▶	**Jason** He's an original. He doesn't buy labels. He buys what he likes.	**Syrus** He's always very conscious of his appearance.	**Me** I was the only one who cooked.	**Elka** She's very polite. She's had home training.
	WORST ▶	**Montana** She did what Jason did. But she couldn't pull it off.	**No one** No one had bad hygiene.	**Sean** When he cooked, he made himself sick.	**Jason** He didn't give a f**k. If he needed to burp, he'd let it rip.
MONTANA	BEST ▶	**Syrus** He's got style and a ton of clothes. And he loves shopping.	**Elka** She's partial to feminine deodorant sprays.	**Kameelah** She did the most cooking of anyone in the house.	**Elka** She's just a little princess.
	WORST ▶	**Me** I never buy clothes.	**Jason** He doesn't wear underwear and he wears clothes over and over.	**Elka** All she knows how to make is macaroni and cheese.	**Jason** He licks knives.
SEAN	BEST ▶	**Syrus** He's always aware of how he looks. And he always looks tops.	**Me** I was pretty clean, except for those hives.	**Kameelah** She was the only one I ever saw *really* cook in the house.	**Me** In terms of manners, I was the best raised of the whole bunch.
	WORST ▶	**Montana** She shops at thrift stores. And her stuff looks like s**t.	**No comment** He knows who he is.	**Elka** The only thing she can cook is macaroni and cheese.	**Jason** He was the pig of the house.
SYRUS	BEST ▶	**Me** The others in the house would wear my clothes.	**Me** I always smell fine. Cleanliness is next to Godliness...and Syrus.	**Kameelah** She left a dinner for me one night that was pretty good.	**Elka and Me** She and I were brought up right.
	WORST ▶	**Sean** But we transformed him. He got 'most improved'.	**No comment** The offenders know who they are.	**Elka** All she could make was macaroni and cheese.	**Jason and Kameelah** Jason curled food on his tongue and Kameelah pulled it out.

WORST

MUSIC	DANCER	PICKUP ARTIST	SEX LIFE	
Me 'Cause my boyfriend, Walter, is the lead singer in the best band.	**Kameelah** She can definitely bust a move.	**Syrus and Sean** They were always arm-in-arm with a new girl each night.	**Montana, Sean, and Syrus** The three little musketeers got plenty.	
Sean and Montana They're still stuck on AM radio.	**Sean** He has two left feet.	**Genesis and Me** We were the ones stuck at home every night.	**Me** I don't know anything about that stuff.	
Elka She has a little bit of everything—from alternative to slow jazz.	**Kameelah** Especially when she does those step shows.	**Jason** He's like a girl, the way he uses his eyes. He just lets it happen.	**Syrus** He got the most action of all of us.	
Jason He only likes male artists and I prefer female ones.	**Sean** He dances like a typical white boy.	**Sean and Syrus** They make a competition out of it.	**Me** Elka's a virgin by choice. I haven't had sex in three years.	
Me 'Cause anyone who listens to Elvis, Ella, and Duke is happening.	**Nobody** No one could cut a rug worth a s**t.	**Syrus** He picked up the most.	**Syrus and Me** We both got it. Me from one woman. Sy from many.	
Elka She lives in the bush.	**Sean** He's from Wisconsin. Need I say more?	**Me** I get really stupid and awkward.	**Elka and Genesis** One's a virgin. The other got none.	
Me I like my music.	**Me** But I never saw Syrus dance.	**No comment** It's nothing I'd be proud of.	**Jason** 'Cause he had a real girlfriend.	
Sean and Montana I don't like their country rock. It's not my cup of tea.	**All the rest** 'Cause I saw the others dance.	**Me** It's something I'm not big on.	**No comment** I don't care to know what other people did in bed.	
Jason He likes all the music I do.	**Kameelah** She can dance!	**Syrus** He's got the rap down pat.	**Tie** I'd say a few of us in the house were in the running.	
Sean His all-time favorite is Meat Loaf.	**Sean** Have you seen him try to dance?	**Elka** She's already got her man.	**Genesis** She didn't seem like she was getting a whole lot.	
Me I have the hippest variety of Top 40 and country.	**Me** I've got the moves of a midwestern boy.	**Syrus** He's so smooooooth.	**Kameelah** She got it all the time from Doug.	
Syrus He listens to that nerdy hip-hop music.	**Montana** She thinks she's so great, when in reality... she sucks.	**Me** I'm not too good at that stuff.	**Genesis** She didn't get any, and she's not even sure who she wants it from.	
Me Definitely!	**Kameelah** She was always dancing around.	**Me** Undoubtedly!	**?** Depends on what you're into.	
Sean Garth Brooks just ain't my cup of tea.	**Montana** She thinks she's a white girl with rhythm... She's just a white girl.	**Jason** His rap needs a little refining.	**Elka** 'Cause she never got any. At least, I don't think so.	

Sean

MOST FAVORITE: I really liked the sequence where we picked up the log in Maine. Jason and I are singing together in the truck with Syrus alongside. That's exactly who I am. A happy-go-lucky guy. The three of us bonded that day.

LEAST FAVORITE: The scene where I called Kameelah a bitch. If you recall, it occurred when we got lost returning from the East Boston Social Center. The reason I hate that scene is not because I called Kameelah a bitch, but because I apologized to her at the end of the argument. After watching that scene on TV, I wish I could go back to that moment and call her a bitch once more, 'cause that's how she was acting. I should not have apologized.

> *The Real World* was truly the best experience of my life. When else in my life would I get to have people walk into my house as guys, and leave as girls?

Like with Genesis' drag friends. When would that ever happen to me? Or when else would I ever get to be cultured in the African-American experience the way Syrus cultured me? Rarely, if at all. All those experiences were wonderful for me. I think I might have been a really stale person had I not done the show. It opened my eyes to a lot of different things.

Before *The Real World*, I'd *piece* people out for a variety of reasons—from the color of their skin to their sexual preference. I won't lie to you and say I've stopped doing that entirely, because everyone does a bit of *piecing*. But I give people more of a chance now, and reserve judgment until I really know what they're like.

If I could do *The Real World* again, I'd even do it with the same six. As time passes, I've softened up toward the other people in the house, including the ones I didn't get along with—namely, Kameelah and Genesis. I arrived in Boston wet behind the ears. I didn't know much about black people and lesbians. Unfortunately, Kameelah and Genesis didn't want to teach me. If I did it a second time, I'd be arriving much more schooled. And much more understanding.

"**I** get recognized just about every day. And it still astounds me every time. I had no idea it would be this way. Sometimes, it's just insane and everyone seems to know my name. The bigger the city, the more I'm spotted. Teenagers mostly. But a lot of 30- and 40-year olds seem to watch the show, too.

And I certainly didn't think people would get so excited meeting us. It's as if we we're TV stars, but of course, we're not! We're just a bunch of kids who were lucky enough to have our lives filmed. We don't have any other skills beyond that. We can't act. We can't play sports. We can't sing. We just lived our lives and had it taped.

I think it's odd, though, that people actually feel like they really know me. I was featured on the show the least, so viewers have only seen a couple moments of my life. In other words, barely any part of what I'm really like. Yet, people feel like they

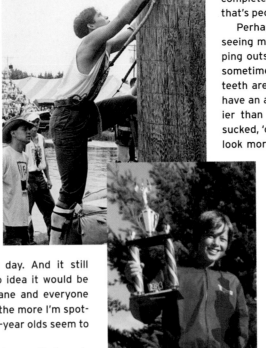

Above: 1983 World Lumberjack Competition, first place, Peewee Division. *Above left:* more lumberjack behavior.

completely understand me. And I think that's peculiar.

Perhaps the weirdest part of it all is seeing myself on TV. It's been like stepping outside myself. I'd watch the show sometimes and think, 'Man, my fang-teeth are big!' Or, 'Holy s**t! I really do have an accent.' I was also a little heavier than I normally am. Which kind of sucked, 'cause it would have been nice to look more fit. But I was in better shape when I did *Road Rules,* so now I don't care so much about looking fat on *The Real World.*

My only major disappointment with *The Real World* was that I barely appeared on the show. Same with *Road Rules All-Stars.* I am a side player whose sole purpose in life, or so it appears, is to instigate conflict. And once I am done instigating, then I disappear. Look, I'm not saying both experiences weren't great for me, they were. But evidently, my experiences were not as interesting to the producers, 'cause I am cut out of most of both shows.

But generally, I'm quite pleased with the way it turned out, especially on *The Real World.* My parents have given me a little s**t, though. After the first episode aired, my mom gave me a hard time. You know the one, the one where we arrive at the Firehouse. I was obviously a bit drunk in that show. And after it aired, my mother said to me, 'I can't believe you'd disrespect yourself like that. I didn't raise you that way.' Well, I felt bad enough about the stuff I did on the show—I didn't need my mom telling me she was embarrassed, too.

So, I sat her down and said, 'Mom, you've got to lighten up. These things happened six months ago. I'm going to have enough trouble dealing with them myself. I need your support, not your slings and arrows.' Well she was real understanding and never gave me a hard time again.

My dad was supportive of me during the show, too, but now he's big on telling me, 'Ten years from now, do you want to be known as the kid who did *The Real World*...but hasn't done s**t since?' He says to me, 'Get the hell on with your life. Don't sit back on this little fame, or let it dictate your life.' And he's right.

So I plan to finish law school next spring. Then, I'll take the Wisconsin Bar, and either go practice law with my dad in Hayward, Wisconsin, where I'm from, or go out to California and look for a job.

Impressions

Impression Given:

I don't think many viewers got much of an impression of me. I was barely featured on any of the episodes. I was more of a secondary character in other people's dramas. I think viewers only knew a few things about me: that I walked around in my underwear; that I fought naked with Montana; and that I did some logrolling.

Other than that, the strongest impression I made was as an instigator. It seemed like I was the one ruffling feathers in the house. They'd show me sticking my head in places where it didn't belong. Yes, I occasionally stick my head in places where it doesn't belong, but viewers have this impression that I do that all the time,'cause that's how I was portrayed on the show.

Impression Desired:

I would have preferred it if they'd shown more of my relationship with Syrus. I think we had a pretty unique friendship. Unfortunately, they only showed a little portion of it.

Celebrityhood

Best Part:

I got to be famous for a year, while the show aired. So I want to enjoy all the attention. Lots of strangers know my name. People come up to me and ask me questions. Frankly, I never thought something like that would happen to me. And since I know it's not going to last much longer, why not enjoy it while it lasts? I feel like I'm the reigning Miss America. After one year, I have to pass the crown to the new cast.

Worst Part:

Sometimes, it's a bit annoying when a stranger interrupts your date to ask a *Real World* question...especially one you've been asked over and over again. But the positives far outweigh the negatives.

Wildest Part:

Jason and I did a public appearance in northern New York, and it was f**king nuts. There were women fighting to get next to us. They were actually pushing each other out of the way. How whacked is that? Some of them were throwing their phone numbers at us. A few practically begged us to screw them. Of course, Jason and I didn't take any of them up on their offers...you know, being the upstanding guys that we are.

Close Encounters

MONTANA and I talk nearly every day, except for those times when she's angry with me. When she and Vaj broke up, I found out from her that day. Well, the next night I did a speaking engagement in northern New York. Someone asked me a question about Montana and Vaj, so I told him that I'd just heard they'd broken up.

Unfortunately, one of the people at the speaking engagement posted the news on the Internet. Vaj came across it online the next day and hit the roof. Montana was pissed at me for a while. And she had a right to be. Sometimes, I blab my mouth more than I should. But now everything between Montana and me is A-OK.

I talk to SYRUS quite often, about once a week. I spent six weeks out in L.A. and we

SEAN & RACHEL

As some of you know, Rachel and I began dating on *Road Rules All-Stars*. But when the show ended last summer, our relationship cooled as I was more into her than she was into me. Then, last January, Rachel was flying through Minneapolis and stayed with me overnight. And, well, I guess Rachel had a change of heart.

Ever since, we've been making regular trips back and forth between Los Angeles, where she lives, and Minneapolis, where I'm in law school. I'd say we've got a really good relationship going now. I really like her. She's got a great personality. She's really intelligent, loves to laugh, can have fun doing anything. And she's very pretty, too.

It's nice having both *The Real World* and *Road Rules* in common. It certainly gave us a strong bond, at first. But, of course, our relationship has grown much deeper and now we rarely talk about the show. Usually, Rachel gets recognized by MTV viewers over-25,

who watched *The Real World – San Francisco.* And I get spotted by everyone under-15.

As for our future together, we're not sure what's going to happen. Rachel is pursuing an acting career out in L.A. And I can't leave Minnesota for another year 'til I'm finished with law school. It's always been my intention to return to Hayward, Wisconsin, where I was born and raised. I just assumed I'd join my dad's law firm and raise a family. But Rachel wants me to move out to California. So as you can imagine, that's been a big topic of conversation.

Will I go to California? Or stay in the mid-West? Sounds to me like an episode of *The Real World.*

hung out together nearly every day. I speak to ELKA and JASON about once a month. GENESIS and I spoke a while back and had a really nice conversation.

KAMEELAH called me once during the past year, which actually freaked me out, 'cause there's no reason for her to call me, unless she has a problem. As it turned out, she was trying to get Syrus' number.

To be honest, I'm perfectly happy to see or speak with anyone in the cast. We'll always share a special bond, having had this amazing and difficult experience together. But as the years go on, Syrus and Montana will be my life-long friends. And I hope Jason and Elka will remain a part of my life as well.

DATING

It's *much* easier to meet girls after doing the show. Somehow, just 'cause I've done a TV show, I'm more desirable in girls' eyes. If I ever wanted to be with a girl any night of the week, basically I could. It has nothing to do with me, honest. Women actually seek me out. It's insane. But now that I'm seeing Rachel, I'm not really dating any other women.

The Creators on Sean

Jon:
Sean complains that we didn't show a lot of him in the Boston episodes. Well, not a lot of dramatic things happened to Sean in Boston. We would've shown more of his relationship with Becky, his girlfriend back home. But when she came to visit him in Boston, they barely talked. We couldn't figure out how to make a story out of it without dialogue. Frankly, their lack of communication was sort of weird. So Becky's visit ended up on the cutting-room floor.

But we did show Sean interacting with the girls in the house. He and Montana had a flirtation going. And he, Kameelah, and Genesis were constantly provoking each other. Furthermore, we portrayed his terrific relationship with Syrus. So, I think we included as much of Sean as we could. And I definitely think it came across that he has a big heart.

Mary-Ellis:
Sean has a great sense of humor. He's a really attractive guy. He has the All-American family, in the All-American town of Hayward, Wisconsin. And yet, even though he may end up moving back there—'cause his family owns the town—I wouldn't be surprised if he took a side step and became an actor or did something in the arts.

Road Rules All-Stars

I have no idea why they picked me out of *The Real World - Boston* cast to do *Road Rules All-Stars*. Perhaps they needed an instigator, since, that's the role I seemed to play on *The Real World*.

At first, I wasn't sure I wanted to do *Road Rules*. It meant missing another semester of law school. But I figured it was an opportunity that would never come along again. And only four other people could say they'd ever done both *The Real World* and *Road Rules*.

I enjoyed doing *Road Rules*. It was definitely a positive experience. But *The Real World* was the best experience of my life. If I were to compare the two, I'd definitely choose *The Real World*. You get a lot more freedom on *The Real World* than you do on *Road Rules*. And I developed a much closer bond with the people in the Firehouse than the people in the Winnebago, of course, with the exception of Rachel! Nothing against Eric, Jon and Cynthia, but the cast of *The Real World - Boston* was together six months and really bonded. The *Road Rules All-Stars* were only together for three weeks.

Kiss and Tell

JASON:
Sean always had gas.

MONTANA:
We all went to Maine on a ski trip, but they never showed it on the air. One reason might be because Sean hooked up with a teenager, who was barely legal. In fact, the girl's mom had to pick them up afterwards and drive them home...'cause the girl didn't even have her license yet.

SEAN:
I definitely got a lot more action than they showed. All of us did—with the exception of Genesis and Elka.

JIM JOHNSTON
(*Real World* producer):
One day, Sean and Montana were walking through Boston's Public Garden and stumbled upon a big crowd. Robin Williams was filming a scene in a movie with an unknown actor. A real dramatic scene taking place on a park bench. The movie turned out to be *Good Will Hunting* and the unknown actor, Matt Damon. Neither Sean nor Montana met either one. But they did steal some food from the crafts service table.

Inquiring Minds

Most frequently asked question
Did you hook up with Montana?

Sean's answer
No, we didn't. But she's a tremendously fine friend.

Most frequent e-mail request
I get nearly five e-mails a week requesting a date. Things like, 'If you ever come out this way, I'll show you a really good time.'

Sean's e-mail reply
I usually don't reply. As of yet, I've never taken someone up on one of those offers.

Syrus

MOST FAVORITE: The scene where Sean and I were doing the calendar at the After School Program. The one where Sean said to me, 'Let's paint a white background,' and I respond, 'Why can't it be black?' That s**t cracked me up.

LEAST FAVORITE: When everyone was talking behind my back about dating a parent in the After School Program. Especially the moment where I walk into the restaurant and Montana is dissing me. I could see 'em all straightening up. I knew they were backstabbing me. That moment sucked!

"I'm so happy I'm me... and not other people in the house. I think there were a lot of pretty **closed-minded people living in the Boston Firehouse.**

The biggest exception was Sean and Montana. To a large extent, Kameelah was the worst offender, especially regarding racial things. She gave me all that s**t about interracial dating, then showed an attraction for Jason. Practice what you preach, girl. 'Cause I always will."

I watched every show. I had to be in tune with it. I needed to know what parts of me were being shown. Usually, I'd watch the episodes with friends. For the premiere, I had a big-a** party at the Beverly Club in Beverly Hills. Over 100 people came, including some of the crew from the show.

Each week, my phone would ring off the hook during the broadcast. After the episode where I cried at the After School Program aired, forget it...that one tear got me hundreds of phone calls. People were talking so much crap. 'Oh, Syrus. You're just sooo sensitive!' Hey, I've got no problem showing my feminine side to the world. Its 1998, man. Brothers can be sensitive, too [laughing.]

In general, I'm pleased with the way I was portrayed on the show. Yes, I think they left out a huge aspect of Syrus. They stereotyped me as the partying-only-white-women-liking-jock. But I think they stereotyped Kameelah, too. She was depicted as the angry black woman. And Montana as the New York feminist.

It's true I partied a lot. I don't think I've ever partied as hard in my entire life as I did in Boston. But I had to escape from that house. Some of the people annoyed me so much. Most of them were a lot younger than me and it showed. I got myself peace of mind by enjoying all the *finer things* that Boston had to offer. Had I not, I might've whooped somebody's a**.

"There's more to me than partying, but you'd have never known it from watching the episodes. Well, other than my dating white women, which they loved to show. And they did that to create conflict with Kameelah. When, in fact, I've always been open to dating all sorts of women, regardless of color.

Since the show aired, I've gotten a lot of slack from black people about the way I deal with white people. Some of them call me a sell-out 'cause I befriend so many whites. Well, that's jack! Selling out to me is not being true to those that are true to me—black, white, blue, or green. I'm open-armed to everyone. I don't live life with blinders on. I have peripheral vision, if you know what I mean.

I've also gotten s**t about the rape argument I had with Montana. I was so scared when that aired, 'cause my side got all twisted. I wish they had shown more of where I was coming from and what I was once forced to go through.

A few years back, I was a college student on a basketball scholarship at the University of Hawaii. I met a girl and was invited up to her place. She greeted me at the door wearing nothing more then a teal G-string. She climbed on top of me and placed *me* inside of her. Now, I ask you ...how do you rape someone when they're on top of you?

Two weeks later, the woman claimed I'd violated her and accused me of rape, and things got whack from there. I was forced to meet with the Dean. My classmates and my teammates started giving me a hard time. Calling me stuff like, 'Mike Tyson,' and other s**t like that. I was freaking out. But charges were

never pressed. And she ended up taking it all back. But the label, 'rapist,' stuck with me for a long time, when bottom line was, I'd done nothing wrong.

So, that's what I was trying to explain to Montana. That if a woman calls you a rapist, you can be labeled one the rest of your life. I'm not saying it's right what women go through to prove they've been raped. But some women throw that word around without realizing the consequences.

In spite of this disagreement with Montana, we were able to mend our relationship. And that, I thought, was a pretty big deal. Unfortunately, they hardly portrayed that on the show. They showed her trying to get me kicked out of the After School Program, but none of my backing her when she was being kicked out herself. I think I deserved some props for that, and believe it would have shown that, at least, some of us were capable of being open-minded enough to overcome our differences.

Still, I'm real cool with the way things turned out on the show. I met some great people in Boston, especially Sean and Montana. I did that town complete, before it did me. I enjoyed watching all the episodes and the exposure on TV. I know a lot of former *Real World* cast members get the TV bug from being on the show. Well, that bug has grown into a big, ol' insect inside of me.

Close Encounters

On average, I speak with SEAN twice a month. I talk to MONTANA about once a month. And I've seen JASON whenever he comes to L.A. But I haven't really spoken with the others all that much. Honestly, I don't really care to. If I ever go to Orlando, I'll look up GENESIS. And in Las Vegas, maybe ELKA, too. But if I head up toward Stanford...well, I might look up KAMEELAH. But it would all depend on what else I had going on.

The Creators on Syrus

Mary–Ellis:
Syrus is walking charisma. I once strolled through Los Angeles Airport with him. People of all ages and walks of life would smile at him and say, 'Hi.' It was as if everyone thought they knew him. But I'm telling you, these were not people who recognized him from the show. He just has this presence, this sweetness. He has a great smile. His eyes twinkle and his face lights up. And he uses it in almost every situation. So people feel, in spite of his imposing size, that he's so accessible. It's a real gift. And I hope he uses that to his advantage.

DATING

A former *Real World* cast member once said, 'I'll never have a problem dating again.' Well, I never had one before. But now, I'm *really* not having any problems.

Since the show aired, women will say or do anything, man. I'll be with Jennifer and a girl will come right up to me and give me a big hug or kiss right in front of her. Girls I've never met before have knocked ice cream and drinks out of my hands jumping into my arms. I guess they feel like they know me 'cause they've seen me on the show. And when I'm on stage speaking at a college...man, the looks I get could kill.

I was always a confident person. I just couldn't get a job. But as far as all this going to my head, don't worry, I'm still as broke as hell [laughing].

I started this clothing company called, GODDOG, with four of my closest friends. We're five guys from very diverse backgrounds. So, GODDOG reflects that diversity. We present a smooth blend of styles, representing all people living in harmony. Most of the designs are mine and fit my lifestyle—surfer dude...meets ball player... meets home-boy...meets reggae hipster...meets hip-hop cat. We're selling T-shirts and soon, a line of nightclub attire. We're available on the Internet, so give us a visit.

Jon:
Syrus originally came into our office looking for a job as a casting coordinator. As we were interviewing him for that position, we suddenly realized, 'Whoa, this guy is perfect to actually be *on* the show.' He was that dynamic. Just by seeing the way the kids at the After School Program responded to him reveals how magnetic he is. I'd have to say Syrus' biggest problem is self-discipline. I think Syrus is in search of what's going to make Syrus a millionaire...without having to get up too early.

SYRUS & JENNIFER

Jennifer and I have gone through a lot of turbulence since the show. Unfortunately, we don't think the relationship is going to continue. I love Jennifer to death, and she knows that, but that doesn't mean we can be together. So, we're doing our separate things now...and we'll see what happens in the future.

People ask me if *The Real World* hurt our relationship. I don't think so. Sure, it was tough for her to watch some of things I did. But she took the show for face value. She said, 'We weren't together at that time. He did what he did. And I did my own thing.'

Right now, I'm finding it hard to maintain any long-term relationships. First, I need to find a career path that'll make me happy with myself. Right now, I'm not exactly sure what I want to do. I don't have an occupation, really. I do odd jobs. My basketball leagues. My clothing line. My club promotions. Jennifer was, and is, in a stable job, making real money. I'm not. And I've got to get my life together before I can commit to a relationship. Because the bottom line is: Syrus must be pleased with Syrus....before Syrus can please anyone else.

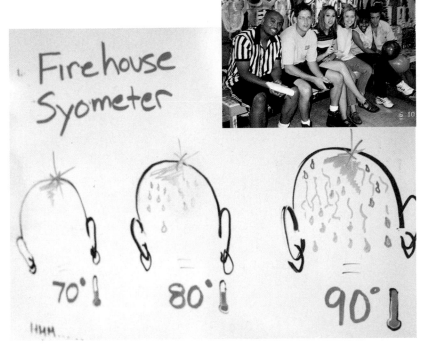

Firehouse Syometer

70° 80° 90°

HMM...

Kiss and Tell

SEAN:
Toward the end of the show, the entire cast got the idea to go sky-diving. So, the whole house drove to Rhode Island. But when we got there, big Syrus wimped out. Genesis didn't jump either, but she had a legitimate excuse 'cause she has a heart murmur. The rest of us jumped, attached to an instructor. They filmed the whole thing, so I'm surprised they never showed it. Perhaps they didn't because just a month after we jumped, the four instructors that escorted us were killed in a plane crash.

SYRUS:
I've done acting work on *Baywatch* for three summers. I've had a blast doing that show. I've mostly been an extra. And if I had extra time, I did extra... [laughing].

Inquiring Minds

Most frequently asked question
Don't I know you from someplace?

Syrus' answer
I always respond, 'What high school did you go to?' 'Cause I don't want to throw the show in their face.

Strangest request
Who slept with more women? You or Eric of *The Real World-New York*?

Syrus's answer
Eric, of course!

Most outrageous request
I've been asked to sign someone's butt cheek.

Syrus' response
I did it, of course!

Celebrityhood

What's It Like?
It's the weirdest thing. It's a hundred times bigger than anything I ever anticipated. I had no clue it would be this way. I get grandparents approaching me at Sunday brunch nearly as often as kids do. Even celebrities recognize *me* now. One of them approached me at a strip joint... Who? Sorry, I'm not giving out any names. The craziest thing is that everyone now assumes I'm loaded with money 'cause I'm on TV. Man, I'm the brokest celebrity in all of L.A.

Best Part:
I get *comped* in Vegas. That's pretty cool.

Worst Part:
It's never that bad. Besides, I'm a social butterfly. I like meeting people. But it also means I can't have a bad day, particularly when kids want an autograph, 'cause I always want to be obliging.

Funniest Celebrity Encounter:
The 'Bud guy' from the Budweiser commercials spotted me in Washington, D.C. He flipped out over me.

Strangest Moment:
One of the DJs on Power 106—the hip-hop radio station in L.A.—put out an A.P.B. for me on the air. He said, 'If anyone sees Syrus from *The Real World*, tell him to call Power 106.' So I'm driving down the street in my Bronco, and all of a sudden, two different drivers yell at me to pull over and call the station.

ENCORE?

Would you do The Real World again?

ELKA:
At the end of our time in Boston, I said I'd never do it again. But I've changed my mind. I'd do it again...either with the same group or a new set. Anything to feel that sense of community again.

GENESIS:
Yeah, especially knowing what I know now. I'd even do it again with the same six people. Jason, Kameelah, and Elka for sure. Syrus and Sean would be fine, too. And I'd like to get inside the head of Montana, just to figure that girl out. Man, she pulled s**t out of her ass sometimes. I'd love to know where she got that stuff from. If I was a psychology major, I'd use Montana as a case study.

JASON:
I wish I'd done it knowing what I know now. But once is enough for a lifetime. I'm glad I did it, though. It was an amazing opportunity.

KAMEELAH:
I'm glad I did it. But I wouldn't do it again. Not at this point.

MONTANA:
I'm glad I did it. But I wouldn't do it again.

SEAN:
Perhaps, if there was a *Real World* for 30-year-old guys. But right now, it's time for me to move on with my life. Finish law school and begin my career.

SYRUS:
I'd do it again in a heartbeat—even with the same people. I'd love to do it again with Sean and Montana.

Would you do a *Real World* Reunion?

ELKA: Yeah, just so I could see everyone again.

GENESIS: Oh, yeah!

JASON: Yeah, I like the whole process. The lights, the cameras and the action. It's all really exciting to me. Hell, I'd do it for free.

KAMEELAH: Yeah, I'll do it.

MONTANA: Yeah, totally!

SEAN: Yeah, when the time comes I'll probably do it.

SYRUS: Hell, yeah!

LEGACY

How will The Real World – Boston *be remembered by viewers?*

 We'll be remembered as the show that saved *The Real World* **from sinking. After the Miami season, the ratings went down. But our cast brought them back up. Or so I'm told.**

The Creators' Response

Mary – Ellis:
The Boston cast saved *The Real World!* Oh, my God. Are you kidding? The ratings went through the roof for the Miami season. Yes, many people loved the Boston cast, including us. But the ratings actually went down during their season. However, I do think the Boston cast was a fascinating group, and really relatable for the viewers. I know a lot of people adored watching them. And I did, too.

Jon:
'Saved *The Real World!*' That's total bulls**t! Probably, someone told them that to make them feel better. And that someone was probably me [laughing]. No, but seriously... I do think the Boston cast had really big hearts. They weren't afraid to show their emotions. They were just fun to watch. Yes, they made mistakes. But they didn't take themselves too seriously, and I think many viewers appreciated that.

 GENESIS:
I have no idea.

 JASON:
I've been told by a lot of people that our season was the best one since New York. And I've heard we were the season that saved *The Real World.* Perhaps they say that to the new cast each year. Nevertheless, I think we all lived together pretty well. There was definitely conflict. But there wasn't as much bickering about stupid things, unlike past seasons. Maybe it's because we had an older cast.

KAMEELAH:
Unlike some previous seasons, everyone on our cast had some type of aspiration. In past years, cast members seemed to be like, 'This is six months of my life. And after that, I've got to find something else to do.' They all seemed kind of aimless. I also think the community service element made our interactions more focused and interesting than prior shows. You didn't find them discussing religion in the L.A. house, for instance. I liked that aspect of our show.

MONTANA:
People seem to think we were a season where we all hated each other. But we didn't really. We just hated some of each other [laughing].

 SEAN:
We'll be remembered for Vaj calling Montana a whore and Genesis crying at the computer.

 SYRUS:
The people I meet tell me *The Real World's New York, San Francisco* and *Boston* are the three best of all.

153

How to get on
The Real World

To apply to be on *The Real World*, you need to show us that you are an open, honest and sincere person, who's dealing with issues of concern to the *Real World* audience. How can you do this? Read on for step-by-step directions.

 Call *The Real World* Hotline: (818) 754-5790.

This number will give you the latest information on applying, the deadlines for next season, and where to send your application.

 Write a cover letter.

We want you to tell us a little bit about yourself. Why do you want to spend six months in a house full of strangers? What activities will you pursue? Please include a snapshot of yourself in this cover letter.

 Make a videotape.

We'd also like to see you as well as hear from you. Make a ten-minute videotape of yourself talking about whatever you think makes you a good candidate for *The Real World*. Remember, we want to see if you are a person who is open and willing to express what's important to you. Sometimes, the best videos are simple—like someone sitting on their bed talking about what makes them tick. Just be honest and sincere. And don't overthink it. (Also, make sure there's enough light on your face and that you're close enough to the microphone to be heard.)

 Fill out the enclosed application.

Answer all the following questions as honestly as you can. Please keep your answers to a paragraph in length. And please be sure to type your answers or write legibly.

DATE RECEIVED:

NAME:

ADDRESS:

PHONE: E-MAIL ADDRESS:

BIRTHDATE: AGE:

SOCIAL SECURITY NO.:

PARENTS' NAMES:

ADDRESS:

PHONE: E-MAIL ADDRESS:

SIBLINGS (NAMES AND AGES):

WHAT IS YOUR ETHNIC BACKGROUND?

ARE YOU OR HAVE YOU EVER BEEN A MEMBER OF SAG/AFTRA? HAVE YOU EVER ACTED OR PERFORMED OUTSIDE OF SCHOOL?

EDUCATION: NAME OF HIGH SCHOOL: YEARS COMPLETED:

NAME OF COLLEGE: YEARS COMPLETED AND MAJORS:

OTHER EDUCATION:

WHERE DO YOU WORK? DESCRIBE YOUR JOB HISTORY:

WHAT IS YOUR ULTIMATE CAREER GOAL?

WHAT ARE YOUR PERSONAL (NOT CAREER) GOALS IN LIFE?

IN YOUR OPINION, WHAT ARE THE GREATEST PROBLEMS AND CHALLENGES FACING KIDS WHO ARE GROWING UP TODAY?

DO YOU EVER PLAN TO HAVE CHILDREN OF YOUR OWN? WHEN AND HOW MANY?

WHAT ABOUT YOU WILL MAKE YOU AN INTERESTING ROOMMATE?

IF YOU'RE LIVING WITH A ROOMMATE, HOW DID YOU HOOK UP WITH HIM OR HER? TELL US ABOUT HIM OR HER AS A PERSON.
DO YOU GET ALONG? WHAT'S THE BEST PART ABOUT LIVING WITH HIM OR HER? WHAT'S THE HARDEST PART ABOUT IT?

HOW WOULD SOMEONE WHO REALLY KNOWS YOU DESCRIBE YOUR BEST TRAITS?

HOW WOULD SOMEONE WHO REALLY KNOWS YOU DESCRIBE YOUR WORST TRAITS?

DESCRIBE YOUR MOST EMBARRASSING MOMENT IN LIFE:

DO YOU HAVE A BOYFRIEND OR GIRLFRIEND? HOW LONG HAVE YOU TWO BEEN TOGETHER? WHERE DO YOU SEE THE RELATIONSHIP GOING?
WHAT DRIVES YOU CRAZY ABOUT THE OTHER PERSON? WHAT'S THE BEST THING ABOUT THE OTHER PERSON?

HOW IMPORTANT IS SEX TO YOU? DO YOU HAVE IT ONLY WHEN YOU'RE IN A RELATIONSHIP OR DO YOU SEEK IT OUT AT OTHER TIMES?
HOW DID IT COME ABOUT ON THE LAST OCCASION?

DESCRIBE YOUR FANTASY DATE:

WHAT DO YOU DO FOR FUN?

DO YOU PLAY ANY SPORTS?

WHAT ARE YOUR FAVORITE MUSICAL GROUPS/ARTISTS?

DESCRIBE A TYPICAL FRIDAY OR SATURDAY NIGHT:

WHAT WAS THE LAST UNUSUAL, EXCITING, OR SPONTANEOUS OUTING YOU INSTIGATED FOR YOU AND YOUR FRIENDS?

OTHER THAN A BOYFRIEND OR GIRLFRIEND, WHO IS THE MOST IMPORTANT PERSON IN YOUR LIFE RIGHT NOW? TELL US ABOUT HIM OR HER:

THE REAL WORLD APPLICATION FORM

WHAT ARE SOME WAYS YOU HAVE TREATED SOMEONE WHO HAS BEEN IMPORTANT TO YOU THAT YOU ARE PROUD OF?

WHAT ARE SOME OF THE WAYS YOU HAVE TREATED SOMEONE WHO HAS BEEN IMPORTANT TO YOU THAT YOU ARE EMBARRASSED BY, OR WISH YOU HADN'T DONE?

IF YOU HAD TO DESCRIBE YOUR MOTHER (OR YOUR STEPMOTHER, IF YOU LIVED WITH HER MOST OF YOUR LIFE AS A CHILD), BY DIVIDING HER PERSONALITY INTO TWO PARTS, HOW WOULD YOU DESCRIBE EACH PART?

IF YOU HAD TO DESCRIBE YOUR FATHER (OR YOUR STEPFATHER), BY DIVIDING HIS PERSONALITY INTO TWO PARTS, HOW WOULD YOU DESCRIBE EACH PART?

HOW DID YOUR PARENTS TREAT EACH OTHER? DID YOUR PARENTS HAVE A GOOD MARRIAGE? WHAT WAS IT LIKE?

DESCRIBE HOW CONFLICTS WERE HANDLED AT HOME AS YOU WERE GROWING UP (WHO WOULD WIN AND WHO WOULD LOSE, WHETHER THERE WAS YELLING OR HITTING, ETC.)?

IF YOU HAVE ANY BROTHERS OR SISTERS, ARE YOU CLOSE? HOW WOULD YOU DESCRIBE YOUR RELATIONSHIP WITH THEM?

DESCRIBE A MAJOR EVENT OR ISSUE THAT'S AFFECTED YOUR FAMILY:

WHAT IS THE MOST IMPORTANT ISSUE OR PROBLEM FACING YOU TODAY?

IS THERE ANY ISSUE, POLITICAL OR SOCIAL, THAT YOU'RE PASSIONATE ABOUT? HAVE YOU DONE ANYTHING ABOUT IT?

DO YOU BELIEVE IN GOD? ARE YOU RELIGIOUS OR SPIRITUAL? DO YOU ATTEND ANY FORMAL RELIGIOUS SERVICES?

WHAT ARE YOUR THOUGHTS ON: ABORTION?

OTHER SEXUAL ORIENTATIONS?

WELFARE?

AFFIRMATIVE ACTION?

DO YOU HAVE ANY HABITS WE SHOULD KNOW ABOUT?

DO YOU: SMOKE CIGARETTES?

DRINK ALCOHOL? HOW OLD WERE YOU WHEN YOU HAD YOUR FIRST DRINK? HOW MUCH DO YOU DRINK NOW? HOW OFTEN?

DO USE RECREATIONAL DRUGS? WHAT DRUGS HAVE YOU USED? HOW OFTEN?

DO YOU KNOW A LOT OF PEOPLE WHO DO DRUGS? WHAT DO YOU THINK OF PEOPLE WHO DO DRUGS?

ARE YOU ON ANY PRESCRIPTION MEDICATION? IF SO, WHAT, AND FOR HOW LONG HAVE YOU BEEN TAKING IT?

HAVE YOU EVER BEEN ARRESTED? (IF SO, WHAT WAS THE CHARGE AND WERE YOU CONVICTED?)

WHAT BOTHERS YOU MOST ABOUT OTHER PEOPLE?

DESCRIBE A RECENT MAJOR ARGUMENT YOU HAD WITH SOMEONE. WHO USUALLY WINS ARGUMENTS WITH YOU? WHY?

HAVE YOU EVER HIT ANYONE IN ANGER OR SELF-DEFENSE? IF SO, TELL US ABOUT IT (HOW OLD WERE YOU, WHAT HAPPENED, ETC.)

IF YOU COULD CHANGE ONE THING ABOUT THE WAY YOU LOOK, WHAT WOULD THAT BE?

IF YOU COULD CHANGE ONE THING ABOUT YOUR PERSONALITY, WHAT WOULD THAT BE?

IF SELECTED, IS THERE ANY PERSON OR PART OF YOUR LIFE YOU WOULD PREFER NOT TO SHARE? IF SO, DESCRIBE (I.E. FAMILY, FRIENDS, BUSINESS ASSOCIATES, SOCIAL ORGANIZATIONS, OR ACTIVITIES)

IS THERE ANYONE AMONG YOUR FAMILY OR CLOSE FRIENDS WHO WOULD OBJECT TO APPEARING ON CAMERA? IF SO, WHY?

ARE YOU NOW SEEING, OR HAVE YOU EVER SEEN, A THERAPIST OR PSYCHOLOGIST?

WHAT IS YOUR GREATEST FEAR (AND WHY)?

IF YOU HAD ALADDIN'S LAMP AND THREE WISHES, WHAT WOULD THEY BE?

PLEASE RATE THE FOLLOWING ACTIVITIES/PASTTIMES USING THE FOLLOWING SCALE: N: NEVER S: SOMETIMES O: OFTEN A: ALWAYS

	RATING	COMMENT
READ BOOKS		
SLEEP 8 HOURS		
WATCH TELEVISION DAILY		
SHOP		
GO OUT/SOCIALIZE		
SPEND TIME WITH FRIENDS		

	RATING	COMMENT
SPEND TIME ALONE		
WORK/STUDY		
TALK ON THE PHONE		
COOK		
CLEAN		
ARGUE		
WRITE		
READ NEWSPAPERS		
ENJOY THE COMPANY OF ANIMALS		
STATE OPINIONS		
ASK OPINIONS		
CONFIDE IN YOUR PARENTS		
VOLUNTEER		
PROCRASTINATE		
EAT		
DRINK ALCOHOL		
DIET		
SMOKE		
CRY		
LAUGH		
MOVIES		
THEATRE		
CLUBS		
PARTIES		

LIST 4 PEOPLE WHO HAVE KNOWN YOU FOR A LONG TIME (EXCLUDING RELATIVES) AND WILL TELL US WHAT A GREAT PERSON YOU ARE:
PLEASE INCLUDE TWO ADULTS AND TWO OF YOUR FRIENDS.

1.NAME   ADDRESS   PHONE   HOW DO THEY KNOW YOU?

2.NAME   ADDRESS   PHONE   HOW DO THEY KNOW YOU?

3.NAME   ADDRESS   PHONE   HOW DO THEY KNOW YOU?

4.NAME   ADDRESS   PHONE   HOW DO THEY KNOW YOU?

HOW DID YOU HEAR ABOUT OUR CASTING SEARCH?

SIGNATURE   DATE

Thank you for your time and effort in completing this form.

THE REAL WORLD APPLICATION FORM

Wanna see how hot it really got in the Firehouse?
Wanna know what else rained down on Pier 70?

BOSTON + SEATTLE

LV 49459 70 min.

Then pick up *The Real World You Never Saw: Boston & Seattle* on home video. Because if you think you've seen it all before, you need a reality check.

This is 70 minutes of never-before-seen clips and footage of outrageous pranks, parties, fights, and romantic nights. Get the inside scoop from your favorite cast members on what it's really like to be watched, followed, and taped 24 hours a day!

Just $12.98 In Stores Now